[Psalms]

folk songs of faith

Ray C. Stedman

EDITED BY JAMES D. DENNEY

[*Psalms*]

folk songs of faith

Discovery House Publishers

Books, music, and videos that feed the soul with the Word of God

Box 3566 Grand Rapids, MI 49501

Psalms: Folk Songs of Faith
©2006 by Elaine Stedman
All rights reserved.

Discovery House Publishers is affiliated with RBC Ministries,
Grand Rapids, Michigan.

Discovery House Books are distributed to the trade exclusively by
Barbour Publishing, Inc., Uhrichsville, Ohio.

Requests for permission to quote from this book should be
directed to: Permissions Department, Discovery House Publishers,
P.O. Box 3566, Grand Rapids, MI 49501.

Interior design by Sherri L. Hoffman

Library of Congress Cataloging-in-Publication Data

Stedman, Ray C.
      Psalms : folk songs of faith / Ray C. Stedman ; edited by
James D. Denney.
            p.   cm.
      ISBN 1-57293-171-X
      1. Bible. O.T. Psalms--Criticism, interpretation, etc.
I. Denney, James D. II. Title.
BS1430.52.S74 2006
223'.206—dc22   2006006435

Printed in the United States of America

06 07 08 09 10 /CHG/ 10 9 8 7 6 5 4 3 2 1

Contents

[Psalms]
folk songs of faith

ᏒᏰᏩᎧ

The Treasury of David

AN OVERVIEW OF THE PSALMS

The healing power of the Psalms became amazingly real to me soon after I entered the pastoral ministry. I had just begun my work at Peninsula Bible Church (PBC) when a young man came to me for counseling. He was in his twenties and his wife had just divorced him, leaving him with a five-year-old son to care for. The burden of these struggles was overwhelming him, leaving him feeling depressed to the point of despair.

One Sunday morning before church, he called and asked me to pray for him. His son was away for the weekend, and he was alone. I prayed with him over the phone and told him that as soon as the church service was over, I would come see him and we would talk.

After the worship service, I went straight to the man's house. I parked at the curb, went up to the door, and knocked. No answer. I knew he had to be there; he promised he would wait for me. I knocked again and again. Still no answer.

I tried the door and found it unlocked. I went inside and called his name but heard only silence. With a sense of dread and foreboding, I went into the bedroom—and I found him dead. Not far from his body was the gun he had used to kill himself.

Dazed and in shock, I went into another room and called the police, and when the officers arrived, I explained what I had seen and answered their questions. At home the rest of that day I felt shaken, and my insides were twisted in knots. I felt angry and sorrowful.

I asked myself repeatedly if there weren't something I could have done, something I could have said, to prevent this man from taking his life. I was so upset that I strongly considered leaving the ministry. The whole idea of being a Christian minister seemed pointless. I thought of all the counseling and prayer I had devoted to this man, yet just a few hours after I had last spoken with him, he killed himself.

I spent the rest of the day praying and talking to people, asking for their counsel. I poured out my soul to my wife Elaine. No matter where I turned or what I did, I found no relief. This man's death haunted and tormented me throughout the day and into the night.

Finally, unable to sleep, Elaine and I took our Bibles and read together from the Psalms. Nothing else could bring peace and consolation to our hearts but the simple beauty and enduring truths of the Psalms. To this day I could not tell you which of the psalms we read that night. They all seemed to flow together. But I do know this: Every word was like a healing salve applied to the open wound in my heart.

Down through the centuries, this great collection of ancient Hebrew poetry has pillowed the heads of millions of believers in times of distress and heartache. It has also given voice to emotions of gladness, joy, and hope. It has turned hearts toward God with its rich expression of deep reverence and worship. Every shade of human emotion and experience finds expression in the words of the Psalms.

If you are happy and want to express your joy in words, read Psalm 66 or Psalm 92. If you are grateful and want to express your thankfulness to God, pray the words of Psalm 40. If your heart is full of inexpressible praise for God, turn to Psalm 84 or Psalm 116.

The Psalms also express the need of a soul that has descended into the valley of shadows. If you are troubled by fear and dread, read Psalm 23, Psalm 56, or Psalm 91. If you feel discouraged, read Psalm 42; if you are lonely, discover God's presence in the words of Psalm 62 or Psalm 71. Oppressed with guilt, shame, and a sense of your own sinfulness? Read Psalms 32 and 51. Feeling worried or anxious? Psalms 37 and 73 will soothe your soul. Even feelings of anger and resentment find expression in Psalms 13, 58, and 94. If you feel forsaken, immerse your afflicted heart in the comforting words of Psalm 88. If you struggle with doubt, dwell in the heart-lifting truths of Psalm 119.

While the Psalms have relieved the troubled souls of millions down through the centuries, we should not view them merely as a source of comfort. Though the Psalms do have a soothing effect on the soul, God never intended His Word to serve as a mere "pain reliever" for the difficult times in our lives. God gave all of the Scriptures, including the Psalms, to enable us to understand life. Through the lens of the Psalms, we learn to see reality.

The Origin of the Psalms

A psalm is a hymn, a sacred song. The word comes from the Greek word *psalmos*, which is derived from *psallein,* meaning "to play music upon a harp." The book of Psalms was the hymnbook of ancient Israel. Many of these songs were written to be sung in public.

People often assume that David, the shepherd-king of Israel, wrote all the Psalms, but, in fact, David wrote only about half of the psalms. Moses and King Solomon each wrote two. King Hezekiah wrote ten psalms. A group called the sons of Korah, who led the worship singing in Israel, wrote others. Asaph, a Levite and leader of David's choir, wrote still others. Unknown authors composed a few.

I like to think of the Psalms as the folk songs of the Bible. I love listening to folk songs—not just American folk songs but the folk music of many cultures and lands. Folk music reflects the heart and soul of a people. The biblical folk songs called the Psalms express not merely the heartbeat of ancient Israel but of all people who worship the God of the Bible.

Commonly passed down by oral tradition, folk songs are intended for the people (or "folk") of a specific community or culture. Folk songs aren't meant to be expertly sung and played by professional musicians. They are to be shared by all of us common folk, even those of us who can't carry a tune in a bucket! Folk songs are for everyone. This is as true of the Psalms as for every other folk music tradition.

There are 150 psalms in the book of Psalms, making it the longest book in the Bible. Composed over a span of a thousand years (from about 1410 BC to 430 BC), it is really five books in one. It divides into five different sections, each with its own general theme. Each of the five sections closes with a doxology, such as "Amen and Amen" or "Praise the Lord!" The five divisions of the Psalms parallel the structure of the Pentateuch, the first five books of the Bible (Genesis, Exodus, Leviticus, Numbers, and Deuteronomy).

Why does God's Word follow the same pattern in both the Pentateuch and the Psalms? I believe it is because God designed both of these sections of Scripture to show us the pattern of His workings. He always follows the same pattern, whether in His dealings with an individual human life or with nations in history or with the whole of creation. He always follows five steps, which He has revealed to us in the first five books of the Bible. The Psalms follow the same five steps, reflecting the response of the human heart to this pattern of God's working in our lives. Let's take a closer look at each of these five sections of the Psalms.

The Structure of the Psalms

Section 1: Psalms 1 through 41. The first section echoes the theme of Genesis, the book of foundations. It serves as an introduction to human life and a revelation of the needs of the human heart. The author and probable compiler of the first section of the Psalms was David. This section was probably compiled during the years from 1020 BC to 970 BC.

The first section begins in Psalm 1 with the picture of the perfect man, just as Genesis begins with man in the Garden of Eden. Then Psalm 2 shows us humanity in rebellion, beginning with these words:

> *Why do the nations conspire*
> *and the peoples plot in vain?*
> *The kings of the earth take their stand*
> *and the rulers gather together*
> *against the LORD*
> *and against his Anointed One.*
> *"Let us break their chains," they say,*
> *"and throw off their fetters" (vv. 1–3).*

Throughout the rest of this first section of the Psalms, you see the anguish of humanity separated from its Creator, exemplified by such passages as Psalm 6:3, 6:

> *My soul is in anguish.*
> *How long, O LORD, how long? . . .*
> *I am worn out from groaning;*

all night long I flood my bed with weeping
and drench my couch with tears.

But also the grace and mercy of God is introduced in this section. Here is the picture of God as a defender, a refuge, a righteous judge. God seeks human beings and calls them out of the darkness they have created for themselves, just as He called out to the first fallen man in the Garden, "Adam, where are you?" Here we see God beginning to restore Adam's lost race. The first book of the Psalms is an expression of our deep-seated longing for God and of the first echoes of God's answer.

Section 2: Psalms 42 through 72. The second section corresponds to the book of Exodus, the book of redemption. This section tells the story of God's activity to redeem His people from their captivity to sin. Written by David and the Sons of Korah, these psalms were probably compiled by Hezekiah or Josiah during the years from 970 BC to 610 BC.

Exodus tells the story of Israel in Egyptian captivity, a story of sorrow, bondage, and slavery to sin. Yet Exodus also tells of the great power of God to deliver His people from their captivity. The second book of the Psalms traces the same theme.

Psalm 45 is the psalm of God the king and His sovereign rule over humanity. Psalm 46 speaks of God's deliverance and help in times of trouble. Psalm 50 extols God's strength, while Psalm 51 reveals God's grace to us in our deepest sin and shame. Psalm 72, the last psalm of this section, pictures God in all His might and conquering power—power to free us from captivity to sin.

Section 3: Psalms 73 through 89. The third section corresponds to the book of Leviticus, the book in which God teaches Israel how to draw near and worship Him. Both Leviticus and the third division of the Psalms deal with the provision God had made to be present among His people, the provision called the tabernacle. Asaph wrote these psalms of worship, and they were probably compiled by Hezekiah or Josiah during the years from 970 BC to 610 BC.

Psalm 75 expresses humanity's awareness of God's judgment. Psalm 78 revels in the light of God's unwavering love; it presents God as infinitely merciful but also relentless in rooting out and destroying the sin in our lives. Psalm 84 portrays the continual, bountiful provision God offers us, just as He strengthened and provided for the needs of ancient Israel.

Section 4: Psalms 90 through 106. The fourth section corresponds to the book of Numbers, the book of wilderness wandering, of testing and failure. These psalms, largely of unknown authorship, were probably compiled by Ezra or Nehemiah up to around 430 BC.

Throughout this section of the Psalms we find victory alternating with defeat. In Numbers we see how God steps in and delivers the Israelites in the desert by working mighty miracles and ministering to their needs. When they are hungry, He feeds them bread from heaven. When they are thirsty, He opens a rock for them so that water flows. Even so, the people of Israel soon begin to murmur and complain so that a great spiritual victory is quickly followed by spiritual defeat. We see this same pattern depicted for us in the poetry of the fourth section of the Psalms.

Section 5: Psalms 107 through 150. The fifth section echoes the book of Deuteronomy, the book of the Second Law—that is, the law of the new life in Jesus Christ, the life that sets us free from the law of sin and death. This final section of the Psalms describes God's way of redeeming, sanctifying, and transforming His people.

This section also deals with the power of God's Word; it contains Psalm 119, the longest of all the psalms. Every verse of Psalm 119 mentions God's Word in one way or another ("Your Word," "Your decrees," "Your commands," "the law of the Lord," "His statutes," and "His ways").

There is yet another important feature of this fifth section of the Psalms: the Songs of Ascent, Psalms 120 through 134. These are psalms of praise and thanksgiving that Hebrew worshipers sang as they marched up to Jerusalem to offer sacrifices in the temple.

The fifth and final section of the Psalms is made up entirely of thanksgiving and praise, from beginning to end. It sounds one triumphant note all the way through, and the closing psalms resound with a shout of "Hallelujah! Praise the Lord!"

Difficulties in the Psalms

Some people have difficulty accepting what they read in certain passages in the Psalms. In addition to the psalms of praise and psalms of comfort, there are also psalms in which David cries out against his enemies or complains about his sufferings. Particularly troubling to many people are those psalms that call down God's wrath upon the enemies of Israel. Such expressions of rage and condemnation, they say, seem inconsistent with the New Testament message that we are to love our enemies.

I think we can understand even these troubling psalms if we remember what the New Testament tells us about the Old Testament. As the apostle Paul tells us, these things were written in the Old Testament for our instruction (1 Corinthians 10:11). The enemies the psalmist faced are the same enemies we face today: "For our struggle is not against flesh and blood, but against the rulers, against the authorities, against the powers of this dark world and against the spiritual forces of evil in the heavenly realms" (Ephesians 6:12).

Sometimes we forget who our real enemy is. We think that the person who opposes our plans or attacks our reputation is our enemy. People may hurt us, but our true enemy is not made of flesh and blood. In reality our struggle is against the evil rulers, powers, and spiritual forces that control this world.

In many cases the worst enemy of all is not without but within. As Jesus said, "What goes into a man's mouth does not make him 'unclean,' but what comes out of his mouth, that is what makes him 'unclean' . . . For out of the heart come evil thoughts, murder, adultery, sexual immorality, theft, false testimony, slander. These are what make a man 'unclean'" (Matthew 15:11, 19–20). In light of Jesus' comments about the potential for evil in the human heart, the severe language we find in parts of the Psalms makes perfect sense. We must deal severely with the evil in our lives. Sin has no place in a Christian's life. The Psalms show us how we must deal with the *real* enemies of our souls: our own sin and the attacks of our ultimate enemy, Satan.

Psalms of Jesus

Though they were written centuries before the birth of Christ, the Psalms are filled with rich insights and instruction regarding the work and character of our Lord Jesus. The gospels tell us that after Jesus was raised from the dead, He appeared to the disciples in

Jerusalem and said to them, "Why are you troubled, and why do doubts rise in your minds? . . . This is what I told you while I was still with you: Everything must be fulfilled that is written about me in the Law of Moses, the Prophets and the Psalms" (Luke 24:38, 44).

There are numerous psalms, called Messianic Psalms, which give us a clear prophetic image of Christ. The Messianic Psalms speak of a number of episodes, circumstances, and crises in the Lord's earthly life. We find these prophetic psalms fulfilled again and again in the New Testament.

Psalm 2 presents Christ as the focal point of all history. In that psalm, God says that every nation, every tribe, every people, and every individual must decide what to do with Christ the Lord: either accept Him and take refuge in Him or reject Him. There is no middle ground.

Psalm 22 records the Lord's anguish as He willingly sacrificed Himself on the cross. This amazing psalm takes you into the depths of the Lord's pain and loneliness with its opening line, "My God, my God, why have you forsaken me?" It goes on to describe the gawking crowd around the foot of the cross and the tormentors who cast lots for His garments. The words are graphic and specific, and there can be no mistake that they clearly prefigure the Messiah's death by crucifixion, even though Roman crucifixion was not invented until centuries later: "They have pierced my hands and my feet. I can count all my bones . . ." (vv. 16–17).

This harrowing, heartbreaking account of the death of the Messiah is quickly followed by the culmination of the Lord's story: the triumph of His resurrection, the glory of His second coming, and the righteousness of His future reign.

Other Messianic Psalms reflect the person of Christ and His coming reign as King over all the earth. Psalm 110, for example, points us to the deity of Christ—the great mystery that He is fully man and fully God. And Psalm 118 describes Him as a stumbling block, rejected by men yet used by God as the cornerstone of His redemptive plan. The following table lists a number of Messianic Psalms and their New Testament fulfillment.

Prophecies of the Messianic Psalms
And Their Fulfillment in the New Testament

PSALM	MESSIANIC PROPHECY	N.T. FULFILLMENT
2:7	God declares Messiah as His Son	Matthew 3:17
8:6	All things placed under His feet	Hebrews 2:8
16:10	The resurrection	Mark 16:6–7
22:1	The Messiah forsaken	Matthew 27:46
22:7-8	The Messiah surrounded by mockers	Luke 23:35
22:16	Messiah's hands and feet pierced on the cross	John 20:25, 27
22:18	Lots cast for His clothes	Matthew 27:35-36
34:20	Messiah's bones unbroken	John 19:32-33, 36
35:11	The Messiah accused by false witnesses	Mark 14:57
35:19	The Messiah hated and persecuted	John 15:25
40:7–8	He comes to do God's will	Hebrews 10:7
41:9	The betrayal of the Messiah by a friend (Judas)	Luke 22:47
45:6	The throne of Messiah is forever	Hebrews 1:8
68:18	The Messiah ascends to God's right hand	Mark 16:19
69:9	His zeal for God's house (cleansing the temple)	John 2:17
69:21	Vinegar and gall upon the cross	Matthew 27:34
109:4	Messiah intercedes for His enemies	Luke 23:34
109:8	The betrayer's function is given to another	Acts 1:20
110:1	His enemies put in subjection to Him	Matthew 22:44
110:4	Messiah is a priest after the order of Melchizedek	Hebrews 5:6
118:22	Rejected stumbling block becomes the cornerstone	Matthew 21:42

The New Testament quotes the Psalms more than any other Old Testament book, and perhaps that is because the Psalms have so much to tell us about Jesus. God gave the Psalms to point us to Jesus and to teach us how to worship Him and experience the fullness and richness of life He brings us.

The Psalms also instruct us in how honestly to offer up the full range of our emotions to God. If you have a problem, don't hide it. Tell God about it. If you are angry with God, tell Him so. If you are happy and glad, express your joy and praise to Him. That's true worship: honestly expressing your heart to God.

As Jesus said to the woman at the well in Samaria, "God is spirit, and his worshipers must worship in spirit and in truth" (John 4:24). God is looking for that kind of worshiper. If you will be honest before God, you will find grace to meet all your needs.

There is a story of a rich old miser who came to Christ late in life. After his conversion, he left his miserly ways and became known throughout the town as a man of uncommon generosity.

One day the rich man heard that his neighbor's house and barn had burned down. The rich man's first thought was, "My neighbor needs food for his family! I'll get a ham from my smokehouse and take it right over!" On the way to the smokehouse, however, the man's miserly old nature whispered to him, "Why give them a whole ham? Half a ham will be plenty." He debated with himself all the way to the smokehouse.

Then the rich man remembered what he had learned in the presence of God. He remembered that having received grace and forgiveness from Jesus Christ, he had resolved to crucify his former self. Suddenly he realized where the temptation to be stingy came from. It was the *tempter* who kept whispering, "Give him half a ham." With that realization, the old man said aloud, "Look Satan, if you don't pipe down, I'll give him the whole smokehouse!"

Where sin abounds, grace abounds much more. Helping us to understand this truth is the purpose of the Psalms: They are God's folk songs of faith, written to comfort us, inspire us, instruct us, and draw us into the sweet, rich depths of His grace.

2

The Psalm of the Righteous

PSALM I

In his poem "The Road Less Traveled," Robert Frost writes that while taking a walk in the woods, he came upon a fork in the road. Standing where the two roads diverged, he saw that the first road was well worn and well traveled while the second was overgrown with grass, covered with leaves, and obviously less traveled than the first. It didn't take him long to decide which way he should go. "I took the one less traveled by," he wrote, "and that has made all the difference."

The poet was not speaking of a literal path through the woods but of the journey through life. We all must make choices in life. If we go to the left, we cannot go to the right. We pick a path and must live with the consequences of our decision. In matters of the spirit and faith, the well-worn, well-traveled, popular path is the one that leads to regret. But the road less traveled leads to life and happiness.

"Wide is the gate and broad is the road that leads to destruction, and many enter through it," said Jesus. "But small is the gate and narrow the road that leads to life, and only a few find it" (Matthew 7:13–14).

Like Robert Frost's poem, Psalm 1 is a poem about two different paths through life—one well traveled and popular, the other less traveled and neglected by the crowds. One road leads to death and regret while the other leads to blessing and life everlasting. One road is the broad, well-traveled path of the wicked while the other road is the narrow, less-traveled way of the righteous.

How to Be Happy and Blessed

Psalm 1 breaks ground for the entire book of Psalms and introduces us to the first section, consisting of Psalms 1 through 41. In the previous chapter, we saw that the first section of the Psalms echoes the theme of Genesis, the book of foundations. It provides us with an introduction to human life, and it reveals the deepest needs of the human heart.

The first psalm is a study in contrasts. It distinguishes between two kinds of people who follow two different paths through life: the *wicked* and the *righteous*. It contrasts the self-centered life with the God-centered life.

When Psalm 1 talks about "the wicked," it is not referring to murderers, thieves, rapists, terrorists, or drug peddlers—the kinds of people we tend to describe as "the wicked." You don't have to be a notorious dictator like Adolf Hitler to be numbered among "the wicked." You don't have to be guilty of a felony to be considered "wicked" by God.

When the psalmist speaks of "the wicked," he simply means the ungodly—those people who have little or no time for God in their lives, who have ruled God out of their affairs and their thinking. They have no heed for the fact that God is the creator of the universe, the One who makes sense out of life. To eliminate God from your thinking and your way of life is to be wicked, to be ungodly.

Psalm 1 is a psalm written by David, and the shepherd-king has given this psalm an elegant artistic form. The beauty of Psalm 1 is its simplicity. The psalm consists of only six verses, and it divides neatly in half. In the first three verses, the psalmist shows us what godly, righteous, God-centered living looks like and the happy results that flow from it. In the last three verses, the psalmist shows us what ungodly, wicked, worldly living looks like and the unhappy results it produces.

First, let's look at what the psalmist tells us about the God-centered life. David writes:

Blessed is the man
who does not walk in the counsel of the wicked
or stand in the way of sinners

or sit in the seat of mockers.
But his delight is in the law of the LORD,
and on his law he meditates day and night.
He is like a tree planted by streams of water,
which yields its fruit in season
and whose leaf does not wither.
Whatever he does prospers (vv. 1–3).

A description of the God-centered life appropriately begins with the word "blessed." "Blessed" is one of those code words that Christians use. It simply means to be happy. So Psalm 1 gives us the secret of happiness!

Do the opening words of Psalm 1 sound familiar to you? You may recall that the Lord Jesus began His great discourse, the Sermon on the Mount, in much the same way—that is, with the word "blessed." Matthew 5 tells us that Jesus went up on the mountainside and began to teach the people, saying, "Blessed are the poor in spirit, for theirs is the kingdom of heaven. Blessed are those who mourn, for they will be comforted. Blessed are the meek, for they will inherit the earth. Blessed are those who hunger and thirst for righteousness, for they will be filled" (vv. 3– 6). And one promise of blessing after another follows. In fact these opening verses of Matthew 5 are known as the Beatitudes, a term that means "the blessings." In the Beatitudes Jesus teaches the secrets of being blessed or happy.

When you read the Beatitudes, you can substitute the word "happy" wherever the word "blessed" appears in Matthew 5. So Jesus is truly giving us the keys to happiness in His Sermon on the Mount: "Happy are the poor in spirit, for theirs is the kingdom of heaven. Happy are those who mourn, for they will be comforted. Happy are the meek, for they will inherit the earth. Happy are those who hunger and thirst for righteousness, for they will be filled."

Similarly the psalmist gives us the keys to true happiness when he tells us, "Blessed [happy] is the man who does not walk in the counsel of the wicked or stand in the way of sinners or sit in the seat of mockers." If we live righteous, God-centered lives, we will be happy and blessed.

Where Do You Walk?

The psalmist uses three key words to symbolize three dimensions of life: "walk," "stand," and "sit." Let's look closely at each of those words, beginning with the word "walk."

When he writes in verse 1, "Blessed is the man who does not *walk* in the counsel of the wicked," he refers to the choices we make each day throughout our lives. Every day, moment by moment, we choose between the world's way and God's way. We choose continually whether we will yield to the temptation to gossip or think hateful thoughts or give in to lust or cheat our neighbor. That is our walk. Will we walk in the counsel of the wicked or in the counsel of God's Word?

In the same verse, the psalmist next comments that we are blessed (happy) if we do not "stand in the way of sinners." The image of standing is a picture of the commitments we make. The wicked stand for the things of the world; the righteous take a stand for God. What do you stand for? Do you stand in the way of God or in the way of sinners?

Then the psalmist observes that we are blessed (happy) if we do not "sit in the seat of mockers." To sit is to be settled in one place. This image refers to having a settled attitude toward God, an attitude of mockery and scorn toward God and His law.

The message of Psalm 1 is that those who have found the secret of happiness can be recognized by the way they "walk," "stand," and "sit." Those who do not walk in the way of the wicked are happy and blessed by God. They have rejected the worldly philosophy of the ungodly. What is that philosophy? It takes a number of easily recognized, self-centered forms: "Me first"; "Get what you want now"; "If it feels good, do it"; "Look out for Number One"; "The end justifies the means"; "Do your thing"; "You have your truth and I have mine"; "All religions lead to the same God"; "God is irrelevant"; and "God is dead."

In their selfishness, the worldlings—those people who live their lives according to the ideologies and "isms" of this dying world— tell themselves and each other that God is either endlessly indulgent and tolerant of their sins or that He is sleeping, dead, or nonexistent. "I can live any way I please," they say, "and nothing bad will happen to me. I am not accountable to God. I answer only to me. I am the master of my fate and the captain of my soul." Isn't that the philosophy of this world? Isn't that the counsel of the ungodly? Isn't that the mindset of the wicked?

Those who know the secret of true happiness have rejected the ideologies and "isms" of this world. They do not make decisions based on self-centered, worldly philosophies, but on the truth of God.

Where Do You Stand? How Do You Sit?

Next, those who know the secret of happiness do not stand in the way of sinners. The Hebrew word that is translated "sinners" is an interesting word. It comes from a root word that means "to make a loud noise" or "to cause a tumult." It conveys a sense of provoking a riot or causing a great disturbance. The psalmist says you can recognize godly people because they do not cause trouble, they don't provoke riots, and they are obedient to the law and civil order.

Those who know the secret of being blessed with happiness are not found in the path where troublemaking sinners are found. They are not found in the company of those who create disturbances. Such people reject the way of sin and trouble; they are on the right side of the law. They are good citizens and good neighbors.

Finally, the person who knows God's secret of happiness does not "sit in the seat of mockers." Other Bible translations render that last word as "scoffers" (NASB) or "the scornful" (KJV). Mockers, scoffers, and scorners are people who ridicule, disdain, and disregard the things of God. They blame God and other people for their own problems and never take responsibility for their own sins and failings.

If we are honest with ourselves, we have to admit that there's at least a touch of the mocker in each of us. We have all been in situations where something went wrong or didn't get done, and our first impulse was to say, "Don't blame me! It wasn't my fault! It was his or her fault!" Or even, "It was God's fault!" Rarely is it our first impulse to shoulder the responsibility; instead, we shift the blame.

Parents blame their children. Children blame their parents. Both blame the schools. The schools blame the politicians. The politicians blame the other party. Nations blame other nations. Everyone blames someone. That is the way of the world. It seems that the seat of power is the seat of the scornful, the scoffer, the cynic, the blamer.

But godly men and women reject that attitude. Those who know the secret of a happy, blessed life are characterized by positive attitudes, words, and behavior. They are selfless in their motivations. Godly people act like cheerleaders, not critics; they cheer others on instead of tearing others down. They respect and obey the law.

When godly people make a mistake, they don't shift the blame. They say, "I take responsibility. It was my fault." That's the kind of godly person the psalmist describes in Psalm 1.

Do you and I meet that description?

The Law of the Lord

In the first verse of Psalm 1, we looked at the issue of godly living from a negative perspective; that is, we looked at what a happy, blessed, godly person is not. "Blessed is the man," writes the psalmist, "who does *not* walk in the counsel of the wicked . . ."

There is a shift of perspective at verse 2. In this verse the psalmist takes the positive view and describes what a godly person is. "But his delight is in the law of the LORD, and on his law he meditates day and night."

Now we begin to see why godly people reject the philosophy of this dying world. It is because they have learned to delight in the law of the Lord. What is the law of the Lord? The psalmist refers here to the Scriptures. He is not merely speaking of the Law of Moses, that is, the Pentateuch, the first five books of the Bible. Rather he refers to the whole revelation of God.

Godly people know that God's Word gives us a completely different view of life than is found in the world. The Bible tells us the truth about life. Godly people delight in the fact that they can meditate in a book that reveals the truth about life and eternity. They know that this book discloses an entirely new way of life, a new philosophy that supersedes the ancient, self-centered philosophy of this world.

More than that the Bible reveals a power by which the godly person can fulfill and live out this new philosophy of life. We cannot live godly lives in our own power. The power to live the godly life is God's own power. It is given to us through faith in the Redeemer whom God has sent.

When Psalm 1 was written, sometime around 1,000 BC, no one knew the name of this Redeemer or when He would come. Today, however, we know that this Redeemer's name is Jesus of Nazareth and that He was crucified on the cross and rose again from the dead. Godly believers who lived before Jesus had to live by the same faith that we do today, faith in the Redeemer who came to die so that we might live. It is His resurrection power that is our strength today and has been the strength of godly men and women down through the ages. God reveals that power to us in His Word, the Bible, which the psalmist calls "the law of the Lord."

When I was pastor of Peninsula Bible Church (PBC), a young man told me how he came to choose our church as his spiritual family. He had committed his life to the Lord during a Billy Graham Crusade in San Francisco. Immediately after that he began looking for a church home. He visited several churches but did not feel at home in any of them. One Sunday morning he attended PBC. I was speaking that Sunday and happened to do something in the course of my sermon that got his attention. First, I read this passage from the New Testament:

> *Do you not know that the wicked will not inherit the kingdom of God? Do not be deceived: Neither the sexually immoral nor idolaters nor adulterers nor male prostitutes nor homosexual offenders nor thieves nor the greedy nor drunkards nor slanderers nor swindlers will inherit the kingdom of God. And that is what some of you were. But you were washed, you were sanctified, you were justified in the name of the Lord Jesus Christ and by the Spirit of our God (1 Corinthians 6:9–11).*

After reading that passage, I said to the congregation, "That's a description of the Christians in Corinth. That's a description of the kinds of lives that the Corinthian believers led before coming to Jesus Christ. Now let me ask you: Are there any here who come from this kind of background? Are there any here who have done the kinds of things that Paul describes? Are there any here who were once sexually immoral, idolaters, adulterers, homosexuals, thieves, greedy, drunkards, slanderers, or swindlers?"

As this young man sat in the congregation that morning, he saw something he had never seen before. One by one, from every part of the sanctuary, people stood to their feet. In fact more than half the congregation was standing. The young man was moved to tears. "These people," he said to himself, "are my kind of people!"

"And that is what some of you were," Paul concluded. "But you were washed, you were sanctified, you were justified in the name of the Lord Jesus Christ and by the Spirit of our God." That is what the godly man or woman discovers in the law of the Lord, the Bible. Godly people have learned that God not only demands perfection from His people but He also provides the means by which perfection is made possible.

No, we can't be perfect by our own effort. But by faith we can receive the perfection of Jesus Christ, which covers our sin and empowers us to live for God. Through the Redeemer whom God has sent, we can receive the power and strength to leave behind our old sinful ways and to live in a new and happy way. We no longer have to walk in the counsel of the wicked or stand in the way of sinners or sit in the seat of mockers. We can live as fruitful trees planted by streams of water.

The Secret of Meditating in God's Word

One of the delights of the Psalms is that through these folk songs of faith, we see that Old Testament saints had to draw upon the power and mercy of God in the same way that we New Testament saints do today. We see throughout the Psalms many expressions of the writer's experience of God's presence through all of the dark and low places of life. Elsewhere in the Psalms, he writes:

> The LORD *is my light and my salvation—*
> *whom shall I fear?*
> The LORD *is the stronghold of my life—*
> *of whom shall I be afraid? (27:1).*

The psalmist repeatedly understands that God's presence is light and hope, a fortress that protects us from fear. How do we experience God's presence? One sure way is by meditating on His Word.

After the death of Moses, Joshua faced the lonely challenge of succeeding him as the leader of the nation of Israel. God spoke to Joshua and told him the secret of experiencing His presence in times of danger and fear. God said,

> *Do not let this Book of the Law depart from your mouth; meditate on it day and night, so that you may be careful to do everything written in it. Then you will be prosperous and successful. Have I not commanded you? Be strong and courageous. Do not be terrified; do not be discouraged, for the* LORD *your God will be with you wherever you go" (Joshua 1:8–9).*

Joshua learned the same lesson the psalmist learned, the same lesson that we discover in psalm after psalm: Meditate in God's Word day and night. This does not mean that we are to mechanically chant Bible verses. Meditating on God's Word is anything but mechanical. It's a vital, exciting experience of dwelling in the rich truths we have learned and of continually exploring and finding new and amazing truths. It means drawing upon God's message for our lives whenever we need wisdom, strength, encouragement, or guidance.

In his book *The Counselor,* A. W. Tozer describes Christians of bygone eras and how they approached God's Word. He wrote:

> They came to the Word of God and meditated. They laid the Bible on the old-fashioned, handmade chair, got down on the old, scrubbed, board floor and meditated on the Word. As they waited, faith mounted. The Spirit and faith illuminated. They had only a Bible with fine print, narrow margins and poor paper, but they knew their Bible better than some of us do with all of our helps.
>
> Let's practice the art of Bible meditation . . . Let us open our Bibles, spread them out on a chair and meditate on the Word of God. It will open itself to us, and the Spirit of God will come and brood over it. I challenge you to meditate, quietly, reverently, prayerfully, for a month. Put away questions and answers and the filling in of the blank lines in the portions you haven't been able to understand. Put all of the cheap trash away and take the Bible, get on your knees, and in faith, say, "Father, here I am. Begin to teach me!"

That is true meditation! That is the secret of the godly life! That is how we learn to become like the psalmist, like the happy, blessed, godly saints of old—selfless, obedient followers of God, confident and cheerful in every circumstance.

A Tree Planted by Streams of Water

Next the psalmist describes in poetic terms what the godly person is like:

He is like a tree planted by streams of water,
which yields its fruit in season
and whose leaf does not wither.
Whatever he does prospers (v. 3).

This verse holds special meaning for me. A short time after I began serving as pastor at PBC, the church held a youth conference at a camp in the Sierra Nevadas. One morning a young man told me he needed to talk, so we went out and stood in the shade of a giant Douglas fir tree.

"Pastor Stedman," he said, looking troubled, "I don't know what's the matter with me. I want to be a good Christian, and I try hard, but I keep failing. Then I feel so guilty. As hard as I try, I just can't live like a Christian."

"Well," I said, "there could be several reasons for that. But first let me ask you: How well do you know the Lord?"

"What do you mean?"

"Do you spend time getting to know Him better? Do you delight in reading His Word? Do you spend time talking to Him in prayer? Do you enjoy His presence?"

He hung his head. "I have to admit, I don't do very much of that."

"Let me tell you, it's not just reading His Word that strengthens you. It's also time spent in His presence, listening for His voice, letting Him touch your heart. That's where we get the strength to live every day as a follower of Christ."

The look on my young friend's face showed that he wasn't convinced, so I quickly asked God for the words to help him understand how to draw on God's strength through prayer and meditation. I looked up to the heavens, and I saw that fir tree towering over me. Then the words of Psalm 1:3 popped into my mind: "He is like a tree planted by streams of water."

I said, "Look at this tree. What does it remind you of? What qualities do you see in this tree?"

"Well," he said, looking up, "it's strong. And it's beautiful."

"Exactly!" I said. "That tree represents strength and beauty. Those are two qualities that we admire about this tree. And aren't those the very qualities you want to see in your own life?"

He nodded. "They sure are."

"Well, tell me this: What makes this tree strong and beautiful? Where do the strength and beauty come from?"

He considered. "From the roots, I guess."

"Can you see the roots?"

"No," he said—then his eyes lit up. "Hey, I get it! That's the hidden part of life: the roots. Yet even though they're hidden, the roots are the secret of the tree's strength and beauty!"

And that is exactly what the psalmist says to us in Psalm 1:3. The person who is godly has learned to draw upon the strength and beauty of God through the inner parts of his or her life. The godly person's roots go deep into the rich, life-giving soil of God's Word and His presence. That person is then like a tree planted by rivers of life-giving water.

What is the godly person's life like? It is fruitful and productive. The godly person's life yields its fruit in season. The fruitfulness the psalmist speaks of probably refers to the fruit of the Spirit, the godly character traits we read about in the New Testament: "But the fruit of the Spirit is love, joy, peace, patience, kindness, goodness, faithfulness, gentleness and self-control. Against such things there is no law" (Galatians 5:22–23). The psalmist adds that the godly person's "leaf does not wither." A godly individual is vital and alive, an exciting person to be around. A person who is truly godly is never dull, dreary, or boring. There is nothing more stimulating than being in continual contact with the living God!

Finally the psalmist says that "whatever [the godly person] does prospers." This person is effective and productive in life because whatever he or she accomplishes is done not in human strength but in the strength of God and His hidden yet infinite resources. That is the godly life. That is the secret of happiness and true blessing.

Those who live truly godly lives are authentically happy people. Their outward circumstances can't shake their faith or diminish their joy because they know that true happiness doesn't consist of an abundance of possessions or worldly pleasures. True happiness is found only in an intimate relationship with our infinite Creator.

The Fate of the Wicked

Next this psalm describes the way of "the wicked," those people who have no time for God and no respect for God's law. Notice how succinctly the psalmist contrasts the wicked and the godly: "Not so the wicked! They are like chaff that the wind blows away" (v. 4).

It took the psalmist two verses to describe the secret of the godly life, but it took only *two words* to describe the life of the ungodly: "Not so!" Here is a statement of stark contrast: "Not so the wicked!" They are not like the godly. The wicked follow the philosophy of this dying world, the counsel of the ungodly. They believe in "me first"; in "Get what you want, and get it now"; in "God is dead"; and "God is irrelevant." The wicked rebel against the laws of God and man, and when they reap the consequences of their rebellion, they blame God, society, and everyone else for their troubles.

The ungodly, writes the psalmist, are like the chaff that the wind blows away. If you are a city dweller, you probably don't know what chaff is. I grew up in Montana, which is wheat country. Every fall the harvesters came around to the various farms with their threshing machines. Threshing is the process of beating the stems and husks of grain plants to separate the valuable grain from the worthless straw. The bundles of wheat stalks would be thrown into the threshing machine. As the machine beat the stalks in its mechanical innards, the straw would be blown out and the wheat would dribble down a chute to be poured into trucks and taken away to the granary.

And what of the chaff? Chaff consists of tiny bits of seed coverings, straw fragments, and dry leaves. It is light and floats on the air. It is a terrible annoyance for anyone who comes in contact with it. It sticks to your sweaty skin. It settles on the back of your neck and gets down inside your shirt. It causes a frightful itching. In every culture around the world and at every point in history, chaff has been regarded as the most worthless stuff imaginable.

Back in David's day, a thousand years before Christ, the only thing farmers could do with chaff was toss it in the air and let the wind blow it away. Today, two thousand years after Christ, that is still the only thing you can do with chaff: Let the wind blow it away.

The wicked, God says, are like chaff. Those who have no room for God are like worthless stubble that blows in the wind. They may be very impressive people by the world's standards. They may be kings and presidents, authors and actors, CEOs and philanthropists—but if they are not on intimate terms with the infinite Creator, they are like chaff. What good are their worldly power, their wealth, and their luxuries if their lives are worthless in the final analysis? They may have their names etched on bronze plaques; they may even have their faces carved on Mount Rushmore. But if they do not know God, then their lives have been wasted. They are, in God's evaluation (The only evaluation that matters!), as worthless as the chaff that the wind drives away. That's why the psalmist adds these fateful words:

> *Therefore the wicked will not stand in the judgment,*
> *nor sinners in the assembly of the righteous.*
> *For the LORD watches over the way of the righteous,*
> *but the way of the wicked will perish (vv. 5–6).*

This is the twofold fate of the wicked: First, they will not stand in the judgment. Second, they have no place in the assembly of the righteous.

What is the judgment that the psalmist speaks of here? This is a reference to the daily judgment of God, the continual evaluation that God makes of our lives. The wicked have no ability to withstand such judgment. Their lives are regarded as worthless in God's judgment. Everything the wicked do is just so much wasted effort.

What is the assembly of the righteous? This is a reference to another judgment, the final judgment at the end of time. When all of God's redeemed people are gathered together, the wicked will be absent. They may have been very religious people, keeping all sorts of religious rules, rites, and traditions. But if they had no relationship with God, then their religion was worthless. Jesus once said,

> *Not everyone who says to me, 'Lord, Lord,' will enter the kingdom of heaven, but only he who does the will of my Father who is in heaven. Many will say to me on that day, 'Lord, Lord, did we not prophesy in your name, and in your name drive out demons and perform many miracles?' Then I will tell them plainly, 'I never knew you. Away from me, you evildoers!' (Matthew 7:21–23).*

Jesus said that many will try to justify themselves on the basis of the religious works they did—amazing and mighty works, even works of prophecy and casting out demons in Jesus' name. Yet Jesus will reply, "I never knew you! Away from me!" There will be very religious people who will not stand in the congregation of the righteous *because they have never put God at the center of their lives.*

Psalm 1 concludes with an explanation for why some people who seem impressively religious on the outside end up as worthless chaff for all eternity: "For the LORD watches over the way of the righteous, but the way of the wicked will perish" (v. 6). God watches over those who cling to Him. He guards them and guides them throughout their lives. But the way of the wicked will perish. Their lives will blow away upon the wind. The lamp of their lives "shall be put out in obscure darkness" (Proverbs 20:20 KJV). Obliteration and obscurity will be their ultimate fate.

This profound biblical principle has been validated many times throughout history, and never more than when the apostle Paul stood as a prisoner before the emperor Nero. Nero was a cruel man, regarded by historians as one of the most vile and evil rulers in human history. He once commanded that the body of his own mother be ripped apart so that he could see the womb that had borne him. He publicly "married" a handsome young man and used him sexually—all against his will.

One day a man came before Nero, an obscure Jew named Paul. This man Paul came from a despised Roman province, and he came as a prisoner in chains. Nero's name was notorious throughout the world; Paul's name was practically unknown. Nero held the power of life and death; Paul was utterly powerless. Paul later wrote to Timothy that when he stood on trial in Rome before Nero, no one stood with him to support him except God alone, who gave him strength (2 Timothy 4:16–17). Though Paul's death is not recorded in the Bible, tradition says he was beheaded by Nero's order in AD 64.

But consider this: Today the words and deeds of Paul continue to affect our lives and impact our society. The life of Nero is scarcely mentioned or remembered. We name our sons Paul; we name our dogs Nero.

Truly the Lord watches over the way of the righteous, but the way of the wicked will perish. That is the promise—and the warning—of Psalm 1. It is the foundational truth that underlies all the rest of the Psalms.

Have you discovered the secret of happiness? Are you cooperating with God in His desire to produce godliness in your life? Will you stand with the assembly of the righteous on the Day of Judgment, or will your life be driven away from God's sight like chaff upon the wind?

God sets before us two paths, and we must choose either the way of the righteous or the way of the wicked. The road to destruction is broad and many enter it, but the narrow road leads to life, blessing, and happiness.

Which way will you choose?

3

A Psalm of Majesty

PSALM 8

In the opening chapter of this book, I called the Psalms "folk songs of faith." Perhaps you thought I used the term "folk song" figuratively, but I meant that quite literally. The Psalms truly are a form of folk music that were composed for singers who would be accompanied by instruments that were much like the guitars that accompany folk music today.

The inscription at the top of Psalm 8 reads, "For the director of music. According to *gittith*." The Hebrew word *gittith* originally referred to a winepress that was used to squeeze the juice from grapes. Later the Hebrews used this same word to refer to a stringed instrument that was shaped like a winepress. The Greeks began using this stringed instrument, but they changed the Hebrew word *gittith* to *kithara*. The Spaniards adopted the *kithara* and called it a *guitarria*; by the time the *guitarria* came to England, it was called a *guitar*.

So the instructions at the beginning of this psalm indicate that singers were to be accompanied by a stringed instrument that is comparable to our modern-day guitar. The Psalms, then, are some of the first folk songs ever written.

The theme of Psalm 8 is easy to find because David states it in the first verse and repeats it in the last verse. Verses 1 and 9 are identical: "O LORD, our Lord, how majestic is your name in all the earth!" (vv. 1, 9).

Most Bible scholars believe that David wrote this psalm early in his adulthood. It seems to reflect his experience as a shepherd boy who had spent many nights alone with his flocks. On those Judean hillsides under the starlit heavens, young David had ample opportunity to observe the glories of God's creation. The psalmist was awed by God's magnitude, but even more by the fact that such a powerful and immense Being would care for these small, finite creatures known as human beings. So awestruck was David that he could only express his feelings in those beautiful words, "How majestic is your name in all the earth!" What a tremendous God! How majestic! How awesome! How excellent is His name in all the earth! Psalm 8 is truly a psalm of majesty.

The Simplicity of a Childlike Heart

How did David come to have such an exalted view of God? The answer unfolds in the next few lines:

> *You have set your glory*
> *above the heavens.*
> *From the lips of children and infants*
> *you have ordained praise*
> *because of your enemies,*
> *to silence the foe and the avenger (vv. 1b–2).*

Here David expresses his amazement that even a child can grasp the transcendent glory of God. We can picture the psalmist struggling to put into words his lofty thoughts about God. He found that all of his rationality, his intelligence, and his learning could not come close to expressing the magnitude of God's glory. Yet this same God, who is glorious and exalted beyond human understanding, had revealed Himself in such marvelous ways that children, babies, and even infants could praise Him. For the ivory-tower intellectual, God might be on the far side of the universe, but for children and infants, God is always near.

This meaning of the passage is affirmed by an incident from the life of Jesus. In Matthew 21:14 Jesus was in the temple in Jerusalem, healing all the blind and lame that came to Him. As He healed, there were children in the temple calling out, "Hosanna to the Son of David!" *Hosanna* means "save us" or "save now" and was a greeting the ancient Hebrews shouted to someone they viewed as a rescuer or liberator. The children were spontaneously praising God because of the healings they saw Jesus doing, and their shouts infuriated the priests and scribes of the temple. So these learned men said, "Jesus, do you hear what these children are saying?"

In reply Jesus quoted the passage from Psalm 8. He said, "Have you never read, 'From the lips of children and infants you have ordained praise'? " (v. 16).

In other words, "These children have grasped the truth that you learned men are too prideful to understand. They know they have seen the healing power of God, so they are shouting in fulfillment of Psalm 8. The glory of God can best be grasped through the simplicity of a childlike heart. To understand the wisdom of God, it is better to have the 'foolishness' of a child than the 'sophistication' of a learned man."

The apostle Paul makes the same point in his first letter to the Christians at Corinth: "But God chose the foolish things of the world to shame the wise; God chose the weak things of the world to shame the strong. He chose the lowly things of this world and the despised things—and the things that are not—to nullify the things that are . . ." (1:27–28).

God has designed life in this way. He has ordained that humble things should expose the barrenness of human pride and that weak things should pull down the strongholds of power. He has ordained that small and simple things should topple mighty towers and strong fortress walls.

God has an amazing ability to convey Himself to the childlike mind. Why? Because children (and childlike adults) are humble. Pride obscures truth. Proud people cannot stand to hear that they are wrong, that there is sin in their life. They sit in judgment over others. If they read God's indictment of their life in the Scriptures, they think, "I'm glad those words don't apply to me! But boy, does my neighbor need to hear this!" Proud individuals are deaf and blind to God's Word; its pages are shut to them.

But if you come to God and His Word as a child comes—humble, curious, teachable, impressionable, willing to inquire and explore God's truth, full of questions instead of knowing all the answers— then God can teach you. Your understanding will be opened wide. Jesus expressed this principle when He prayed to God the Father, "I praise you, Father, Lord of heaven and earth, because you have hidden these things from the wise and learned, and revealed them to little children" (Matthew 11:25).

The psalmist tells us that childlike humility is not only a mark of the greatness of God but it is also a powerful defense against the enemy of our souls. When God speaks through children and the childlike, He thwarts the sophisticated strategies of His ruthless, calculating enemies.

If you have ever read books like J. R. R. Tolkien's *The Lord of the Rings* or C. S. Lewis's *The Lion, The Witch, and the Wardrobe*, then you have seen this principle illustrated in story form. In *The Lord of the Rings*, Tolkien describes how hobbits—short, small, childlike people who live in an isolated corner of the world, forgotten and ignored by the wise and the powerful—become the instruments of the Divine Will that bring down the strongholds of the Dark Lord Sauron and the forces of evil. And Lewis, in *The Lion, The Witch, and the Wardrobe*, tells the story of a family of four children who, by acting in simple childlike obedience to the powerful and loving lion-king Aslan, help to defeat the wicked and powerful White Witch of Narnia.

These fictional stories illustrate real-life truths. Powerful enemies who take pride in their wise strategies and defenses are often sent fleeing by the simple, childlike faith of a humble and seemingly insignificant believer.

From the Lips of a Child

If you were to visit our secular universities today, you would find many atheist professors whose mission in life is to tear down the faith of any believers in their classes. It doesn't matter what the course is; it might be a course in biology or literature or psychology or even religion. Whatever the field of study might be, those professors will find some way to attack God and undermine the faith of their students.

I once heard of a university professor who was lecturing, and again and again in his talk he would state with absolute insistence, "There is no God!" There happened to be a Christian student in the back of the classroom. He was young and earnest in his faith, but he was an intellectually unsophisticated freshman.

Though the professor had a lengthy list of degrees, the student detected a flaw in the professor's intellectual position. So the student raised his hand and said, "Professor, the next time you say, 'There is no God,' would you mind adding, 'as far as I know'? After all, you once told us that no one can prove an absolute negative. So when you say, 'There is no God,' it seems you're violating the rules of logic you've been teaching us."

The professor tried to hem and haw and harrumph his way around the student's objection, but everyone in that classroom saw that the professor had been caught in his own trap. He had violated the very principles he himself had taught, and an intellectually unsophisticated freshman student had pointed it out to him. A prideful intellectual was laid low by a young man with a childlike faith and a child's simple logic.

Some years ago there was a Sunday school teacher who was theologically liberal. Though he didn't believe in a literal God or miracles, he thought it was a good idea for young people to have religious rules to guide their behavior. So as he taught his class of boys, he told them the story of Jesus' feeding the five thousand.

After telling the story, he added, "You know, boys, this isn't really a miracle. Jesus never actually performed miracles. What really took place here was that the crowd was hungry, so a little boy decided to share his lunch with Jesus. He brought his lunch to Jesus, and when the crowd saw the boy's generosity, they realized they should all share their lunches so everybody would have enough. If there was any miracle at all, it was a miracle of sharing."

The Sunday school teacher leaned back, satisfied that he had drawn a positive lesson from the Bible while explaining away the miracle. Then a boy raised his hand. "Sir," he said, "what did they fill the twelve baskets with afterwards?"

The teacher, of course, had no answer!

God often uses children to teach those truths that adults will not face in order to demonstrate His love and wisdom. Human beings continually make the mistake of thinking that a vast education and profound knowledge are required in order to reach God. But God replies, "No. To reach Me, simply come to me in the simplicity of a childlike faith."

Yes, God is in favor of knowledge, for He is a God of truth and knowledge. But the path of knowledge is not the path to God. It is humility, not knowledge, that leads us to true intimacy with our infinite Creator. We find God by listening with the simple humility of a child. That is why Jesus said, "I tell you the truth, unless you change and become like little children, you will never enter the kingdom of heaven" (Matthew 18:3).

Saint Augustine was one of the most revered and respected theologians of church history. Before he converted to Christianity in AD 386, however, he was a young philosophy student in Rome who lived a wild and immoral life. He caroused and partied until all hours of the night. He later wrote in his autobiography that he became sick of his sinful life. Yet even though he wanted to follow God, he felt powerless to do so. A part of him wanted to continue living the old life of sin.

He cast himself down on the ground in the shade of a fig tree and wept aloud, crying out, "How long, how long? Why can't I stop living such an unclean life?" As he lay on the ground weeping over his sins, he heard the voice of a child coming from a neighboring house. The child chanted over and over, "Take up and read! Take up and read!" Augustine paused and listened. What did the chant mean?

He stood up and went to a bench where he had left a scroll of Paul's letter to the Christians at Rome. With the child's chant of "Take up and read!" ringing in his mind, he took up the scroll and read these words from Romans 13:13–14: "Let us behave decently, as in the daytime, not in orgies and drunkenness, not in sexual immorality and debauchery, not in dissension and jealousy. Rather, clothe yourselves with the Lord Jesus Christ, and do not think about how to gratify the desires of the sinful nature."

After reading those verses, Augustine put the scroll down. His doubts and confusion were instantly dispelled, and his heart was filled with the light of clarity and certainty. Augustine committed himself to putting God first, and he never returned to his old ways again.

What an impressive God we have—a God who is able to convey life-changing truth through a simple, humble child!

Do We Matter to God?

Next the psalmist expresses his wonder and amazement over the depth of God's wisdom:

> *When I consider your heavens,*
> *the work of your fingers,*
> *the moon and the stars,*
> *which you have set in place,*
> *what is man that you are mindful of him,*
> *the son of man that you care for him? (vv. 3–4).*

Imagine young David out under the stars at night, watching his sheep. In those days before industrial pollution, the sky would blaze with millions of stars, and the moon would cross the heavens like an orb of pure silver. Looking heavenward night after night, David must have felt an overwhelming awe as he considered the work of God's hands.

Thirty centuries after David wrote these words, we feel the same sense of awe whenever we get away from the lights and smog of the city and see the starry heavens that God has made. Even though human beings have left footprints on the moon, sent robots to Mars, and launched probes beyond the orbit of Pluto, we are no less impressed with God's creation today than David was when he wrote Psalm 8.

Today we have a much greater understanding of our universe than anyone had in David's time. We know, for example, that our own Milky Way galaxy (which contains 100 billion stars) is so vast that it would take a ray of light 150,000 years to traverse its diameter. And our own galaxy is just one of more than 200 billion galaxies in the known universe. How unsearchable is the power that designed, created, and sustains it all! That's the truth that so amazed the author of Psalm 8.

Having contemplated the vastness and complexity of the universe, David confronts the question that the universe evokes: "How could God possibly have any interest in human beings? Aren't tiny, feeble human beings utterly beneath the notice of a God who could create such a universe? What is our purpose? Why do we exist? Do we matter to God?" These ancient questions are still uppermost in the minds of people today.

There are really only two possible answers to the question of human meaning in the universe. One answer comes from God's Word, the Bible. The other comes from rationalist philosophers and materialist science. Rationalists believe that human reason is the only guide to truth; they reject the authority of God's Word. Materialists believe that physical matter is the only reality; they reject the existence of the soul and spirit. Rationalists and materialists look at the world and see nothing but cosmic forces, random chance, and blind evolution. The human race is an accident, and human beings are mere cogs in a mindless cosmic machine.

Philosopher Bertrand Russell expressed this bleak view when he wrote, "Brief and powerless is Man's life; on him and all his race the slow, sure doom falls pitiless and dark. Blind to good and evil, reckless of destruction, omnipotent matter rolls on its relentless way." Or, as Shakespeare put it, "Life is but a tale / Told by an idiot, full of sound and fury, / Signifying nothing." The idea that life is meaningless and human beings are doomed to despair has spread throughout our society like a spiritual plague. The result: rising rates of suicide, drug abuse, alcoholism, and violence throughout our society.

But contrast the despairing view of life with the view we find in God's Word. In verse 4 the psalmist asks, "What is man that God is mindful of him?"—but he doesn't end there. He goes on to answer his own question by revealing God's plan and purpose for the human race as a whole and for each individual human life:

> *You made him a little lower than the heavenly beings*
> *and crowned him with glory and honor.*
> *You made him ruler over the works of your hands;*
> *you put everything under his feet:*
> *all flocks and herds,*
> *and the beasts of the field,*
> *the birds of the air,*
> *and the fish of the sea,*
> *all that swim the paths of the seas (vv. 5–8).*

The psalmist says that God's greatness is revealed by His plan for humanity. This plan involves a twofold relationship: First, humanity has a unique relationship to God. Human beings were created to be a little lower than God. If you are familiar with the King James Version of this passage, you know that it reads, "For thou hast made him a little lower than the angels." The Septuagint, a Greek translation of the Old Testament dating from the third century BC, influenced this translation.

The New International Version renders this phrase, "You made him a little lower than the heavenly beings." God is certainly a "heavenly being," but the phrase is still not specific enough to do justice to the text. The original Hebrew text actually reads, "You made him a little lower than Elohim." What does *Elohim* mean? It is one of the Hebrew names for God, and it is interesting to note that it is a *plural* form of God's name. Why is a plural form used? Some Bible scholars suggest that this is the "plural of majesty," as when a queen would refer to herself in the plural ("We are not amused!"). But I believe that the plural form of God is used here because even in the Old Testament God revealed Himself to be one God in three Persons.

Psalm 8 tells us that God made human beings to be a little lower than Elohim, a little lower than God Himself. We were made in God's image, which means that (at least in our unfallen form) we are a miniature reflection of what God is, what the divine life is like. The invisible God made Himself visible through human beings, which He made to be a little lower than Himself. God's plan was for humanity to be the instrument by which God would do His work in the world; humanity would be the expression of the character and being of God.

Human beings are the creatures that are nearest to God. There is none other nearer, for God designed human beings to be His dwelling place. That is what the Bible reveals to us. Human beings are unique and remarkable because God Himself intends to live in us and shine through us. It's amazing but true: Human beings are the bearers of God.

In Psalm 8 we see why God loves humanity—yes, even *lost* humanity! God sees in every man and woman His own image, that which He created to be the bearer of His glory. That is why every human being is inexpressibly important to God. That is why He is patient with us, not wanting anyone to perish but wanting everyone to come to repentance, as 2 Peter 3:9 tells us. God longs to reach every man, woman, boy, and girl, because each is made and designed for Himself.

The psalmist goes on to say that because of that special relationship between God and humanity, we are designed to be in dominion over all other things. Humanity is to rule the animal creation and all the natural forces in the world.

You made him ruler over the works of your hands;
You put everything under his feet:
all flocks and herds,
and the beasts of the field,
the birds of the air,
and the fish of the sea,
all that swim the paths of the seas" (vv. 6–8).

"Yes," you might say, "that's true, because human beings can assert their will over the animals of the world. We can use our intelligence and our weapons to control the animals and make them obey us." But that's not what David is saying to us. He is describing the relationship God intended for us to have with the animal kingdom—a relationship in which animals would naturally and willingly serve humanity. We catch a glimpse of this relationship whenever we see animals tamed and domesticated. There are animals that willingly submit to human beings and are easily tamed.

This is a small reflection of what David describes in Psalm 8. It is an example of the willingness of the created order to obey humanity. Of course not all of the created order obeys us. We can housebreak a dog and domesticate a cat. But in the New Testament book of Hebrews, the writer notes that there is a breakdown in the created order. The writer quotes this same passage in Psalm 8: "You made him [humanity] a little lower than the angels; you crowned him with glory and honor and put everything under his feet." Then the writer to the Hebrews adds this commentary: "In putting everything under him [humanity], God left nothing that is not subject to him. Yet at present we do not see everything subject to him" (Hebrews 2:7–8).

And that is the reality we see all around us, isn't it? The created order is only partially subjected to us. Humanity has been tragically perverted by the fall. The image of God that was stamped on us at creation has been marred and distorted by sin. We are like cracked mirrors that still reflect the image of God but in a broken and distorted way. Because of the fall, we are no longer good stewards of God's creation. Instead of running the creation, we ruin it. We pollute the air and water. We consume natural resources at a prodigious rate. We destroy the life-giving soil with chemical pollutants. We cause species after species to disappear from the planet, never to return.

Each breath of smoggy air we take convinces us of the truth written by the writer of Hebrews: We do not yet see everything subject to humanity. But the writer of Hebrews didn't stop there. He went on to write: "But we see Jesus, who was made a little lower than the angels, now crowned with glory and honor because he suffered death, so that by the grace of God he might taste death for everyone" (Hebrews 2:9).

Because Jesus suffered death, God has crowned Him with the glory and honor that He had intended for humanity at the beginning. Through Jesus God shows that He still intends to fulfill His original plan for humanity and creation. Follow the life of the Lord Jesus in the gospel accounts. The first thing He does is change water into wine at a wedding feast. Grapevines turn water into grape juice season after season, and yeast converts grape juice into wine on a daily basis, but Jesus short-circuited the processes of nature, changing water into wine in a single instant of time. We are mistaken if we think that Jesus performed that miracle as God. He performed it as a man—in his humanity as God intended humanity to be.

With the command, "Quiet! Be still!" Jesus calmed the winds and the waves. The disciples then looked at one another and said, "Who is this? Even the wind and the waves obey him!" (Mark 4:39–41). They didn't realize that what He had done was accomplished not by His inherent deity but by His perfect humanity indwelt by God.

Jesus said, "Don't you believe that I am in the Father, and that the Father is in me? The words I say to you are not just my own. Rather, it is the Father, living in me, who is doing his work" (John 14:10). When Jesus broke the loaves and fishes and fed the five thousand, He did not do that as God; He did that as a man, as humanity

44

ruling over creation, fulfilling God's intention for the human race. He did not perform any of His many other miracles as God but as a man, representing a perfected and restored humanity.

So the writer of Hebrews says, "But we see Jesus . . ." We see the beginning of God's newly restored and re-created humanity. So we know the answer to the most profound questions asked by the human race: "What is the purpose of life? Why am I here? Why do I go on getting up every morning, working hard, making money— what is it all for?" The answer is that our purpose is to become what God intended us to be from the beginning. We can only fulfill that purpose by becoming part of God's new, restored humanity through faith in Jesus Christ, God's Son.

God is fulfilling His original intention for humanity right now. He is beginning a new humanity by teaching us lessons we could never learn in any other way through the struggles and difficulties of life. He does this in order to prepare us for the day when He will pull aside the curtain of history so that the whole world will suddenly see what He has been working on all along: His new creation, His new humanity.

The apostle Paul wrote, "The creation waits in eager expectation for the sons of God to be revealed" (Romans 8:19). God cannot be defeated by the wickedness and foolishness of humanity. Even though we are destroying the world in which we live, God will not be defeated. The most exciting news of our day is not what we read in *USA Today* or watch on CNN or Fox News. The headlines of today are lining birdcages tomorrow; a week, a year, a decade from now, they are forgotten.

But there are events unfolding behind the scenes of history, right at this very moment, that will affect all of eternity. These exciting events are taking place in your life and mine as God is creating a new humanity in us through the experiences we go through every day. Our pain and problems are transforming us into people who know Jesus Christ, who reflect His character, who are truly the children of God. As Paul writes, "I consider that our present sufferings are not worth comparing with the glory that will be revealed in us" (Romans 8:18). Elsewhere he adds, "For our light and momentary troubles are achieving for us an eternal glory that far outweighs them all" (2 Corinthians 4:17).

You see, there is a purpose to life—if you know Jesus Christ! Apart from Him life is just as bleak and meaningless as Bertrand Russell said. There is no reason to live if you do not know Jesus Christ. But if your life is joined to His, then you are part of a new creation that God is fashioning behind the scenes of your life. One day the glory of your re-created life will be revealed, and the entire universe will sing in a great intergalactic chorus the final verse of this psalm: "O LORD, our Lord, how majestic is your name in all the earth!" (v. 9).

What a magnificent God we serve, a God who could design and create a complex universe that is billions of light-years wide, who chooses to work His will through children and infants, and who is deeply, intimately concerned about each of us. Human sin and human folly cannot thwart His plan. God's beautiful goal of a restored and perfected humanity shall one day come true, and you and I will be a part of it if we make Jesus the Lord of our lives.

4

Two Volumes of Revelation

PSALM 19

Famed agnostic Robert Ingersoll once visited the equally famed minister Henry Ward Beecher. Despite the vast gulf between their views, Ingersoll and Beecher were close friends who occasionally met together over dinner for good-natured debates.

During one particular visit, Ingersoll noticed a beautiful globe on the desk in Beecher's study. It was not a globe of the earth but of the stars and constellations of the heavens. Ingersoll admired the globe and wanted to purchase one. "That globe is exquisite!" he said. "Who made it?"

"Why, nobody made it," Beecher replied. "It just happened."

To this day the debate still rages between those who say that God created the universe and those who say that the universe "just happened." As we continue our study of the Psalms, we come to a passage that deals directly with this age-old controversy. Psalm 19 tells us that we can know with certainty that God created the universe because the knowledge of God has been written for us in two volumes of revelation. There is the revelation of the creation itself, and there is the revelation of God's written Word. Both forms of revelation are essential to understanding God accurately.

Here in the opening words of the psalm, David sets forth the first volume of revelation, the "book" of His creation:

The heavens declare the glory of God;
the skies proclaim the work of his hands.
Day after day they pour forth speech;
night after night they display knowledge.
There is no speech or language

where their voice is not heard.
Their voice goes out into all the earth,
their words to the ends of the world (vv. 1–4).

This is a declaration of God's greatness as displayed in nature. Every night since the beginning of time, the stars have appeared in the night sky, declaring the glory of God. The sun, moon, and stars are like headlines spelling out God's revelation of Himself to the human race. But in recent years, we have learned not only to read the headlines but the fine print as well. Today we not only know about the sun, moon, and stars but we find our amazing Creator revealed in nebulas, galaxies, and black holes. The complex and delicately balanced design of the cosmos speaks resoundingly of God and His wisdom, intelligence, and power.

Only He Who Sees

The rich abundance of this natural revelation is underscored in verse 2 where we read, "Day after day they pour forth speech; night after night they display knowledge."

David tells us that the day pours out information about God, and the night spreads the knowledge of God before us. The truth about God is pouring in upon us at all times from every direction—if we have eyes to see it. When I read this psalm, I'm reminded of the words of Elizabeth Barrett Browning in *Sonnets from the Portuguese*:

Earth's crammed with heaven,
And every common bush afire with God;
But only he who sees, take off his shoes.
The rest sit round it and pluck blackberries.

It takes a seeing eye to perceive what God has said about Himself in nature, but once we begin to see, the truth of God seems to rain down upon us. We have all had this sense of awe in the presence of God's creation. That's why a hush falls upon a group of people who step out under the stars and see them shimmering in their glory. We feel the mystery of the Infinite reaching down to us, calling to our spirits. A silence descends upon us. We know we are in the presence of God and His wonders.

In the same way, we fall silent before the ebb and flow of the sea because we sense the irresistible power of the tides. We glimpse the face of God when we gaze upon the sea. We hear the voice of God in the crashing surf, in the roar of a storm, in a display of lightning and thunder.

Our Lord is the creator and sustainer of the galaxies, stars, and planets. He is the Lord of the mountain heights and the ocean depths. He is the Lord of the pink morning, the white noon, and the blue evening. In verses 3 and 4, David declares the universality of nature's revelation of God:

> *There is no speech or language*
> *where their voice is not heard.*
> *Their voice goes out into all the earth,*
> *their words to the ends of the world.*

All people everywhere have been exposed to this revelation of God in nature. In the book of Acts, we read how the apostle Paul and his traveling companion Barnabas came into a pagan city and were received as gods because they performed a miracle. The people thought these two men were Jupiter and Mercury and began to worship them.

Paul and Barnabas stopped them and said,

> *Men, why are you doing this? We too are only men, human like you. We are bringing you good news, telling you to turn from these worthless things to the living God, who made heaven and earth and sea and everything in them. In the past, he let all nations go their own way. Yet he has not left himself without testimony: He has shown kindness by giving you rain from heaven and crops in their seasons; he provides you with plenty of food and fills your hearts with joy (Acts 14:15–17).*

Paul and Barnabas were speaking of the witness of nature, the testimony of creation to the Designer, Planner, and Creator of all.

Lost, Alone, and Alienated

Next the psalmist uses the sun as a specific illustration of how nature testifies to the wisdom and power of God:

In the heavens he has pitched a tent for the sun,
which is like a bridegroom coming forth from his pavilion,
like a champion rejoicing to run his course.
It rises at one end of the heavens
and makes its circuit to the other;
nothing is hidden from its heat (vv. 4b–6).

To an earth-bound observer, the sun appears to move across the sky. As people see the sun make its transit of the heavens, they are exposed to its testimony, yet many do not receive that testimony. They do not grasp the meaning of the sun as a symbol of God in nature. In many cultures, in fact, human beings have so completely missed the message of nature that instead of worshiping the God whose light and strength are symbolized by the sun, they worship the sun itself!

Why do people worship the sun instead of the One who created it? Because the message of God, as proclaimed through nature, has become obscured and clouded. Human beings look at the universe but do not understand what it says to them. As a result the reality and power of God are displayed throughout the earth and across the heavens, and people go about their business without taking any notice of the message.

This is the great issue at stake in the controversy over creation and evolution. I have no quarrel with scientists who come up with hypotheses to explain how the universe was formed and how life developed. That is what people of science are supposed to do. Darwin's theory of evolution by natural selection is an attempt to explain the abundance and variety of plants and animals in the world based on an interpretation of certain types of evidence.

Where Darwinism goes wrong is when so-called "authorities" use his theory as a wedge to divide God from His creation. "Since evolution explains how life came to be," they say, "we no longer need God as an explanation." Thus God's testimony is silenced. We are told what to think about nature: that the universe is the result of random collisions and chaos and that life is the product of millions of years of mutation, competition, and natural selection. We're told that belief in God is an outmoded, ignorant superstition.

In Romans 1 the apostle Paul tells us that people are exposed to the natural revelation of God through creation, yet they deliberately reject it. Because they reject the truth, God allows certain consequences to take place, which Paul lists for us. One of those consequences is, "Since they did not think it worthwhile to retain the knowledge of God, he gave them over to a depraved mind, to do what ought not to be done" (v. 28). What does Paul mean by "a depraved mind"? He is saying that the thinking of those who reject God becomes distorted and disordered.

All around us we see the results of distorted, depraved thinking. It was depraved thinking that caused our courts to remove prayer, Bible reading, and the Ten Commandments from our public schools. It is depraved thinking that attempts to remove the words "under God" from the Pledge of Allegiance. Anti-God forces have been trying to remove all mention of God from public view in our society and to revise history so as to pretend that God had no role in founding the United States. It's hard to believe, but true; some school textbooks have actually falsified American history by teaching that at the first Thanksgiving observance in 1621, the Pilgrims gave thanks to the native Americans—not to God. These textbooks alter the facts and deliberately leave God out of the picture.

The distorted thinking of depraved minds is also evident in the realm of science and technology. Many of the discoveries and developments of science—from the genetic engineering of "designer babies" to the horrors of nuclear, biological, and chemical weapons—are creating insoluble problems for our society. Because human beings do not want to retain God in their thinking, because there is an unwillingness to acknowledge that God is in the laboratory as well as the sanctuary, God gives people over to a demented, depraved science that produces technological nightmares that may one day destroy us.

That is the judgment of God upon a world that distorts the revelation of nature. God designed His creation to tell us not only how things happened but who is behind them. While it is perfectly proper for a scientist to investigate the realm of nature, it is a tragic error to exclude God from that realm. Behind this universe, behind the mystery of our own existence, are God's own wisdom, intelligence, and power. When we refuse to acknowledge Him, we are left feeling alone and alienated in a dead and mechanistic universe.

The Second Volume of Revelation

Question: What was the first food consumed on the moon? Answer: The bread and wine of Holy Communion.

On Sunday, July 20, 1969, at 3:17 p.m. Eastern Standard Time, astronauts Neil Armstrong and Buzz Aldrin landed on the moon. Aldrin had brought with him a gift from his church: a small silver cup, a vial containing less than an ounce of wine, and a packet of unleavened bread. During a rest period, Aldrin radioed Mission Control in Houston and said, "This is the lunar module pilot speaking. I would like to request a few moments of silence . . . to contemplate for a moment the events of the last few hours." Then he opened the packages and poured the wine.

He later recalled,

> In the one-sixth gravity of the moon, the wine slowly curled and gracefully came up the side of the cup. Then I read the Scripture,
>
> 'I am the vine; you are the branches. Whosoever abides in me will bring forth much fruit.' I ate the tiny wafer of bread and swallowed the wine. I gave thanks for the intelligence and spirit that had brought two young pilots to the Sea of Tranquility. It was interesting for me to think: The very first liquid ever poured on the moon, and the very first food eaten there, were the elements of Holy Communion.

To me, that historic moment symbolizes the joining of the two halves of Psalm 19, the joining of the two volumes of revelation. The book of nature is only volume one. But there is another book, volume two, which answers all the deepest questions of human existence: Why are we here? Who is behind the creation of the universe? What is the meaning of it all? If nature is volume one of the revelation of God, volume two is a deeper, clearer, and more detailed revelation of God: His Word, the Bible.

When Buzz Aldrin landed on the moon and walked upon its airless surface and looked out at the stars that surrounded him, he was reading from volume one; when he read from the Bible those words of Jesus, "I am the vine; you are the branches" (John 15:5), he was reading from volume two.

In the next few verses of Psalm 19, we will see how David brings these two volumes of God's revelation together, answering the great "Why?" and "Who?" questions of human existence: "Why are we here?" and "Who made us?" It is important that we read both volumes, the second as well as the first, because the answers to these deep questions of our existence can only come from the lips of God Himself. So God has given us a Book, and it is to that Book that the psalmist now turns:

> *The law of the* LORD *is perfect,*
>   *reviving the soul.*
> *The statutes of the* LORD *are trustworthy,*
>   *making wise the simple.*
> *The precepts of the* LORD *are right,*
>   *giving joy to the heart.*
> *The commands of the* LORD *are radiant,*
>   *giving light to the eyes.*
> *The fear of the* LORD *is pure,*
>   *enduring forever.*
> *The ordinances of the* LORD *are sure*
>   *and altogether righteous.*
> *They are more precious than gold,*
>   *than much pure gold;*
> *they are sweeter than honey,*
>   *than honey from the comb.*
> *By them is your servant warned;*
>   *in keeping them there is great reward (vv. 7–11).*

Here David describes the resource that God designed for the inner life of human beings. Nature feeds and strengthens our outer life. But the Word of God touches the inner life. Whereas nature is all about "outer space," God's Word conquers the "inner space" of our humanity, the soul and spirit.

The psalmist examines the characteristics of God's revealed Word one by one and shows us what it can do. In verse 7 David tells us, "The law of the LORD is perfect, reviving the soul." What is "the law of the LORD"? That is a broad term used by many Old Testament writers to describe all the written revelation that God has given us.

Why is the law of the Lord perfect? Because it is complete and comprehensive. There is no part of your life and no problem that you will ever face that the Word of God does not adequately address.

Next David writes that the statutes of the Lord, God's Word, are dependable. You can count on the Bible to be a true and reliable guide to life. You don't need a lot of education in other areas if you are a student of God's Word. Even if you are "simple" and unsophisticated in worldly knowledge, the Bible can make you wise.

David's next assertion deals with the precepts of the Lord. There are few things that bring greater joy to the heart than knowing that you have found the truth. God, the source of all reality and truth, gave the Bible to us; when we read the Bible, we read about life as it really is.

Next we read in verse 8, "The commands of the Lord are radiant, giving light to the eyes." The word translated "radiant" can also mean "pure." This passage suggests the image of God's Word as a source of pure radiance that lights the path before us.

Some people have attacked the Bible, claiming that it is a "dirty" book because it sometimes deals with dark and even disgusting subject matter. It speaks candidly about adultery, fornication, incest, homosexuality, bestiality, murder, human sacrifice, and the slaughter of infants. Some have even charged that the Bible is immoral and have tried to ban it or burn it on that basis.

But there is a great difference between the Bible and truly immoral and obscene literature: The Bible never depicts the dark side of life without shining a pure and radiant light upon it. The Bible never portrays evil as if it were good, as immoral literature does. It never makes sin look attractive, as obscene books do. It is a realistic Book that portrays sin as it really is: sordid, shameful, and destructive to sinners and to those around them.

More Precious Than Gold

David next considers what it means to fear the Lord. The word *fear* is sometimes misinterpreted, as if God expects us to cower in terror from some dreadful Being who might strike us dead at any moment. That is not what "the fear of the LORD" means. This kind of fear is a solemn respect for God. This respectful fear of the Lord is pure, says the psalmist, and it will keep you pure as well. It endures forever. Once you enter into the fear of the Lord in its rightful sense, you find that this produces a quality of life that keeps you from defiling yourself.

Finally David sums up everything he has said about God's Word:

> *The ordinances of the LORD are sure and altogether righteous.*
> *They are more precious than gold, than much pure gold;*
> *they are sweeter than honey, than honey from the comb.*
> *By them is your servant warned;*
> *in keeping them there is great reward.*

The thoughts and words of God, as expressed in His ordinances, are enriching and wealth producing, more desirable than gold; they are sweeter than the drippings of the honeycomb. If we, God's people, will keep His ordinances, we will experience a lifetime of great rewards.

You might say, "I read my Bible, but I don't find all of these riches and rewards that are supposed to be there!" Do you know why? Look again at what David has been saying in this psalm: "The law *of the* LORD; the statutes *of the* LORD; the precepts *of the* LORD; the commands *of the* LORD; the fear *of the* LORD; the ordinances *of the* LORD" (emphasis added).

"Of the LORD" is the most important phrase in this passage. The laws, statutes, and precepts should *not* be viewed as a good luck charm: "If you keep God's law, you'll have good luck!" That is not what David is saying at all. He is saying that the law, statutes, precepts, commands, fear, and ordinance of the Lord are the channels that point us to the Lord. Through these channels we find the Lord and know the Lord, and it is the Lord Himself who does all of these wonderful things in our lives. It is the Lord who forgives, revives, cleanses, and enlightens us so that we can know Him personally and rejoice in Him.

The Cure for Hidden Faults

But there is something that can interfere with the process of reading God's Word. David asks: "Who can discern his errors? Forgive my hidden faults" (v. 12).

If you cannot read God's book of nature or His book of the Word, it is not because there is anything wrong with either volume. The error is within the reader, not the book. David asks, "Who can discern his errors?" And that is the crucial question. Aren't we are all victims of our own errors and hidden faults and failures? We can't see our own errors, yet our flawed thinking constantly affects the way we interpret reality. If our thinking is distorted, we will misunderstand much of what we read in God's Word. That is why we desperately need to be delivered from hidden errors. As the apostle Peter writes in his first book: "Therefore, rid yourselves of all malice and all deceit, hypocrisy, envy, and slander of every kind. Like newborn babies, crave pure spiritual milk, so that by it you may grow up in your salvation (2:1–2).

The sin in our lives hinders our desire for the Word. These sins can be hidden errors and faults that cause distortion and misunderstanding when we read God's Word. So in Psalm 19, David addresses the fact that something is wrong within us, and he concludes with a prayer that should be on your lips and mine:

> *Keep your servant also from willful sins;*
> *may they not rule over me.*
> *Then will I be blameless,*
> *innocent of great transgression (v. 13).*

Is that your prayer? If so, what do you think God will do in response? You might think that God will take a sponge and cleanse those inner corners of your life where your faults hide from view. But no, God doesn't do that. His way of dealing with hidden faults is much more uncomfortable than that. He might send someone into your life to point your faults out to you. He might bring about some circumstance in your life that will expose your faults so that you can see how truly ugly and hurtful they are.

Having our errors and faults corrected is an unpleasant experience. It's often painful, and it can be embarrassing. God has to open up the secret places in our lives, and He often must use other people to reflect back to us the way we really are because we cannot see ourselves clearly. Other people can, but we cannot. Our faults are hidden from us but not from others.

Think about it. You know that there are people you can name who have faults that you can clearly see. You look at them and think,

"How can they be so blind?" Well, guess what? Someone is thinking the very same way about you! We do not see ourselves clearly.

So when you pray, "Lord, cleanse me from my hidden faults, and keep me from willful sins," expect God to act in unexpected ways. Expect to be uncomfortable and embarrassed when your faults are exposed. But afterwards, when you see how God has answered your prayer, you'll know the joy that comes from being cleansed and perfected for His service.

The cure for hidden faults and willful sin is dependence upon God's active presence in our lives. "Everything that does not come from faith is sin," wrote the apostle Paul (Romans 14:23). Everything we do in our own self-confidence is sin. Everything we do in our own strength and wisdom is sin. So we must go to God and say, "Lord, I can't live a holy life in my own power. I can't serve you in my own power. I can't become what you want me to be in my own power. Come live Your life through me." Then and only then can we truly live in dependence on God.

"Lord, Show Me Your Secrets"

David closes with these often-quoted words, which are such a powerful and penetrating prayer:

> *May the words of my mouth and the meditation of my heart*
> *be pleasing in your sight,*
> *O LORD, my Rock and my Redeemer (v. 14).*

In other words, "Let everything I say and everything I think be acceptable to God. May all my thoughts and conversations reflect the light and love of God. May my heart be so pure and righteous before God that no sinful thought would dare to dwell in it and no sinful word escape it." When we pray that kind of prayer before exploring nature's wonders (volume one) or the wonders of the Bible (volume two), then we will find that God is able to speak to us in a clear and powerful way.

George Washington Carver was a brilliant African-American chemist, botanist, former slave, and a sincere, humble Christian. As a scientist he went to God and prayerfully said, "Lord, there are so many secrets in the universe. Please open them up to me." He sensed

God telling him, "George, the universe is too big for you. I want you to start with a peanut."

So George Washington Carver investigated the mysteries of the peanut. He discovered over 325 new uses and products that could be made from peanuts, plus additional uses and products derived from sweet potatoes, soybeans, and pecans. His discoveries revolutionized the technology and economy of the South, and he was a tremendous benefactor to all humanity. George Washington Carver's rich legacy began where yours and mine must begin—with a humble prayer to God: "Lord, please show me your secrets."

When we ask God to make our thoughts and words acceptable in His sight, then we can become a source of blessing to everyone around us. We will begin to see nature as it is. We will begin to understand what God's Word truly says to us, and God can lead us into His truth. We can trust the Word of our Lord, our Redeemer, for He is the Rock we stand upon.

5

The Warrior's Psalm

PSALM 20

Throughout history war has always been a rich (though tragic) source of folk music. One such song is the tune called "Shule Agra," which came from the so-called Glorious Revolution of 1688, an uprising against England's King James II. Some ninety years later, heartsick wives and sweethearts on both sides of the American Revolutionary War still remembered and sang that song, but by then the song had been given new words:

Here I sit on Buttermilk Hill
Who could blame me, cry my fill,
Every tear would turn a mill,
Johnny's gone for a soldier.

I sold my flax, I sold my wheel,
To buy my love a sword of steel,
So it in battle he may wield,
Johnny's gone for a soldier.

Now as we come to Psalm 20, we discover an ancient folk song of war, a song that the people of Israel sang when the king went forth to battle. This psalm is a prayer for the king's safety and for victory over the enemy. It is an expression of faith in the power of God to give the armies of Israel victory over the foe. It is a folk song of faith for times of battle.

Psalm 20 falls into three natural divisions: Verses 1 through 5 record the prayer of the people of Israel for their king. In verses 6 through 8, we read the king's response. Then in verse 9, there is a shout of benediction from the people. Let's take a closer look at the themes of each of these divisions of Psalm 20.

Protected by the God of Jacob

The apostle John, in the book of Revelation, tells us that our Lord Jesus "has made us to be a kingdom and priests to serve his God and Father" (1:6). And the apostle Peter tells that we are "a chosen people, a royal priesthood" (1 Peter 2:9). We are kings and priests— a royal priesthood. To be royal is to reign, to be kingly, noble, and majestic. And to be a priesthood is to have access to our Holy God so that we can offer to Him sacrifices of service, worship, praise, and thanksgiving.

The Bible tells us that we believers are kings and priests. So when we read in the Old Testament about kings and priests of old, we are justified in applying the lessons of those stories and psalms to ourselves. God gave those passages of Scripture to us to teach us how kings and priests ought to behave. They instruct us and prepare us for the spiritual battles that we face every day as followers of Jesus Christ.

The first five verses of Psalm 20 consist of a prayer of the people of Israel for their king as he goes to war. The psalmist writes: "May the LORD answer you when you are in distress" (v. 1a).

Right from the start, we see that to be a king is to face trouble. Every kingdom has enemies, and sooner or later those enemies will wage war. It is not easy to fight battles whether in the physical realm or the spiritual realm. The battles that you and I face are fraught with peril. As kings and priests of God, we know that days of trouble and distress lie ahead for us. We cannot escape our trials. We can only face them in God's strength with His sword in our fists as we fight our way through them.

How can we fight our way to victory in the battles we face? David the king—himself a man of battle—gives us the answer in the next line: "May the name of the God of Jacob protect you" (v. 1b).

There is only one refuge for our souls in the day of distress, and that refuge is the name of the God of Jacob. Only God is adequate for every situation. Only He can tell what dangers lay ahead. Only He has the wisdom and foresight to steer a course through all of life's battles. If you are not resting upon the God of Jacob, you will never survive the battle.

Why does David refer to God as "the God of Jacob"? I'm glad he chose that title. There are two men in the Bible who have always encouraged me because God greatly used them despite their serious character flaws. In the New Testament that man is Peter, with his tendency of speaking rashly and impulsively without prayerfully choosing his words.

In the Old Testament the man who most encourages me is Jacob—Jacob the manipulator, the schemer, the big-time operator. He deceived his dying father and tricked his brother in order to obtain a blessing. He wanted to be blessed by his father and by God, yet he thought that trickery was the way to obtain that blessing. God had to teach Jacob one painful lesson after another in order for Jacob to see that the pathway to blessing was one of trusting and worshiping God—not trickery and deceit.

Hebrews 11 tells us, "By faith Jacob, when he was dying, blessed each of Joseph's sons, and worshiped as he leaned on the top of his staff" (v. 21). The staff symbolized the record of Jacob's entire life. At the end of his life, looking back over all that God had brought him through and taught him, Jacob acknowledged God and worshiped Him with his dying breath. Jacob had learned that all of his schemes were for nothing. To receive God's blessing, Jacob needed do nothing more than worship God and wait on Him to act. That's why God is called "the God of Jacob."

What do you and I do when we face a day of distress and trouble? We panic! Like Jacob we try to manipulate events so that we can come out on top. But our refuge does not lie in schemes and plans. The God of Jacob is our only refuge.

Help from the Sanctuary, Support from Zion

How does God's help come to us? Look at the next verse: "May he send you help from the sanctuary and grant you support from Zion" (v. 2).

Notice that phrase, "help from the sanctuary." In the Old Testament the sanctuary is always a picture of the place where we meet with God. In Israel it was the temple, the place where the Israelites came to get their thoughts straightened out, to get their attitude toward life corrected. There they met with God, heard the Word of God, and learned the thoughts of God.

In Psalm 73 we get a glimpse of how entering the sanctuary of God changes our perspective on life. In that psalm the writer Asaph is deeply troubled because the wicked seem to prosper and the righteous seem to suffer. "I envied the arrogant," he writes, "when I saw the prosperity of the wicked" (v. 3). He goes on at length to describe the life of ease and abundance that the wicked seem to enjoy.

But then at verses 16 and 17, we see a sudden shift in the psalmist's attitude:

When I tried to understand all this,
it was oppressive to me
till I entered the sanctuary of God;
then I understood their final destiny (73:16–17).

What caused Asaph's change of attitude? He entered the sanctuary of God. Upon entering the presence of the Lord, Asaph began to see the wicked person's life from God's perspective. He understood the final destiny of those who reject God. Yes, they may seem to prosper for a time, but God knows the end of their story. When we enter the sanctuary of God, we gain God's view of life; our thoughts are illuminated and attitudes are corrected. We see the world as it truly is.

If you have spent many years at all on this planet, one thing you have certainly learned by now is that life is rarely as it seems to be. We are surrounded on all sides by illusion and delusion. Just when we think we understand what is going on around us, we find that we have been deceived. Only God sees reality as it is. So if we want to understand what life is truly all about, we must enter His sanctuary and learn to see reality from His eternal perspective.

What is this sanctuary the psalmist speaks of? Is it a church building made of stone and stained glass? No, a building is just a building. God's sanctuary is a storehouse of truth where our eyes are enlightened and our minds gain understanding. In other words the sanctuary of God is the Bible. It is there, in the sanctuary of God's Word, that we find help. That is the provision the God of Jacob has made so that He can come to you and help you. "May he send you help from the sanctuary," says the psalmist, and the sanctuary he speaks of is found in the pages of God's Word.

It amazes me how many Christians fail to enter the sanctuary of the Scriptures when they find themselves in trouble. If your tooth aches, you call the dentist; if your water pipes break, you call the plumber; if you are slapped with a lawsuit, you call a lawyer. Yet when you experience problems and pain in your soul or spirit, when you are sick with shame or guilt, when your sleep is robbed by anxiety or fear, what do you do? If you are like most people, you leave your Bible unopened, its promises unread and unclaimed. Why?

Our twenty-sixth president, Woodrow Wilson, was a man of great wisdom and faith. He led our nation through the difficult years of World War I and introduced the idea of the League of Nations, the forerunner of today's United Nations. He once said,

> I am sorry for men who do not read the Bible every day. I wonder why they deprive themselves of the strength and of the pleasure. It is one of the most singular books in the world, for every time you open it, some old text that you have read a score of times suddenly beams with new meaning. There is no other book that yields its meaning so personally, that seems to fit itself so intimately to the very spirit that is seeking its guidance.

The psalmist not only promises that the believer can receive help from the sanctuary but also "support from Zion." Zion is another name for the kingdom of Israel. In the Scriptures Zion symbolizes the invisible kingdom of God that surrounds us. This invisible Zion is made up of ministering angels who are sent forth to support the heirs of salvation. In other words, all the invisible help that God can give you in the day of trouble is made available by prayer.

Jesus suffered tremendous agony in the garden of Gethsemane. He prayed and great drops of blood fell from his brow. At that point an angel appeared and strengthened Him. That was an angel from the invisible realm of Zion, made visible to Him in order that we might be taught a lesson of what happens when we pray.

I have never seen an angel, but I know that I have experienced the ministry of angels. I have gone into prayer depressed, downcast, discouraged, and defeated, but while I have prayed, I have felt my spirits caught up and strengthened. I have received help from Zion, from the invisible kingdom of angels waiting to minister to those who are going through a time of trouble.

The Great Sacrifice

In verse 3 the psalmist reveals the basis of God's guarantee of help from the sanctuary and support from Zion: "May he remember all your sacrifices and accept your burnt offerings. *Selah.*"

The offerings of Israel were the meal offerings, the cereal offerings, and the sacrifices of bulls, goats, lambs, calves, pigeons, and other animals. These sacrifices, of course, were symbolic pictures of the coming work of the Lord Jesus Christ upon the cross. He is the Great Sacrifice, and these offerings foreshadowed His sacrificial death, which took place a thousand years after these words were written. The sacrifice of Christ is the basis on which God answers our prayers and sends us help and support.

How do you know that God will help you in the reading of Scripture and in prayer? Because of the sacrifice of the Son of God. He has given Himself upon the cross to remove all barriers between God's love and us. In the sacrifice of the Lord Jesus, our sins and guilt have been completely removed. Now as we confess our sin and receive God's forgiveness and grace, He can pour His blessing out upon us without restraint, no matter what we have done.

Notice that the psalmist adds a special Hebrew word at the end of this verse: *Selah.* That word means, "Stop and think." The psalmist is saying, "Pause for a moment and reflect on what this means." The apostle Paul puts it beautifully in Romans 8:32: "He who did not spare his own Son, but gave him up for us all—how will he not also, along with him, graciously give us all things?" Isn't that an amazing truth to reflect upon? God did not spare His own Son but sacrificed Him for us, and if God would give us the gift of His Son, He will surely give us every other good gift! That is what God makes available to us when we pray in Jesus' name.

Please understand that "in Jesus' name" is not a little magic formula you tack on at the end of a prayer to make it work. "In Jesus' name" means that you are praying on the basis of His sacrifice. You are resting on the finished work of Christ, and that is why you expect God to answer your prayers. And that is why the psalmist writes, "May he remember all your sacrifices and accept your burnt offerings." Those sacrifices and offerings are symbols of the great sacrifice that Jesus made on our behalf upon the cross of Calvary.

Character Displayed in a Crisis

In verse 4 the psalmist reveals the extent to which this help is available to us as we face the battles of life: "May he give you the desire of your heart and make all your plans succeed."

When our hearts have been thoroughly cleansed by the Word of God and by prayer, then what is left in our hearts is what God wants for us. Every genuine believer in Jesus Christ wants what God wants. We want His will to be done. What do we want? What is the deepest desire of your heart? Many superficial answers come to mind: a new car, a new house, a bank account overflowing with money. But after a moment's reflection, you realize that these "wants" are not really your deepest desire. What you truly desire is to be a joyful, whole human being. You want to be confident, courageous, full of faith and love, ready to do God's will, able to face any situation, even the battles of life.

Isn't that what we truly want? That is our heart's desire! And the good news of Psalm 20 is that God has promised to grant you the desire of your heart. He has promised to fulfill your God-inspired plans. He has promised to give you victory in the battles you face.

What are your plans? They are the ways by which you achieve your heart's desire. They are the day-to-day choices you make in life. The psalmist is not writing here of the snap decisions we make in times of pressure and crisis; rather he is writing of the strategic plans we make as we live out our lives.

It has been said that character is not *made* in a crisis; it is *displayed* there. That is true. We build our character in the decisions we make, day in and day out, moment by moment. Then when the times of crisis come, we act according to the character pattern we have been building over the years. If we have been building a character of obedience, faith, and godly wisdom, we will respond in a Christlike way in the time of crisis; if we have been building a character of selfishness and foolish self-reliance, the character we have made will crumble in the heat of crisis.

It is important that we align our hearts with the heart of God so that we will desire what He desires for our lives. Then we will commit ourselves anew to the Lord, day by day, moment by moment. Our plans will be God's plans. Our deepest desire will be God's own desire for our lives. God will grant our desire by fulfilling our plans, by giving us the grace to present ourselves to Him daily. Then He will make our plans succeed.

In verse 5 the psalmist reminds us that with victory in battle comes rejoicing: "We will shout for joy when you are victorious and will lift up our banners in the name of our God. May the LORD grant all your requests."

The psalmist portrays for us a great gathering of victorious believers. Victory is never a solitary accomplishment. We do not win victories by ourselves. You might think you do, but you don't. Others have had a part in it. They have entered into the battle with you, standing at your side, guarding your back, wading into the fray, mingling their own blood, sweat, and tears with yours. They have earned the right to share in the joy of victory.

So when you experience victory in your life, share it with other believers. Share it with those who have supported and encouraged you. Share it with those who have prayed for you. Rejoice with them and let them enter into your joy. Raise up a banner together in God's name.

A celebration of victory! That is what a church meeting should be. That is what a home Bible study should be. That is what we should experience whenever two or more believers are gathered in the name of Jesus Christ. We have gained a great victory through Him, and we are experiencing more and more victories on a daily basis. Yes, there are setbacks and trials, and we must support each other through those times. But we should also share those times of rejoicing when God leads us triumphantly through the battles of life and awards us the victory.

Victory in Life, Victory in Death

Verses 6 through 8 give the king's response to what the people have prayed in the opening verses. The king makes a statement that is confident and full of faith:

Now I know that the LORD saves his anointed;
he answers him from his holy heaven
with the saving power of his right hand.
Some trust in chariots and some in horses,
but we trust in the name of the LORD our God.
They are brought to their knees and fall,
but we rise up and stand firm.

Notice that the king has not even gone to battle, yet he is declaring with confidence what is going to happen! That's the mark of a Christian. My definition of a Christian is "a person who is completely fearless, continually cheerful—and constantly in trouble."

In this passage the king refers to himself as the "anointed" of the Lord; in ancient Israel, kings were always anointed when they ascended to the throne. Anointing the king's head with oil was a sign of consecration and sanctification for his office as ruler of the people. The Hebrew word for "anointed" in verse 6 is the same word that is translated "messiah." Since the New Testament tells us that we, as followers of Christ, are kings and priests of God, we should also see ourselves as God's anointed. In other words, we are, in a very real and biblical sense, God's "messiahs" in the world today.

Do these words shock you? Do they seem to verge on arrogance and even blasphemy? Obviously we are not "messiahs" in the same sense that Jesus, the Son of God, is *the* Messiah, but we are God's anointed in the world today. We are His kings and priests, fighting the battles of spiritual warfare in the world today. We are in the world representing Jesus Christ.

In these verses the king, the anointed one of God, declares that he is not afraid because he has not placed his trust in earthly armament and weaponry, such as chariots and horses. He puts his trust solely in the name of the Lord God. That is where our hope, confidence, and trust lie as well.

Does this mean that God will always deliver us from enemies, pain, tragedy, or death? No, clearly not. What is victory from God's perspective does not always look like victory from a human perspective. Those who were martyred for their faith have won some of the greatest victories for God.

I never tire of reading the wonderful words the apostle Paul wrote to his friends in Philippi from a prison in Rome. He was scheduled to appear before the cruel emperor Nero, who would sentence him to death. Yet this is what Paul wrote:

> For I know that through your prayers and the help given by the Spirit of Jesus Christ, what has happened to me will turn out for my deliverance. I eagerly expect and hope that I will in no way be ashamed, but will have sufficient courage so that now as always Christ will be exalted in my body, whether by life or by death (Philippians 1:19–20).

Read those last few words again: "whether by life or by death." Paul was confident that God would give him the victory, whether he *lived* victoriously or *died* victoriously. Paul is expressing his supreme assurance that God is in control of all of our circumstances and that He will be honored and glorified no matter what happens in our lives. That is a wonderful outlook for an anointed priest and king of God to have.

In the motion picture *The Return of the King*, based on the book from J. R. R. Tolkien's *Lord of the Rings* trilogy, there is a scene that takes place after a terrible battle. The soldiers of the kingdom of Rohan have won the battle, but many brave men of Rohan have fallen on the battlefield. The ruler of the land, King Theoden, stands before his army in a great hall and raises his cup. "Tonight," he says, "we remember those who gave their blood to defend this country. Hail the victorious dead!"

That is the attitude of the apostle Paul. Those who fight bravely, even though they fall in battle, are the victorious dead—victors in Christ. The Lord Jesus Christ will be magnified in the bodies of His followers, whether by life or by death. Those who live will rejoice together. Those who die a martyr's death will be remembered as the victorious dead. In *The Saint's Call to Arms*, the seventeenth-century believer William Gurnall wrote:

> As part of Christ's army, you march in the ranks of gallant spirits. Every one of your fellow soldiers is the child of a King. Some, like you, are in the midst of the battle, besieged on every side by affliction and temptation. Others, after many assaults,

repulses, and rallyings of their faith, are already standing upon the wall of heaven as conquerors. From there they look down and urge you, their comrades on earth, to march up the hill after them. This is their cry: "Fight to the death and the City is your own, as now it is ours! For the waging of a few days' conflict, you will be rewarded with heaven's glory."

That is the confident, victorious attitude of the psalmist and of the apostle Paul. Those believers who have died are the victorious dead who have already marched up the hill and now line the walls of heaven, cheering us on. Those believers who still live are conquerors and comrades, battling their way into the City, fighting the good fight of faith in the name of Jesus the Lord. Living or dead, we are all conquerors in Christ. That is our confidence. That is our joy.

Like the king in Psalm 20, we place no confidence in weapons or armaments, in chariots or horses. Our confidence is in God alone. There is nothing wrong with chariots or horses; when warriors go to war, they need to be properly fitted for battle. But if chariots and horses (or missiles and tanks) are your sole source of confidence, you will not stand a chance. You dare not go to war unless the Lord of Glory is behind you.

As you face the battles of your life, do not put your confidence in your education, wealth, family name, position in the community, church connections, reputation, skills, talents, or personality. When the chips are down, your confidence must be in the Lord. He alone brings you the victory.

The Shout of Triumph

Finally we have a triumphant shout of benediction, which the people offer to God for their king: "O LORD, save the king! Answer us when we call!" (v. 9).

Here the people call upon God to save and protect their king in battle. In the words "Answer us when we call," the people imply that they will continue to pray for their king.

In a broader sense, this is the prayer that we as Christians pray for one another. We ask God to protect our fellow Christians in their battles and their struggle against the enemy, and we promise to continue in prayer for one another. As we pray for one another, God will continue to supply us with everything we need to fight our way through the perils ahead.

We don't know what battles we face in the days ahead, but God knows. As the psalmist promises us in this "Warrior's Psalm," the God of Jacob will answer us in the day of distress. He will protect us and send us support from the invisible realm of Zion. He will grant us the victory over our enemies, both in life and in death. And we will shout for joy and raise our banners high, because the Lord of Glory is with us.

6

The Psalm of the Cross

PSALM 22

On November 22, 1963, President John F. Kennedy was assassinated in Dallas, Texas. This is a matter of historical fact.

Now suppose there was a document that predicted this event, and we knew it had been written a thousand years earlier, in AD 963. That was about the time of the Byzantine Empire, when Constantinople ruled most of the Western world and barbarian tribes inhabited much of Europe. America would not be discovered for another five hundred years.

Suppose that this document predicted that a man would come into prominence as the head of a great nation, that he would be riding in a metal chariot not drawn by horses, and that he would be violently murdered by a lead pellet fired from a rod-shaped weapon made of wood and iron, aimed from the window of a tall building. Suppose that this document also predicted that the news of the man's death would be instantly carried around the world, and millions would mourn him.

Such a document would be viewed with awe and wonder today. Why? Because it would have made a startlingly detailed prediction of President Kennedy's death fully a thousand years before the invention of the automobile or firearms or the instantaneous communication media of the mid-twentieth century. The prediction would be regarded as fantastically accurate, so accurate that it would be absurd to dismiss the prediction as a mere coincidence. Clearly such a prediction could not be made except through supernatural means.

That is exactly the kind of prediction we find in Psalm 22.

Forsaken and Despised

Psalm 22 is an amazing psalm in its prophetic accuracy. It gives a picture of the crucifixion and resurrection of the Lord Jesus, as portrayed by David the psalmist. Written one thousand years before Jesus Christ was born, it is one of the most precise and accurate predictions ever penned. At least nine specific aspects of the crucifixion are described here in precise detail. All were fulfilled during the six hours in which Jesus hung upon the cross, from nine o'clock in the morning until three o'clock in the afternoon. It is important to remember that Psalm 22 not only describes the agonies of the cross in exacting detail but does so *more than five centuries before Roman crucifixion was even invented*!

Moreover, the latter part of Psalm 22 clearly depicts Jesus' resurrection from the dead. The probability that the predictions of these nine events would be fulfilled by chance in one person, on one afternoon, is inconceivably small. The chance that all this could occur by accident is beyond the remotest possibility.

Psalm 22 falls into two major divisions: In part one, verses 1 through 21 recount the experience of an unknown Sufferer who is alone and crying out to God in agony. These first twenty-one verses represent the stream of thoughts and emotions that went through the Savior's mind as He hung upon the cross.

The second division, verses 22 to 31, provides a different view of this same individual. We see Him no longer alone but in the midst of a large company. His suffering is over, and He is praising God and shouting in victory. The psalm ends with this individual claiming the worship of the entire world.

The simplest way to approach this psalm is simply to read it through, making observations as we go. The conclusions to be drawn from Psalm 22 are so clear and unmistakable that they hardly require comment.

> *My God, my God, why have you forsaken me?*
> *Why are you so far from saving me,*
> *so far from the words of my groaning?*
> *O my God, I cry out by day, but you do not answer,*
> *by night, and am not silent (vv. 1–2).*

The psalm begins strikingly with the words Jesus uttered from the cross: "My God, my God, why have you forsaken me?" The rest of the opening words add what has come to be called "the cry of dereliction"—the desolate cry of abandonment as the Sufferer becomes aware that His God has forsaken Him.

In the gospel account, Jesus uttered these words at the end of a strange period of noonday darkness that settled upon the land. For the first three hours as He hung upon the cross, the sun had shone brightly. But at high noon, a strange and frightening gloom settled over the landscape. No one has ever explained that darkness, which lasted for three hours. It was not an eclipse of the sun because the totality (completely dark phase) of a solar eclipse never lasts more than about seven-and-a-half minutes.

There have been similar periods of darkness in recorded history. For example, on May 19, 1780, a strange darkness settled across central New England, beginning at around ten in the morning. The event was reported in a dozen newspapers across Massachusetts, New Hampshire, Rhode Island, and Connecticut. It was so dark that a person couldn't read except by candlelight. Those who experienced it likened it to the ninth plague that Moses called down upon Egypt— or the darkness at the crucifixion. Many New Englanders were so frightened that they left their normal activities and gathered in churches to pray. So though days of darkness are rare in history, they have happened before, and the darkness that covered Jerusalem and the surrounding area on the day of the crucifixion was such a day.

Notice how Psalm 22:2 suggests this period of darkness: "O my God, I cry out by day, but you do not answer, by night, and am not silent." The sufferer cries out in the day and in the night, in the light and the dark, but God does not answer.

Here we have the strange mystery of the abandonment of the Son of God, what some have called "Immanuel's orphaned cry." Jesus spoke these words in the Aramaic language: *"Eloi, Eloi, lama sabachthani?"* ("My God, my God, why have you forsaken me?") Because He cried out with a loud voice, passersby misunderstood Him. When they heard the words *"Eloi, Eloi,"* they thought he was crying for Elijah. But he was calling out for God from the depths of His being because of His sense of abandonment.

The strangeness of God the Father's rejection of our Lord seems to be an inconsistency, as the Sufferer states His awareness of God's faithful character:

Yet you are enthroned as the Holy One;
you are the praise of Israel.
In you our fathers put their trust;
they trusted and you delivered them.
They cried to you and were saved;
in you they trusted and were not disappointed (vv. 3–5).

He remembers the history of God's people and the fact that God never abandoned any of them. Even though they were sinful, God saved them when they cried out to Him. Yet the Sufferer of Psalm 22 feels completely abandoned by God. For some strange reason, God does not treat him as He treated past people of faith. In His abandonment and His sense of rejection by God, the Sufferer feels that He is a worm, not a man:

But I am a worm and not a man,
scorned by men and despised by the people.
All who see me mock me;
they hurl insults, shaking their heads:
"He trusts in the Lord;
let the Lord rescue him.
Let him deliver him,
since he delights in him" (vv. 6–8).

In both Psalm 22 and the gospel account of the crucifixion, we see that the spectators treated the Sufferer (Jesus) like a despised and hated criminal, as though He had lost His right to be considered a human being. Matthew's gospel records that the crowd actually used these very words in taunting Jesus: "He trusts in God. Let God rescue him now if he wants him, for he said, 'I am the Son of God'" (27:43). These words echo the words of Psalm 22:8: "He trusts in the Lord; let the Lord rescue Him." What an amazing prediction this is! The crowd had no intention of fulfilling prophecy when they spoke, yet their taunts were foretold a thousand years earlier.

The Mystery of His Abandonment

We are faced with the strange mystery of why the Father abandoned His Son. The Sufferer of Psalm 22 presses the point, making the case that there is no justifiable reason for God to abandon Him:

> *Yet you brought me out of the womb;*
> *you made me trust in you*
> *even at my mother's breast.*
> *From birth I was cast upon you;*
> *from my mother's womb you have been my God.*
> *Do not be far from me,*
> *for trouble is near*
> *and there is no one to help (vv. 9–11).*

See how utterly forsaken this man is! There is no one to help. This is how Jesus felt when His friends betrayed Him, denied Him, and fled. Only God the Father was left, and then, as Jesus hung upon the cross, He realized that even God the Father had forsaken Him. He was truly alone.

The Sufferer of Psalm 22 knows no explanation for this strange sense of abandonment. He says that from the very moment of His birth He was in fellowship with God. This of course was true of Jesus Himself. When Jesus began His public ministry, the Father spoke from heaven and put His seal of approval upon Jesus' life, saying, "You are my Son, whom I love; with you I am well pleased" (Mark 1:11).

There is absolutely nothing that Jesus ever did to merit such total abandonment by the Father, yet He was forsaken. In His human weakness, Jesus didn't even understand it, so He cried out this strange cry of dereliction, "My God, my God, why have you forsaken me?"

The Father turned away from Jesus because the Son of God was being sacrificed as an offering for the sins of the world. All the ugliness and horror of our sin was laid upon Him. As another great prophetic Old Testament passage tells us,

> *But he was pierced for our transgressions,*
> *he was crushed for our iniquities;*

the punishment that brought us peace was upon him,
and by his wounds we are healed (Isaiah 53:5).

The psalmist prophetically describes the scene from the cross:

Many bulls surround me;
strong bulls of Bashan encircle me.
Roaring lions tearing their prey
open their mouths wide against me (vv. 12–13).

Here the psalmist describes the onlookers in poetic metaphors. These spectators are compared to strong bulls and roaring lions—frightening images of bestial ferocity. Who could survive being surrounded by enraged bulls or hungry lions? The Sufferer's situation is hopeless, an image of absolute despair. He is surrounded by enemies from which there is no hope of escape, no chance of mercy. The horrors of death by torture await Him.

The Dust of Death

Next the psalmist reaches deep within his being and describes his despairing emotions:

I am poured out like water,
and all my bones are out of joint.
My heart has turned to wax;
it has melted away within me.
My strength is dried up like a potsherd,
and my tongue sticks to the roof of my mouth;
you lay me in the dust of death (vv. 14–15).

What a description of the agony and exhaustion of the cross! Having hung for five to six hours with massive nails through His wrists and feet, the Sufferer feels that his bones are pulled out of joint. His diaphragm is compressed, and the only way He can breathe is by pushing against the nails with His legs to force air into His lungs. The simple act of breathing itself causes an awful sense of weariness and fatigue. Burned and dehydrated by the heat of the sun, His heart feels like melted wax within Him, and He experiences a throat-cracking, ravaging thirst.

When these words were written, no one had ever been put to death this way. It would be five centuries before the invention of crucifixion as a form of capital punishment. The Jews would have known nothing about crucifixion as a form of capital punishment since their method of execution was stoning. Yet it is clear that Psalm 22 refers to death by crucifixion. This description could fit no other form of execution, and it is certainly a prophetic description of the death of Jesus Christ:

> *Dogs have surrounded me;*
> *a band of evil men has encircled me,*
> *they have pierced my hands and my feet.*
> *I can count all my bones;*
> *people stare and gloat over me.*
> *They divide my garments among them*
> *and cast lots for my clothing (vv. 16–18).*

The psalmist says that he is surrounded by "dogs," which was the term the Jews used to describe their Gentile enemies, especially the Romans. When Jesus hung upon the cross, His Roman executioners surrounded Him—indeed, they encircled Him.

The Romans pierced His hands and feet; this piercing dislocated His bones, a fact that is reflected in the striking phrase, "I can count all my bones." Roman crucifixion is the only form of execution that involves piercing both the hands and feet, so this passage specifically describes Roman crucifixion.

The Sufferer decries the fact that He has been stripped naked. His enemies stare at His nakedness, and they gloat over His shame and suffering. The crowning indignity is that the Gentiles actually sit at the foot of the cross, casting lots for the Sufferer's garments while He hangs above them in His torment and death agony.

The gospel writers record that the unfeeling Roman soldiers gambled for Jesus' clothing as He hung dying. Obviously the Romans had no idea that in doing so they were helping to fulfill the thousand-year-old Hebrew Scriptures. But that is in fact what they were doing.

The Final Prayer

Next we come to the final prayer of the Sufferer of Psalm 22:

But you, O LORD, be not far off;
O my Strength, come quickly to help me.
Deliver my life from the sword,
my precious life from the power of the dogs.
Rescue me from the mouth of the lions;
save me from the horns of the wild oxen (vv. 19–21).

"Deliver my life from the sword," writes the psalmist. The "sword" is a symbol of government authority—specifically, in a prophetic sense, the authority of the Roman government. The "mouth of the lions" refers to invisible powers and satanic forces. The "horns of the wild oxen" present a picture of the Sufferer impaled upon two widespread horns. In all of this we see a picture of Jesus crying out in His death throes for help from God.

This of course is exactly what Jesus expressed in His last words upon the cross. Luke's gospel tells us: "Jesus called out with a loud voice, 'Father, into your hands I commit my spirit.' When he had said this, he breathed his last" (23:46).

In other words Jesus says, "If anyone is going to save me, Father, it has to be You. If anyone is going to raise me up out of the dust of death, it must be You. I commit my spirit to You, Father."

A Sudden Change of Tone

In verse 22 the psalmist's voice takes on a different tone. Clearly this is the same speaker—the Sufferer—but now His suffering has ended. Without a word of explanation, the Sufferer describes a very different scene. He no longer hangs dying from a cross, despised and forsaken. He is in a different place, and He is no longer alone: "I will declare your name to my brothers; in the congregation I will praise you" (v. 22). What has happened? There is only one explanation for this abrupt shift in tone, scene, and emotional content: the resurrection.

The individual who in verses 1 through 21 has been tortured, pierced, humiliated, abandoned, and killed now stands in the midst of a company of people, a congregation of His brothers. We see this scene echoed by the writer to the Hebrews in the New Testament. In

Hebrews 2, the writer applies these very words to Jesus: "Both the one who makes men holy and those who are made holy are of the same family. So Jesus is not ashamed to call them brothers. He says, 'I will declare your name to my brothers; in the presence of the congregation I will sing your praises'" (vv. 11–12).

Here we see a wonderful result of the resurrection of Jesus: Those who are called by God and saved by Jesus Christ become joint heirs with Him. They share in His resurrection life, and He calls them brothers. Both the saved and the Savior are members of the family of God.

In the next verse the resurrected Sufferer says,

> *You who fear the* LORD, *praise him!*
> *All you descendants of Jacob, honor him!*
> *Revere him, all you descendants of Israel!"* (v. 23).

Why does the Sufferer, speaking through the psalmist, call upon the people to praise God the Father? Because God is the One who has answered the prayer of a dead man, a crucified man; God has raised the Sufferer out of the dust of death. The resurrection is the ground of Christian worship. As the psalmist goes on to say:

> *For he has not despised or disdained*
> *the suffering of the afflicted one;*
> *he has not hidden his face from him*
> *but has listened to his cry for help (v. 24).*

Again, the writer of Hebrews adds his commentary to Psalm 22 when he writes:

> *May the God of peace, who through the blood of the eternal covenant brought back from the dead our Lord Jesus, that great Shepherd of the sheep, equip you with everything good for doing his will, and may he work in us what is pleasing to him, through Jesus Christ, to whom be glory for ever and ever. Amen (13:20–21).*

This is the basis of praise for all Christians: Our living Lord has been raised from the dead. His life is now our life, and our lives belong to Him. The psalmist goes on to say:

From you comes the theme of my praise in the great assembly;
before those who fear you will I fulfill my vows.
The poor will eat and be satisfied;
they who seek the LORD will praise him—
may your hearts live forever! (vv. 25–26).

Here is the promise of the Lord Jesus that out of the resurrection power that He now possesses He will meet all of our needs, and we will be satisfied. We will praise Him, and our hearts will live forever. As the apostle Peter writes, "His divine power has given us everything we need for life and godliness through our knowledge of him who called us by his own glory and goodness" (2 Peter 1:3). There is not a single thing we need that He has not already made available to us.

So it is true, as Hebrews 7:25 tells us, "He is able to save completely those who come to God through him, because he always lives to intercede for them."

The next verses go on to show how the resurrection power of our Lord moves out across the entire world, drawing together all people in obedience and worship to Jesus Christ:

All the ends of the earth
will remember and turn to the LORD,
and all the families of the nations
will bow down before him,
for dominion belongs to the LORD
and he rules over the nations (vv. 27–28) .

Here we see the fulfillment of the Great Commission that Jesus gave to His followers before He ascended to heaven after His resurrection. He commanded His followers to preach His gospel to all nations so that people would respond and come to Him out of every tribe and culture of the world. Today we live in an age when men, women, and children from every tribe and nation are hearing about Him, and they are coming to Him.

The closing words of Psalm 22 show that all people and all creatures throughout the universe will ultimately be subject to Him:

All the rich of the earth will feast and worship;
all who go down to the dust will kneel before him—

those who cannot keep themselves alive.
Posterity will serve him;
future generations will be told about the Lord.
They will proclaim his righteousness
to a people yet unborn—
for he has done it (vv. 29–31).

The rich and the living will kneel before Jesus the Lord. The poor and even the dead will kneel before Him. Generations unborn will hear that Jesus was crucified and raised again and that He brings them His righteousness and deliverance.

The passage ends with the words, "for he has done it." In the original Hebrew language, this phrase literally says, "It is finished."

"It is finished!" That was the victory shout Jesus spoke from the cross as recorded in John 19:30. Isn't that amazing? Psalm 22 begins with the words of Jesus from the cross: "My God, my God, why have you forsaken me?" And it ends with the words of Jesus from the cross: "It is finished."

The work of Jesus is done. It is finished. There is nothing left to do. Through His death and resurrection He has granted to us all the things we need for life and godliness. What a prophetic passage this is, and what a Lord and Savior we have who willingly endured so much to fulfill it!

Thank God for our suffering and resurrected Savior.

7

The Psalm of the Shepherd

PSALM 23

I was checking out at a local department store when the sales clerk looked at me and said, "You're Pastor Stedman from Peninsula Bible Church, aren't you?"

"Yes, I am," I said.

"I don't know if you remember me, but my name is—" And the moment she said her name, I remembered this woman and her family.

It had been about three years earlier. Her family had just moved to the area. They didn't know anyone in town and were staying at a motel. One day the woman and her husband decided to go house hunting, but their twelve-year-old son wanted to stay behind, so they left him in the room. Hours later they returned to find their son dead. He had hanged himself in the closet.

These grieving parents didn't know where to turn for comfort, but as they thumbed through the phone book they came across the listing for our church and they called me. I went to the motel and found the woman and her husband white-faced with shock. I didn't know them, and I didn't know what to say. But I asked God for wisdom and sat down with them. We talked for a while, and then I felt God leading me to open my Bible to Psalm 23. We read those beautiful words together, and the psalm seemed to give them a measure of peace. The couple asked me to officiate at the funeral, and I based my talk on that wonderful Twenty-Third Psalm.

All of those memories flooded back to my mind the moment the sales clerk said her name. And there in the store, tears came to her eyes and she said, "Pastor, you'll never know how much comfort our family received from that psalm. We've talked about it many times since, and we return to Psalm 23 whenever the hurt becomes too great to bear. Those words have brought us peace when nothing else could. We have gotten through the past three years by leaning on the truth that 'the Lord is my shepherd.'"

Down through the centuries, Psalm 23 has been a source of amazing comfort and encouragement to generations of believers. The Puritan writer James Janeway, author of the Christian young reader's classic *A Token for Children*, was thirty-eight years old as he lay dying in 1674. His only request was that the words of Psalm 23 be read to him. After hearing those words he said, "I can now as easily die as close my eyes. Here I am, longing to be silent in the dust so that I may enjoy Christ in glory. Don't weep for me. I long to be in the arms of Jesus."

The Twenty-Third Psalm is the most often quoted and memorized of all the psalms. Because of its comforting tone, it is read at more funerals than any other passage of Scripture. In its sweet, rich imagery, we find the comforting reassurance that our Lord is like a Good Shepherd who protects us and provides for us throughout our lives, and even in death.

Dr. Charles L. Allen, author of *God's Psychiatry*, once observed, "If people would repeat Psalm 23 seven times before they go to sleep each night, we would rarely see an emotional breakdown."

The nineteenth-century Congregationalist minister Henry Ward Beecher wrote,

> David has left no sweeter psalm than the short Twenty-Third . . . It is the nightingale of the Psalms. It is small, of a homely feather, singing shyly out of obscurity; but, oh! It has filled the air of the whole world with melodious joy, greater than the heart can conceive. Blessed be the day on which that Psalm was born! . . .
>
> It has comforted the noble host of the poor. It has sung courage to the army of the disappointed. It has poured balm and consolation into the heart of the sick, of captives in dungeons, of widows in their pinching griefs, of orphans in their loneliness. Dying soldiers have died easier as it was read to them; ghastly hospitals have been illuminated; it has visited

the prisoner, and broken his chains, and, like Peter's angel, led him forth in imagination, and sung him back to his home again. It has made the dying Christian slave freer than his master, and consoled those whom, dying, he left behind mourning, not so much that he was gone, as because they were left behind, and could not go too.

Bible teacher Charles H. Spurgeon called Psalm 23 "the pearl of psalms." Spurgeon noted that God seems to have carefully placed Psalm 23, the "Psalm of the Shepherd," immediately after Psalm 22, the "Psalm of the Cross." In the first twenty-two psalms, Spurgeon observes, there are no green pastures or still waters. "It is only after we have read, 'My God, my God, why hast thou forsaken me?' that we come to 'The Lord is my Shepherd.' We must by experience know the value of blood-shedding, and see the sword awakened against the Shepherd, before we shall be truly able to know the sweetness of the Good Shepherd's care."

The Man after God's Own Heart

Psalm 23 is, of course, a psalm of David, the shepherd-king. Yet David writes this psalm not from the shepherd's perspective but from the viewpoint of the sheep. As a shepherd David understands the gentle heart of the Good Shepherd, and that is why he is able to write so beautifully and trustingly as a mere sheep of the Lord's flock.

You might say, "I don't think being a sheep of the Good Shepherd is comforting at all. After all, weren't sheep sacrificed in ancient Israel? Weren't they slaughtered and eaten? Didn't the shepherds of Israel only look after the sheep so they could turn them into lamb shanks and mutton stew?"

No! It is true that there were a few flocks maintained for ceremonial sacrifices, cared for by priestly shepherds. But that's not the kind of shepherd David was, and that's not the kind of shepherd he describes when he writes here of the Good Shepherd. The sheep of the Good Shepherd's flock were raised for wool, not meat. These sheep lived long lives and were part of the family. They were loved—not eaten! That's why the image of the sheep and the Good Shepherd is such an apt metaphor to describe our relationship to the Lord. The Good Shepherd loves and cares for His flock.

The strong assurances and comfort of the Shepherd's Psalm come straight from the trials of David's own life. The story of David (which you can read beginning in 1 Samuel 16 and continuing through 2 Samuel 24) is the story of the man after God's own heart.

David was chosen to be king from among the eight sons of Jesse. The seven eldest sons passed before Samuel, and each one looked like a king in the making until God said to Samuel, "This is not the one I have chosen." Last came the youngest of all: David. God put His seal upon this young shepherd boy because He didn't judge according to outward appearance but according to the heart. Like God Himself, David had a shepherd's heart.

David was not set on the throne immediately. He was tested and proven by struggle and adversity. This is the principle God often follows with those who learn to walk by faith. They are put through a time of testing in obscurity. The purpose of this testing is to enable them to understand how God works through people: human beings can do nothing of themselves. They can only achieve great things through utter dependence upon the God who indwells them.

This is what David learned even as a shepherd boy so that he could say in Psalm 23, "The LORD is my shepherd, I shall not be in want" (v. 1). The shepherd boy was tested in combat against the Philistine champion, Goliath. When young David came into the camp of Israel to bring food to his older brothers, he found the whole camp plunged into gloom and fearful of Goliath's great strength. David demanded to know, "Who is this uncircumcised Philistine that he should defy the armies of the living God?" (1 Samuel 17:26). That is always the outlook of faith. Genuine trust in God is never shaken by circumstances.

David faced Goliath without armor, wielding nothing but a sling and five smooth stones as a weapon. (Why five stones? Later in the account we find that Goliath had four brothers. David had armed himself to take on Goliath's whole family!) David went out, swung the sling around his head, launched the stone—and Goliath fell to the ground with a stone lodged between his eyes.

David's encounter with Goliath is a symbolic picture of the Lord Jesus and His battle against death and Satan. Hebrews 2:14 tells us that by dying upon the cross, the Lord Jesus slew the one who had the power of death, the devil himself. David portrays for us not only Christ in His battle against death but also the believer through whom Christ now lives.

Beginning in 1 Samuel 18, we see that King Saul—the man David would succeed as king—increasingly persecuted David. Saul became jealous, full of rage and bitterness, and he ultimately tried to kill David. It was during this time of persecution and exile that David wrote so many of the psalms—the folk songs of David's own faith in God during times of peril and distress.

David survived the murderous schemes of King Saul, who eventually took his own life after his sons were slain by the Philistines. David ascended to the throne left vacant after the death of Saul. King David had many sons, including one notorious son named Absalom.

In 2 Samuel 15 we read that Absalom plotted to kill his father so that he could seize the throne of Israel. To save his life, David had to flee into the Judean wilderness—an exiled king made a fugitive by his own rebellious offspring! David was hunted for months and was forced to live as a nomad in the same wilderness he had once roamed as a shepherd boy. Many Bible scholars believe it was there in the wilderness, while David hid from his murderous son and feared for his life, that he composed Psalm 23.

Finally in 2 Samuel 18 we read how the rebellious Absalom came to a bad end. Despite all the suffering that Absalom had put him through, David was heartbroken when he learned of his son's death. "O my son Absalom!" he mourned. "If only I had died instead of you!" (v. 33).

Psalm 23 comes to us from the depths of a soul that has known fear, terror, betrayal, grief, and depression. It is a psalm of comfort, yet it is also a psalm of real experience and genuine emotion. David wrote this folk song for people like you and me—people who are going through the trials of life. He wrote it for those who feel hunted, betrayed, and afraid. He wrote it for those whose most important relationships are crumbling. He wrote it for those who are heartbroken over rebellious children. He wrote it for those who are in the valley of the shadow of darkness and death.

Let's take a closer look at this beloved psalm, the "Psalm of the Shepherd," and let's hear what its ancient words say to us today.

We Are Like Sheep

David opens this passage with a strong affirmation that forms the underlying theme of the entire psalm: "The LORD is my shepherd, I shall not be in want" (v. 1).

The psalmist tells us that because Jehovah is our shepherd, we have everything we truly need. We may not have everything we might wish for or covet, but we have all that we need to be happy and satisfied. We tend to think, "If I just had X, then I would be happy." But when we get X, we find that we want Y and Z as well. We will never be happy until we can say, "The Lord is my shepherd. *He* is all I want."

God wants to bring us to the place where He is our all-sufficient supply, the place where we need nothing but Him. My friend and colleague in ministry, David Roper, once put it this way:

> There are really only two options in life. If the Lord is my shepherd, then I shall not want. But if I am in want, then it is obvious that the Lord is not my shepherd. It's that simple! If there's emptiness, loneliness, dissatisfaction, and frustration in our lives, then the Lord is not our shepherd. If we look to anyone or anything other than God as our shepherd, we will never be satisfied.

True happiness and joy in life begin with the recognition that we are sheep in need of a shepherd. This is not a very flattering picture of us because sheep are not the most intelligent of animals. Sheep are, in fact, rather stupid. They can't provide for themselves. They can't defend themselves. They are prone to wander off and get lost. The prophet Isaiah put it this way: "We all, like sheep, have gone astray, each of us has turned to his own way" (Isaiah 53:6a). We must begin by admitting that we are like stupid sheep in need of a shepherd.

David goes on to explain how the Good Shepherd satisfies our needs. In the next two verses he writes, "He makes me lie down in green pastures, he leads me beside quiet waters, he restores my soul" (vv. 2–3a).

The Good Shepherd satisfies our need for rest and the restoration of our souls. When David wrote these lines, he was probably exhausted, having spent weeks or months hiding from his rebellious son Absalom. He was physically, emotionally, and spiritually spent. Yet he knew that the Good Shepherd was with him, guiding him to a place of rest, a place of cool green pastures and crystal-clear waters. In the presence of the Good Shepherd, David's soul and spirit were refreshed.

That's how God meets the needs of our innermost being. Why do sheep need green pastures? Because that is what they feed on. And once they have fed, sheep lie down and rest. Why do sheep need quiet waters? Because they are easily frightened by splashing, running water. They can drink only from still waters.

Green pastures and still waters are a picture of a spiritual reality that we are to feed upon day by day. What is that spiritual reality? What are we to feed upon, drink, and rest ourselves in? The Lord Himself and His Word. God is the resource in whom we are to eat, drink, and rest.

The apostle Paul understood what David went through. Paul knew persecution, betrayal, exhaustion, and struggle. But Paul, like David, also knew where to find spiritual food, drink, and rest. That's why he wrote, "Therefore we do not lose heart. Though outwardly we are wasting away, yet inwardly we are being renewed day by day" (2 Corinthians 4:16).

Light in the Deep Darkness

Next the psalmist shows us another way the Good Shepherd provides for us: He gives us guidance and directs us toward righteousness. He writes, "He guides me in paths of righteousness for his name's sake" (v. 3b).

As we have seen, sheep tend to go astray. They need a shepherd to guide them along the right paths, a shepherd who knows where the dangerous cliffs and rocks are; where the good, green pastures are found; and where the pools of still, quiet water await. The sheep know they can trust the wise guidance of the Good Shepherd.

The wife of physicist Albert Einstein was once asked if she understood her husband's theory of relativity. "No, I don't," she replied, "but I know my husband. If he says it's true, you can trust him." We are in the same situation as Mrs. Einstein. We don't understand the thoughts and intentions of our Good Shepherd, but we know Him and we can trust Him. If the Good Shepherd says it, we know it's true. He will guide us in the right paths, and He will never lead us astray.

What is our assurance that we can trust the guidance of the Good Shepherd? He has staked His reputation—His good name—on it. He guides us in the paths of righteousness, the psalmist says, "for his name's sake." That's His seal, His guarantee. God has promised to lead and guide us, and He has put His reputation on the line. God faithfully keeps His promises. We have His name on it.

Next the psalmist assures us that we are always under the strong, dependable protection of the Good Shepherd, so that we have nothing to fear. He writes:

> *Even though I walk*
> *through the valley of the shadow of death,*
> *I will fear no evil,*
> *for you are with me (v. 4a).*

God never intended the believer to be ruled or troubled by fear. As Paul told his spiritual son Timothy, "For God has not given us a spirit of fear, but of power and of love and of a sound mind" (2 Timothy 1:7 NKJV). When we have confidence in the Good Shepherd, there's no room for fear.

The late Martin R. DeHaan, founder of Radio Bible Class, used to tell the story of a Christian man he knew who was troubled by fear. Every night as this man began to drift off to sleep, he would suddenly be awakened by a sense that he was tumbling into a bottomless pit.

One day this man was walking through a cemetery when he noticed a gravestone with an inscription that captured his attention: "Underneath are the Everlasting Arms." This inscription reminded him that when a Christian believer dies, the Lord carries that one safely to an eternal home in heaven. As he reflected on that inscription, the man was reminded of this verse in Psalm 23: "Even though I walk through the valley of the shadow of death, I will fear no evil, for you are with me" (v. 4a).

This man immediately lost his anxiety and terror. He rested in the everlasting arms of the Good Shepherd. "That night," concluded Dr. DeHaan, "he was able to sing the song he had learned in childhood: 'Teach me to live that I may dread the grave as little as my bed!' At last he could fall asleep without fear."

Take a closer look at the phrase "the valley of the shadow of death." In the original Hebrew language, that phrase conveys an emphatic sense of deep, impenetrable darkness. A more accurate translation might be, "the sunless valley of deathly shadows" or "the valley as dark as death." Why is this an important point? Because so many people think of Psalm 23 as a passage to be read at a funeral after someone has died—after someone has, so to speak, entered "the valley of the shadow of death."

Though I agree that it's an appropriate passage to read when a Christian dies, I believe Psalm 23 is even more applicable to life than it is to death. It is a passage of comfort and assurance for the times when we are passing through life's shadows, through dark valleys of hurt, betrayal, doubt, fear, loss, sadness, and sorrow.

If you lose a relationship due to betrayal or divorce, you are going through the dark valley. If you lose your career or your reputation, then the sun has been blotted out of your world. If your parents, children, or friends turn against you, then that is certainly a dark place in your life. If you have just been diagnosed with cancer or AIDS, then you probably feel the darkness closing in.

You may not be at death's door, but you are going through a time of darkness. If so, then claim these beautiful, comforting words. Dwell in the glowing images of Psalm 23 and let it be a light in your darkness.

The Shepherd's Rod and Staff

David goes on to write about two implements of the shepherd's profession: the rod and the staff. "Your rod and your staff, they comfort me" (v. 4b).

The rod was a pole the shepherd used as a weapon to ward off predatory animals. It was a comfort to the sheep because the shepherd used it to protect them.

The staff was also a pole, but it was fashioned with a hook at the end. Whereas the rod never made physical contact with the sheep, the staff was often used to touch the sheep. The shepherd might tap or prod the sheep with the staff to guide them in the right direction. He might use the hook to catch a sheep by the leg if it strayed or to lift a lamb that had fallen among the rocks.

In short, the staff might be used to rescue a lamb or point a sheep in the right direction, but the Good Shepherd would never use either the rod or the staff to beat or hurt a sheep. That is why the rod and staff are always sources of comfort to the sheep—never a source of fear or pain.

If the shepherd's rod and staff in Psalm 23 are symbols, what do they symbolize? The rod symbolizes the Word of God. It is a weapon that wards off enemies and predators. The Good Shepherd wields it to protect us and warn us of danger. And the staff? It symbolizes the Spirit of God. Like the shepherd's staff, the Holy Spirit provides guidance by applying a prod here, a bit of gentle pressure there; the Spirit rescues us, pulls us back onto the path of righteousness, and lifts us up out of the rocks that we fall among.

"Your rod and your staff, they comfort me," says the psalmist. The believer is certainly comforted by the Good Shepherd's "rod," the Bible. And the believer is also comforted by the Spirit of God, the one whose very name is the Comforter. As believers, we need never fear the "rod" or "staff" of the Good Shepherd: the Bible and the Spirit. These are God's implements of guidance, protection, and comfort in our lives.

From Good Shepherd to Good Host

A major transition takes place at verse 5. The psalmist switches metaphors. Instead of writing as a sheep describing the Good Shepherd, he now writes as a guest who is directly addressing the Good Host who offers him His hospitality and protection:

You prepare a table before me
in the presence of my enemies.
You anoint my head with oil;
my cup overflows (v. 5).

David writes here as if he were a traveler who has journeyed through dangerous lands, finally reaching the tent of the Good Host. The Good Host prepares a table before the traveler. The "table" is a symbol of blessing and abundance, which is underscored by the image of the cup that overflows with wine. Taken together, these metaphors supply an apt image of the life of the believer. We are sojourners in this world, yet God, the Good Host, provides us with an abundance of blessings in His presence.

The phrase "in the presence of my enemies" tells us that the traveler's enemies are all around, yet he has nothing to fear because the Good Host protects him. Again, this is an apt image, for we are surrounded by enemies of all kinds: physical enemies, spiritual enemies, and enemies of our emotional well being. We live in a dangerous world, and the unseen world of spirits and demons is even more dangerous than the world we can see. Yet God, the Good Host, offers us His protection and hospitality.

"You anoint my head with oil," the psalmist says. "My cup overflows." What does the anointing with oil mean? In ancient Israel people were anointed with oil for a number of reasons. Oil was sometimes applied for medicinal purposes, as in Jesus' parable of the Good Samaritan in Luke 10 when the Samaritan treats the wounds of the injured man with wine and oil. Kings and priests were anointed with oil as a sign that they had been consecrated to God's service (see Exodus 29:7; 30:30; 1 Samuel 16:13). The anointing of oil also has a symbolic meaning: Oil symbolizes the presence and activity of the Holy Spirit.

David closes this psalm with a beautiful expression of his confidence in God's loving kindness and his hope of eternal life: "Surely goodness and love will follow me all the days of my life, and I will dwell in the house of the LORD forever" (v. 6).

There are very few things in this life that we can count on. We can't always count on our wealth or our health or our friends and relatives being there for us when we need them, but we can always count on the goodness and love of God, now and throughout our lives.

Does that mean that we will never face pain or illness? Poverty or persecution? Loss or sorrow? Betrayal or abandonment? No, these trials are a part of life. Yet when the Lord is truly our Good Shepherd and our Good Host, when He is all we want, then there is no trial, no disaster, no medical diagnosis that can separate us from the love of God. No matter what happens to us, we know that God's goodness, love, and mercy will follow us wherever we go, throughout our lives, and even into death itself.

Any great saint who has lived in close fellowship with God will tell you that the closer we grow to God, the more clearly we can see His goodness, love, and mercy. There is no place in Scripture where God promises that the righteous will not undergo suffering. But there are many passages in Scripture where God promises that He will transform our suffering into glory and that He will walk alongside us through the valley of the dark shadows. Through the prophet Isaiah He tells us:

> *"Fear not, for I have redeemed you;*
> *I have summoned you by name; you are mine.*
> *When you pass through the waters,*
> *I will be with you;*
> *and when you pass through the rivers,*
> *they will not sweep over you.*
> *When you walk through the fire,*
> *you will not be burned;*
> *the flames will not set you ablaze.*
> *For I am the* LORD, *your God,*
> *the Holy One of Israel, your Savior"* (Isaiah 43:1b–3a).

Psalm 23:6 clearly gives us an image of eternal life: "I will dwell in the house of the LORD forever." Some people will tell you that the Hebrew people of Old Testament times did not believe in eternal life or the resurrection; they will suggest that eternal life is an idea that originated in New Testament times. In this passage the phrase "the house of the Lord" does not refer to the temple or the tabernacle, places of worship, but to God's eternal dwelling place. So David is writing here of *living forever* in the dwelling place of the Lord.

Those who claim that the ancient Hebrews did not have a conception of a heavenly afterlife seem to be unaware of this and other passages that clearly speak of a glorious life that follows this one. In Psalm 133:3, David tells us that God bestows His blessing to us, "even life forevermore." Job, that suffering Old Testament saint, speaks explicitly of resurrection and eternal life when he says:

> *I know that my Redeemer lives,*
> *and that in the end he will stand upon the earth.*
> *And after my skin has been destroyed,*
> *yet in my flesh I will see God;*
> *I myself will see him*
> *with my own eyes—I, and not another.*
> *How my heart yearns within me! (19:25–27).*

The Old Testament prophet Daniel put it this way:

> *Multitudes who sleep in the dust of the earth will awake: some to everlasting life, others to shame and everlasting contempt. Those who are wise will shine like the brightness of the heavens, and those who lead many to righteousness, like the stars for ever and ever (12:2–3).*

Another Old Testament prophet, Isaiah, spoke plainly of the resurrection and eternal life in two prophetic passages:

> *But your dead will live;*
> *their bodies will rise.*
> *You who dwell in the dust,*
> *wake up and shout for joy.*
> *Your dew is like the dew of the morning;*
> *the earth will give birth to her dead (26:19).*

Later in Isaiah, God describes a new heaven and a new earth, a place where there will be no tears and no sorrows—only endless rejoicing because sorrow and death will be gone and forgotten:

> *"Behold, I will create*
> *new heavens and a new earth.*
> *The former things will not be remembered,*
> *nor will they come to mind.*
> *But be glad and rejoice forever*
> *in what I will create,*
> *for I will create Jerusalem to be a delight*
> *and its people a joy.*

I will rejoice over Jerusalem
and take delight in my people;
the sound of weeping and of crying
will be heard in it no more" (65:17–19).

If anyone tries to tell you that the ancient Hebrews did not believe in everlasting life, point them to these passages. Eternal life has always been God's plan for the righteous, for those who believe and trust in Him as their Redeemer and Good Shepherd. If the Lord is your Good Shepherd, if He is all you want, then His goodness, love, and mercy will follow you all the days of your life, and you will dwell in the house of the Lord forever.

God's home is our home. It is appropriate that Psalm 23 closes on a note of longing for our eternal home with Him. We know that we are mere sojourners on this planet; we are just passing through. We have not truly had a place we can call home since our first parents, Adam and Eve, were exiled from the garden.

Throughout the history of our literature, the stories that touch our hearts most deeply are those that reflect our universal longing for a place called home. Odysseus, the hero of Homer's *Odyssey*, was defined by his intense longing for home. Our Lord's most famous parable—the story of the loving father and his prodigal son—is about a young man who discovers (nearly too late!) that all he truly wants out of life is to go home and be with his father.

A more recent tale is L. Frank Baum's children's classic *The Wizard of Oz*, the story of a little girl from Kansas who is carried off to a strange and wonderful land only to discover in the end that "there's no place like home." And finally there's *The Lord of the Rings* trilogy, in which a fellowship of little people called hobbits have the adventure of a lifetime, meeting elves and wizards and talking trees; they witness epic battles and even help to save the world. Yet throughout their adventure, all they can think of is how much they yearn to go back to the Shire and the comfort of home.

In *The Rock That Is Higher*, Madeleine L'Engle wrote, "We are all strangers in a strange land, longing for home, but not quite knowing what or where home is. We glimpse it sometimes in our dreams, or as we turn a corner, and suddenly there is a strange, sweet familiarity that vanishes almost as soon as it comes." That home we long for is heaven.

We are no different from Odysseus or the prodigal son or Dorothy or the hobbits of the Shire. We yearn for our eternal home. We are homesick for heaven. And that is why Psalm 23 is so rich in comfort and reassurance for us all. This precious psalm promises us that our fondest wish will one day come true: We will dwell in the house of the Lord forever.

Sooner or later we all must die, but that is not the end of the story. A grave is not just a hole in the ground that we drop a coffin into. For those who love God, a grave is an open doorway—a doorway to eternity, a gateway to heaven.

That's the promise of the "Psalm of the Shepherd."

8

⟨⟨⟨⟨⟩⟩⟩⟩

A Song of Confidence

PSALMS 42 AND 43

F olk music takes many forms. One form, which came out of the injustice and misery of the slavery of the Old South, is the spiritual. These spirituals include songs such as "Swing Low, Sweet Chariot," "Pharaoh's Army Got Drowned," and "Ain't Got Time to Die." From these spirituals evolved a form of music we call the blues.

Blues music had its beginnings in the Mississippi Delta region in the late 1800s. It was a sorrowful, soulful music that bemoaned the misery and injustice of life. It was music about hard times and harsh realities. Many preachers condemned it as "the devil's music" and warned their parishioners to avoid the roadhouses and juke joints where it was played. Yet the blues dealt with real emotions and real human struggles: broken hearts, broken dreams, broken lives. Blues music gave voice to the pain of the African-American experience during a time of great poverty and injustice.

As we come to Psalms 42 and 43, we find a folk song of faith that was written long before the birth of the blues. Yet this psalm could well be called "The King David Blues." It was written to show us how to respond to our blue moods, how we should think and pray in those times when we say to ourselves, "Why are you downcast, O my soul?"

A Psalm of Confidence and Comfort for the Blues

We have already noted that there are 150 psalms in the book of Psalms, and the book divides into five sections or divisions. The first section, Psalms 1 through 41, echoes the theme of Genesis, the book of foundations.

Now we come to the second section, Psalms 42 through 72, which corresponds to Exodus, the book of redemption. These psalms, written by David and the Sons of Korah, tell the story of God's activity in human history to redeem His people from their captivity to sin. In this section of the Psalms, as in the book of Exodus, we see the work of God on behalf of humanity as He calls Israel out of Egypt and redeems the people by the blood of the Passover lamb. Psalms 42 and 43 introduce this section.

We are looking at Psalms 42 and 43 together because Psalm 43 is clearly part of Psalm 42. In many ancient Hebrew manuscripts, these two psalms were combined into one psalm. At some point in history, a scribe or copyist mistakenly divided the one psalm into two. But if you read Psalms 42 and 43 together, it's clear that they belong together as one psalm.

It would be beneficial at this point to pause and briefly explore the history of how our Bible came to be divided into verses and chapters. Some Christians are under the impression that the verse and chapter divisions of the Bible are inspired by God. In fact they are not. These divisions are artificial, and sometimes they unfortunately interrupt the flow of God's Word. An Englishman named Stephen Langton, who was then a theology professor at the University of Paris, invented the chapter divisions in your Bible in 1205. He placed these chapter divisions into a Latin edition of the Bible.

Rabbi Mordecai Nathan invented the verse divisions in the Old Testament in 1445, and a Paris book publisher, Robert Estienne, added the verse divisions in the New Testament in 1551. When we understand that men, according to their own judgment, determined these divisions, it becomes understandable how some chapter and verse divisions in the Bible seem more haphazard than logical.

Here, at the division between Psalms 42 and 43, we encounter another seemingly haphazard and illogical division. These two psalms should be read as one psalm, which I call "A Song of Confidence." The key to understanding this psalm is found in a refrain that repeats three times:

Why are you downcast, O my soul?
Why so disturbed within me?
Put your hope in God,

for I will yet praise him,
my Savior and my God (42:5; repeated in 42:11 and 43:5).

It is also important to notice the inscription with which this psalm opens: "For the director of music. A *maskil* of the Sons of Korah." Though we tend to pass over these inscriptions without noticing, they are part of the inspired record, and they indicate something important about the psalm.

The word *maskil* is Hebrew for "teaching." This psalm is intended to teach us something—but what? Judging by the repeated refrain, it is intended to teach us how to handle our blue moods, the times when we get up in the morning and say, "Why are you downcast, O my soul?" The answer to each blue mood is, "Put your hope in God." In other words, "Wait for God. He is working out His plan for your life. If you trust in Him during this blue time, you will yet have reason to praise Him."

Who were the Sons of Korah? They were a family of outstanding singers and musicians in Israel who passed their musical office from generation to generation. The Sons of Korah wrote several of the psalms, including this one. But even though David did not personally write this psalm, it clearly reflects his experience. Psalms 42 and 43 were based on the trials and tragedies that King David experienced, and they were put to music by the Korah Family Singers and dedicated to the Director of Music (or Royal Choirmaster).

Previously we have examined only psalms King David wrote, and when we referred to "the psalmist," we were writing specifically of David. In this passage, however, when we use the phrase "the psalmist," it refers to the Sons of Korah, who are writing here from the point of view of King David.

How to Find the Sunshine

Some Bible scholars believe that the incident of David's life that this psalm memorializes is David's exclusion from the temple at the time of his son Absalom's rebellion. As we saw in the previous chapter, there was a time late in David's reign when his son Absalom temporarily seized control of the kingdom. David was toppled from power and driven into exile outside Jerusalem.

Though the psalm does not specifically mention these events, it clearly reflects a time of depression and discouragement in life. But it reflects more than just a time of the blues. The psalmist doesn't accept depression as inevitable. He chooses to do something about his mood. The purpose of this psalm is to help us learn how to handle these dark and discouraging times in our lives.

The fact that we are followers of Christ does not make us immune to depression. The blues will come. When they come we need to do something about them. Unfortunately all too many Christians simply succumb to them. And not only do these Christians give in to their own misery and gloom, but they make sure everyone around them is as miserable as they are.

Many of the greatest saints of the faith have struggled with the blues. Famed evangelist and Christian author Charles Haddon Spurgeon once confessed to his congregation, "I am the subject of depressions of spirit so fearful that I hope none of you ever get to such extremes of wretchedness as I go to." And another nineteenth-century preacher, John Henry Jowett, once wrote to a friend, "I wish you wouldn't think I'm such a saint. You seem to imagine that I have no ups and downs, but just a level and lofty stretch of spiritual attainment with unbroken joy and equanimity. By no means! I am often perfectly wretched, and everything appears most murky."

This psalm teaches us how to overcome the blues that are common to all believers at one time or another. It traces three stages of the psalmist's experience. At the end of each of these three stages, we read the refrain that describes what has brought the psalmist through his struggle with the blues:

Put your hope in God,
for I will yet praise him,
my Savior and my God (42:5, 11; 43:5).

Longing for God

How do we master the blues? How do we begin to put our hope in God so that we can be sustained through a time of discouragement and depression and come to a place where we can yet praise Him? The answer begins with an intense longing and desire for God:

As the deer pants for streams of water,
so my soul pants for you, O God.
My soul thirsts for God, for the living God.
When can I go and meet with God? (42:1–2).

The psalmist expresses his love for God with a beautiful poetic metaphor: Like the deer running through the woods longs for a drink of cool water, so the psalmist's soul thirsts for God. He has reached a place in his experience where he knows that only God can meet his soul's deepest need. He longs to come into a relationship of freshness and revitalizing fellowship that will quench the thirst of his soul.

We learn why he thirsts for God at the close of verse 2: "When can I go and meet with God?" In other words the psalmist is experiencing a sense of God's delay. There is no doubt that there is help for him in God. He expects to find it. He knows God has met his need in the past, and he expects God to meet his need again. But for some reason God's help is delayed, and this is hard for the psalmist to bear. You may have experienced this same sense of God's delay in your own life.

It's wonderful when God immediately answers your prayers and lifts your dejected spirit. But if we are honest, we must admit that there are times when we pray and God seems slow to answer. He appears to let us wait. These periods of waiting and delay test our faith. The psalmist's time of testing and waiting is made worse by the taunting of enemies and memories of past joys. He writes:

My tears have been my food
day and night,
while men say to me all day long,
"Where is your God?" (42:3).

In other words, the psalmist can't eat or sleep. The only "food" he has in the day or in the night is the "food" of his tears. He continues:

These things I remember
as I pour out my soul:
how I used to go with the multitude,
leading the procession to the house of God,
with shouts of joy and thanksgiving
among the festive throng (42:4).

Here the psalmist recalls the past. He remembers going to the temple, leading the crowd, and shouting with joy. Why does he dwell on this memory? Because by recalling past joys, the psalmist finds therapy for his blues. This is a strong expression of his determination to fight his depression and gain the victory over it. He is determined to remember how God has helped him in the past. That's one of the most effective ways to fight the blues: Remember the goodness of God!

Some people tend to dwell on the bad experiences of their lives. Their lives are marked off tragedy by tragedy: "That was the time the garage burned down." "That was the year I went bankrupt." "That was the week of the big earthquake." There are no good memories—just disasters!

Here the psalmist shows how a memory of positive experiences can help change our moods. He says in effect, "I'll remember the times when God caused my heart to sing! I'll remember the times of worship and praise and fellowship with other believers in God's house!"

Remembering the Goodness of God

Longtime missionary leader of OC International Dr. Ed Murphy has a fascinating Christian testimony. He was raised in a Roman Catholic family and was fourteen years old before he even met a Protestant. (He expected to see horns sprouting from the Protestant's head and a tail waving behind.) He came to know Jesus Christ as his Lord and Savior after a young man at a lumber camp gave him a New Testament to read.

Sensing God calling him into missionary work, Ed enrolled at Biola University. When his family heard that he was planning to go to a Protestant school, they told him he was not welcome in the family unless he returned to Catholicism. Ed could not be dissuaded, so he went to Biola and began his studies. Near the end of his first year, he found himself sixty dollars short of paying his bills for the semester. The school rules required that he pay the sixty dollars or he would not be allowed to take his final exams. He tried to find some way to earn or borrow the money, but to no avail.

In desperation Ed wrote to his mother saying, "I know you don't like it that I'm training to be a missionary, but I feel God has led me to do this. Things are tough right now, and I lack sixty dollars to pay my school expenses. I have a summer job lined up, and if you'll lend me the money now, I promise to pay you back this summer."

His mother wrote back, "Son, when you left this house to attend a Protestant college, I told you that you were never to come back as long as you remained in the Protestant faith. You said God would take care of you. Well, now you're in trouble so you're running back to me. If your God is really the God you say He is, then let Him take care of you. Otherwise, let me know when you're ready to drop all this foolishness."

With that Ed began a time of intense testing in his faith. He prayed and asked God to supply, but God delayed in answering his prayer. No money came in. Finally Ed packed his bags and prepared to go home and admit defeat. Just as Ed was getting ready to leave the campus, someone called his name. He turned and saw the dean of education approaching. "Ed," said the dean, "could you come to my office for a moment?"

Ed went to the dean's office, and the dean said, "The other day you told me you owed sixty dollars to the school and couldn't pay it. I was just looking at your account, and our records show that you don't owe the school a dime. In fact, your account shows a credit of forty dollars."

"How can that be?" Ed asked.

"Well, just this morning a person who wishes to remain anonymous has made a hundred-dollar donation to your account."

Ed went to see his mother and she said, "Well, son, you've finally given up your Protestant faith, have you?"

"No mother," he said, "I haven't."

Surprised, she said, "But you can't go back to school!"

"Yes I can," he said. "God supplied. He not only gave me the sixty dollars I needed, but forty dollars more."

His mother didn't know what to say, but sometime later she wrote him and said, "Son, I want to know this kind of God." That incident has been a source of strength to Ed Murphy down through the years. Whenever he is discouraged, whenever God seems to delay in answering prayer, Ed remembers the time when God met his need in a remarkable way.

That is what the psalmist does in Psalm 42:4. He looks back and remembers a time when the goodness of God filled his soul with exultation and joy. He hopes that this memory of God's goodness will relieve his sense of depression. Sometimes the memory of God's blessing in the past will relieve our blues, but not always. At times we need to go deeper with God in order to conquer the blues, as the psalmist does in the next few verses:

Why are you downcast, O my soul?
Why so disturbed within me?
Put your hope in God,
for I will yet praise him,
my Savior and my God (42:5).

But the psalmist's trial is not over. Having reached a deeper stage of depression, he goes to a deeper level of remembering God's goodness:

My soul is downcast within me;
therefore I will remember you
from the land of the Jordan,
the heights of Hermon—from Mount Mizar.
Deep calls to deep
in the roar of your waterfalls;
all your waves and breakers
have swept over me (42:6–7).

The psalmist is still despondent. Remembering the past has not worked. It usually does but now it does not, so the psalmist seeks help by remembering an experience he had when he was in the northern part of Israel near Mount Hermon at the head of the Jordan River. There on a little mountain peak called Mount Mizar (which means "little mountain"), he listened to the thundering waterfalls. He became aware of how the waterfalls and the ocean waves seemed to call to each other, deep calling to deep. It reminded him of how the deep places in the spirit of God call out to the deep places within people.

One of the amazing things about nature is the way silent voices seem to call to one another across vast spaces. The moon calls to the deeps in the sea, raising the tides. The sun and the rain call to the depths of a seed, causing it to stir and send a green shoot out of the ground. There is something in nature that calls to the deep in wild birds, causing them to migrate across trackless wastes to lay their eggs; that same something calls to the deep in salmon, telling them it is time to swim up-river to spawn.

In this way the psalmist thinks about God's creation, and he is reminded that God also calls to the "deeps" within people. There are deeps in God that correspond to the deeps in human nature, and He calls to us and reaches our innermost being. The psalmist specifically names two of the deeps within God: the deeps of His love and the deeps of His joy. These divine deeps call out to the deeps of prayer in the believer.

> *By day the* LORD *directs his love,*
> *at night his song is with me—*
> *a prayer to the God of my life (42:8).*

God's love and joy reach out to the psalmist, calling forth from his spirit a prayer to the God of his life. Remembering that the nature of God is intimately linked to the nature of the believer helps dispel the gloom and depression the psalmist feels. He realizes that though his feelings and moods are changeable, his relationship with God never changes.

But sometimes, the psalmist discovers, even this is not enough to dispel the blues. He expresses his continuing and perplexing depression:

> *I say to God my Rock,*
> *"Why have you forgotten me?*
> *Why must I go about mourning,*
> *oppressed by the enemy?"*
> *My bones suffer mortal agony*
> *as my foes taunt me,*
> *saying to me all day long,*
> *"Where is your God?" (42:9–10).*

The psalmist is still deeply troubled. He has turned to the first two reliable means for dispelling depression, yet they have not helped him this time. He cannot shake the sense that God has been unreasonably late in coming to his aid. Now his earlier depression has grown into a full-blown attack of doubt and despair. He says to God, who has been his Rock, "Why have you forgotten me?"

One Sunday when our daughter Laurie was only seven years old, I preached at the morning worship service, then I went home. My wife, Elaine, had come to church in another car, and she also went home after the church service. Elaine thought I had taken Laurie home with me. I thought Laurie was with Elaine. When we both got home, Laurie wasn't with either one of us! Where was she? She was in children's church, waiting for someone to pick her up.

When I realized that we had left Laurie behind, I jumped in the car and rushed back to church. I found Laurie at the door of the children's church classroom. She had two big tears glistening in her eyes, and there was a tone of reproach in her voice as she said, "Daddy, you forgot me!"

What a horrible feeling to be forgotten! Laurie was upset—not because I was a little late or because she felt unsafe. She was hurt because she felt I had forgotten her! That's the feeling the psalmist expresses: "I say to God my Rock, 'Why have you forgotten me?'" (42:9).

The psalmist goes on to say, "My bones suffer mortal agony as my foes taunt me, saying to me all day long, 'Where is your God?'" (42:10). The taunts of an enemy are like a dagger in the heart. Worse, these enemies don't merely insult the psalmist but they insult his God as well. They tell the psalmist he is a fool to rely on a God who delays, who seems absent and uncaring. In the face of such taunts, faith can only reply:

> *Why are you downcast, O my soul?*
> *Why so disturbed within me?*
> *Put your hope in God,*
> *for I will yet praise him,*
> *my Savior and my God (42:11).*

A Word of Triumph

Now we reach the third phase of the psalmist's battle against depression. His next cry gives voice to feelings of despair:

> *Vindicate me, O God,*
> *and plead my cause against an ungodly nation;*
> *rescue me from deceitful and wicked men (43:1).*

You probably know what it feels like to be mistreated, betrayed, and lied about. You probably know the sting of gross injustice. When we are treated unfairly, something within us wants to scream out to God and demand an explanation. That is exactly how the psalmist responds:

> *You are God my stronghold.*
> *Why have you rejected me?*
> *Why must I go about mourning,*
> *oppressed by the enemy? (43:2).*

The psalmist has fallen into absolute despair. God has always been his stronghold, his fortress. Yet now, inexplicably, God seems to have rejected him and abandoned him to his enemies. He continues to cry out, "Why?"

Have you ever felt like this? The psalmist has entered that greatest of all tests of faith. He has entered a period of sorrow and suffering, he has prayed for help, and God's response is—nothing.

But the psalmist is a man of faith and character. He does not give up on God. He still clings to the One who has been his rock of salvation:

> *Send forth your light and your truth,*
> *let them guide me;*
> *let them bring me to your holy mountain,*
> *to the place where you dwell.*
> *Then will I go to the altar of God,*
> *to God, my joy and my delight.*
> *I will praise you with the harp,*
> *O God, my God (43:3–4).*

What a word of triumph! Now the psalmist understands what God has been doing in his life. Step by step God has been driving him to the ultimate refuge of any believer in a time of testing: the Word of God. "Send forth your light and your truth," he says. "Let them guide me." God's Word is light and truth, and the psalmist cries out for the light of God's promises to shine forth and strengthen his heart.

Then the psalmist describes what will result when God's light and truth shine in his heart:

Then will I go to the altar of God,
to God, my joy and my delight.
I will praise you with the harp,
O God, my God" (43:4).

What a revelation this is! For each of us as believers, there comes a time when we discover for ourselves that the God of the universe is our own personal God, our intimate Friend, and our Refuge.

You may have seen one of the movies based on the true story of the sailing ship HMS *Bounty,* but you've probably never heard the entire story. The ship sailed from England in 1787 with Captain William Bligh and a crew of forty-five men. The *Bounty's* mission: Collect breadfruit plants to be transplanted in the Caribbean isles as a cheap food source for slaves. During the voyage the crew mutinied and set Captain Bligh and eighteen officers adrift on a small boat. The mutineers took the *Bounty* to Pitcairn Island, an isolated place that was barely a dot on the sea charts. They scuttled the ship and founded a settlement on Pitcairn, along with a number of Polynesian women.

One of the mutineers had the knack of distilling alcohol from fermented island fruit. The men of Pitcairn Island had little to do but eat, drink, and cohabitate with the Polynesian women. Their boredom led to brawling and murder. After ten years all but one of the mutineers was dead. Most had died violently at the hands of shipmates. The one man left alive was named John Adams. The rest of the population consisted of the Polynesian women and the twenty-three children fathered by the mutineers.

The lone survivor, John Adams, had become a brutal savage. The women and children of Pitcairn feared and hated him. What's more, John Adams hated himself. Plagued by guilt, he spent his days in a drunken stupor or a suicidal depression.

One day Adams was pawing through an old sea chest that had been brought ashore before the ship was scuttled. In the bottom of the chest, he found a Bible. With trembling hands Adams opened the Bible. He read from the Psalms and discovered the mercy and forgiveness of God. He read the gospel story and learned of a Savior who had died to save him. He read the letters of the apostles and learned about godly living. The power of God's Word struck him like a bolt from heaven, completely transforming his life.

John Adams began teaching the women and children of Pitcairn Island about the God of the Bible. Before he died, every woman, girl, and boy on that island had committed her or his life to the Lord Jesus Christ. Today Pitcairn Island has a population of fewer than a hundred people. It is reported that all the citizens of that island, all the living descendents of the mutineers, are committed followers of Jesus Christ to this day.

That's the power of God's Word to send forth light and truth into lives filled with darkness. That's the power of the Bible to transform a wretched sinner into a godly saint. That's the power of God's Word to enter our gloom and depression and to lift us up to the holy mountain where God dwells.

That's what the psalmist is saying. When you can't shake the blues and you suffer from a depression that nothing relieves, then there's only one thing to do: Rest upon God's Word. Let Him send forth His light and truth into your soul. Listen to the sweet and soothing words of the Bible, and especially the Psalms. Let those words guide you, lift your spirit, and heal your heart.

Finally the psalmist closes with the refrain we have heard twice before—the refrain that so comfortingly sums up the "Song of Confidence," Psalms 42 and 43:

Why are you downcast, O my soul?
Why so disturbed within me?
Put your hope in God,
for I will yet praise him,
my Savior and my God (43:5).

9

The Psalm of the Messiah-King

PSALM 45

A Muslim will tell you, "The prophet Jesus, peace be upon him, is one of Allah's holiest prophets." A Jehovah's Witness will say, "Jesus is another name for Michael the Archangel, who was created by Jehovah." A Mormon will tell you, "Jesus is the Elder Brother of the fallen angel Lucifer." A Christian Science practitioner or a New Ager will say, "Jesus was a mere human being who lived out a divine ideal." A Bible-believing Christian will say, "Jesus Christ is my Lord and Savior, God the Son, the Messiah, whose coming was promised throughout the Old Testament."

Who is Jesus? Your answer to that question will affect your entire life and determine your eternity. How do *you* answer that question?

How can you know who Jesus is? You find His story in the New Testament and especially the four gospels: Matthew, Mark, Luke, and John. But you might be surprised to discover that Jesus is also revealed in a surprisingly clear and detailed way in the Old Testament, particularly in the Psalms. In fact Jesus is the central figure of the Psalms, just as He is the central figure of the entire Bible.

Of all the Old Testament books, the one most quoted by New Testament writers is Psalms. Why? Because the Psalms have so much to say about Jesus. This book is a treasury of prophecies about the promised Messiah—prophecies that were fulfilled again and again in the life of Jesus.

Prophetic Psalms of the Messiah

The psalms that portray the life of Jesus in a prophetic way are called Messianic Psalms. In chapter 6 we looked closely at one of them, Psalm 22, the "Psalm of the Cross." There we are told that Jesus' executioners would pierce His hands and feet, and they would part His garments and gamble for them. All of this was fulfilled when Jesus was crucified.

Other Messianic Psalms include Psalm 2, in which God declares the Messiah to be His Son; Psalm 16 (especially verse 10), a wonderful description of the resurrection of the Messiah; Psalm 34 (especially verse 20), which predicts that the Messiah's bones would not be broken; Psalm 41 (especially verse 9), which predicts Judas's betrayal of Jesus; Psalm 69, which portrays the Messiah as being hated for no reason (in John 15:25 Jesus quotes this psalm, applying it to Himself) and describes His being given vinegar and gall upon the cross; Psalm 110, which points us to the deity of Christ, the great mystery that He is fully man and fully God; and Psalm 118, which portrays Him as a stumbling block, rejected by men but used by God as the cornerstone of His redemptive plan.

It's not just Christian writers and commentators who see that these psalms refer to the Messiah. Scholars of the Judaic faith agree that these psalms are unquestionably messianic prophecies. Though Judaic scholars do not see the historic Jesus as the fulfillment of these prophecies, they agree that these psalms are prophecies of the Jewish Messiah. The Messianic Psalms describe various facets of the life and ministry of the Messiah.

Jesus Himself told us that the book of Psalms spoke of Him: "This is what I told you while I was still with you: Everything must be fulfilled that is written about me in the Law of Moses, the Prophets and the Psalms" (Luke 24:44).

There are three psalms that specifically portray the Messiah as the King. First, Psalm 2 portrays the Messiah as the King in His authority:

Why do the nations conspire
and the peoples plot in vain?
The kings of the earth take their stand

and the rulers gather together
against the LORD
and against his Anointed One.
[*Note:* Messiah *literally means "the anointed one" in Hebrew.*]
"Let us break their chains," they say,
"and throw off their fetters."
The One enthroned in heaven laughs;
the Lord scoffs at them.
Then he rebukes them in his anger
and terrifies them in his wrath, saying,
"I have installed my King
on Zion, my holy hill" (2:1–6).

Psalm 72 provides another beautiful description of the Messiah as King. This is a picture of a day that is still in our future when the Messiah will reign as King throughout the earth. All the earth will be restored in beauty and splendor. Peace will fill the earth as the waters fill the sea.

Finally, Psalm 45 portrays Messiah as the King in all of His beauty and splendor. It is a glimpse of the majesty and perfect character of Jesus Christ. This psalm was written to mark an historic occasion, the marriage of one of the great kings of Israel, probably King Solomon's marriage to an Egyptian princess (see 1 Kings 3).

Even though this passage was written for an earthly wedding service, it is clear from the lofty and worshipful description of the King that this psalm depicts someone far greater than any earthly king. Both Jewish and Christian Bible commentators readily acknowledge that Psalm 45 presents a picture of Messiah, the Anointed One of God.

The Most Excellent of Men

Note the inscription at the top of Psalm 45. We learn first that this psalm is dedicated to the director of music and is to be performed to a tune (now lost to us) called "Lilies." The psalm was composed by the Sons of Korah, a family of outstanding singers and musicians in Israel who passed their musical office from one generation to the next.

The inscription also tells us that Psalm 45 is a *maskil*, a teaching psalm. It was written to teach us something important about the King, the Messiah. And the inscription also tells us that this psalm is a wedding song, a romantic love song. The psalmist writes:

My heart is stirred by a noble theme
as I recite my verses for the king;
my tongue is the pen of a skillful writer (v. 1).

This statement is a lyrical expression of how inspired the psalmist feels because of the perfection and nobility of the King. The writer is overcome with a sense of adoration. He is eager to write down these emotions, so eager that words flow easily and the writer's tongue is metaphorically compared to the pen of a skillful writer. Feelings of awe and adoration can transform a tongue-tied oaf into a paragon of eloquence!

I recall how my son-in-law Steve was shipped out to Vietnam just a week after his marriage to my daughter. Steve had never been much of a letter writer before. But soon after he shipped out, my daughter began receiving letters—lots and lots of letters. Steve wrote on almost a daily basis. I don't know what he wrote because my daughter said the letters were for her eyes only! But I do know that feelings of love and adoration can utterly transform a young man.

The psalmist writes as one who is awestruck and inspired by the majesty of the King. In verse two, he describes his impression of the King:

You are the most excellent of men
and your lips have been anointed with grace,
since God has blessed you forever (45:2).

I believe we get a hint of the physical appearance of Jesus Christ in this verse. If you have read the four gospels, you know that they do not describe His physical appearance at all. The many paintings we have of Jesus are created from sheer imagination, for the gospels do not even hint at what He looked like.

Some commentators have suggested that Jesus was physically unattractive or disfigured, and they base this conclusion on the words of the prophet Isaiah:

His appearance was so disfigured beyond that of any man and his form marred beyond human likeness . . . He grew up before him like a tender shoot, and like a root out of dry ground. He had no beauty or majesty to attract us to him, nothing in his appearance that we should desire him. He was despised and rejected by men, a man of sorrows, and familiar with suffering. Like one from whom men hide their faces he was despised, and we esteemed him not (52:14b; 53:2–3).

I don't agree with the commentators who say that these words from Isaiah are a physical description of Jesus. Instead I'm convinced that these words describe the disfigurement He suffered when He was beaten and flogged, when a crown of thorns was crushed into his scalp, and when he was crucified. But I believe that before He was so brutally beaten, our Lord Jesus was a strong and attractive man with an appealing personality.

Multitudes flocked to Jesus everywhere He went. I believe they were drawn not only by the beauty of His words but also by His striking personal presence. As the psalmist writes, "You are the most excellent of men."

Lips Anointed with Grace

Next note what the psalmist says about the speech of the King, the coming Messiah: "Your lips have been anointed with grace, since God has blessed you forever" (v. 2). Luke tells us of an incident in the life of Jesus that parallels this statement from Psalm 45.

On this occasion Jesus went to the synagogue in Nazareth, his hometown. Standing before people who had watched Him grow up since childhood, Jesus asked for the scroll of the prophet Isaiah. When it was handed to him, He opened it and read from Isaiah 61:1–3a:

"The Spirit of the Lord is on me, because he has anointed me to preach good news to the poor. He has sent me to proclaim freedom for the prisoners and recovery of sight for the blind, to release the oppressed, to proclaim the year of the Lord's favor" (Luke 4:18–19).

After reading this passage, Jesus rolled up the scroll and said, "Today this scripture is fulfilled in your hearing." Then Luke adds this important observation: "All spoke well of him and were amazed at *the gracious words that came from his lips*" (Luke 4:22a, emphasis added).

The gracious words that came from his lips! Here is an echo of the words the psalmist wrote to describe the Messiah: "Your lips have been anointed with grace." The words of Jesus captivated people, and they saw that He was the One who held the secrets of life. That's why the crowds sought Him out. People would leave their fields and shops, forget to eat or sleep, and walk for miles over the countryside just to hear Him. "Never did anyone speak like this man!" they said.

Down through the centuries, His gracious words, as recorded in the gospels, have continued to attract armies of followers. People are still being freed from the bondage of sin and death because of the gracious words He spoke. The lips of Jesus the Messiah have been anointed with grace so that we might become the people God intended us to be.

Many writers have tried to capture the incomparable character of Jesus Christ. One of the best attempts was that of Dr. James Allen Francis, who served as pastor of the First Baptist Church of Los Angeles. He described the unique life of Jesus in his book *The Real Jesus and Other Sermons.* Dr. Francis's words have often been quoted, though they were frequently ascribed to an anonymous or unknown author. Dr. Francis writes about Jesus:

> A child is born in an obscure village. He is brought up in another obscure village. He works in a carpenter shop until he is thirty, and then for three brief years is an itinerant preacher, proclaiming a message and living a life. He never writes a book. He never holds an office. He never raises an army. He never has a family of his own. He never owns a home. He never goes to college. He never travels two hundred miles from the place where he was born.
>
> He gathers a little group of friends about him and teaches them his way of life. While still a young man the tide of popular feeling turns against him. The band of followers forsakes him.

One denies him; another betrays him. He is turned over to his enemies. He goes through the mockery of a trial; he is nailed on a cross between two thieves, and when dead is laid in a borrowed grave by the kindness of a friend. Those are the facts of his human life. He rises from the dead.

Today we look back across nineteen hundred years and ask, "What kind of a trail has he left across the centuries?" When we try to sum up his influence, all the armies that ever marched, all the parliaments that ever sat, all the kings that ever reigned are absolutely picayune in their influence on mankind compared with that of this one solitary life.

Jesus is, in short, exactly as the psalmist proclaimed Him to be: He is the most excellent of men, and His lips have been anointed with grace because God has blessed Him forever. He stands upon the highest pinnacle of human history and heaven's glory, proclaimed by God, acknowledged by angels, adored by saints, feared by devils—the living Lord Jesus Christ, the Savior of all who have placed their trust in Him.

The Victories of the King

Next the psalmist pictures the Messiah as the victorious King:

> Gird your sword upon your side, O mighty one;
> clothe yourself with splendor and majesty.
> In your majesty ride forth victoriously
> in behalf of truth, humility and righteousness;
> let your right hand display awesome deeds.
> Let your sharp arrows pierce the hearts of the king's enemies;
> let the nations fall beneath your feet (45:3–5).

Notice the sudden transition at verse 3. The psalmist moves from extolling the graciousness of the King's words to picturing Him as mighty in battle—a warrior and a destroyer of nations and enemies. Here is a startling contrast: the grace of Jesus the Messiah alongside His majestic, invincible power as the Warrior-King.

It is important to remember that the psalms use figurative language and metaphors to describe spiritual reality. This passage is not a description of bloody physical warfare but of spiritual warfare, which is far more intense and involves much higher stakes. The psalmist speaks here of enemies more dangerous than armies of mere flesh and blood. As the apostle Paul reminds us, "For our struggle is not against flesh and blood, but against the rulers, against the authorities, against the powers of this dark world and against the spiritual forces of evil in the heavenly realms" (Ephesians 6:12).

Dr. Charles Habib Malik (1906–1987) was a Lebanese philosopher and statesman and served as president of the General Assembly of the United Nations. He once said, "We must remember that we are still living, as the Germans say, *zwischen den zeiten*, between the times, when demonic forces can quickly soar very high, and can bring about conditions wherein men are no longer able to control the events of their lives."

Dr. Malik understood the spiritual reality of our age and the reality of our struggle against the spiritual forces of evil in the heavenly realms. These spiritual forces are the enemies who hold humanity enslaved. They are the enemies over whom Jesus, our King and Messiah, has won the victory. They are the ones He has trampled, destroyed with the sword of his right hand, and pierced to the heart with arrows.

When the psalmist writes of the victories of the King, he is not writing about clashing swords and blood-soaked battlefields. He is picturing for us the great battle that the Messiah has waged against unseen forces of evil, of the powers of darkness that have been driven back, of enslaved souls now set free. These are the victories of our Messiah-King.

In the New International Version, verse 4 reads, "In your majesty ride forth victoriously in behalf of truth, humility and righteousness." This is not the most accurate translation of the original Hebrew. What the psalmist actually says in this verse is, "In your majesty ride forth victoriously [by means of] truth, humility, and righteousness." In other words, the Messiah uses truth, humility, and righteousness *as His weapons*. This is an important distinction.

Here the psalmist describes the character of Jesus: He is truth incarnate, He is humble, and He is righteous. The psalmist also tells us that these character qualities are the very weapons Jesus the Messiah uses in His battle against the spiritual forces of evil controlled by Satan.

The righteousness that Jesus wielded as a weapon against the spiritual forces of evil was not *self*-righteousness, the kind of so-called righteousness that says, "I am right and you are wrong." That's the false and arrogant righteousness of the Pharisees. One of the great ironies of the life of Christ is that He was the One most qualified to behave in a "holier than thou" way, yet He never did. He dealt graciously and kindly with sinners, adulterers, prostitutes, beggars, tax collectors, and other outcasts. Sinners never felt condemned or shamed in His presence.

Jesus fulfilled the messianic prophecy of Psalm 45:4—the prophecy of a coming King who would vanquish His enemies with weapons of truth, humility, and righteousness. The psalmist didn't know what name this King would be known by, but we know His name: Jesus of Nazareth, the promised Messiah, the King of kings and Lord of lords.

The Great Mystery of Our Faith

The psalmist goes on to describe this King, making it abundantly clear that he is no mere mortal king upon an earthly throne. Without question this King is Jesus the Messiah:

> *Your throne, O God, will last for ever and ever;*
> *a scepter of justice will be the scepter of your kingdom.*
> *You love righteousness and hate wickedness;*
> *therefore God, your God, has set you above your companions*
> *by anointing you with the oil of joy (45:6–7).*

These verses are quoted in the opening chapter of Hebrews to prove the deity of the Lord Jesus Christ and His superiority to any of the angels (Hebrews 1:8–9). Jesus is not an angel; He is not the highest of the created beings; He is God, God who became a man. And how does the psalmist address the King in verse 6? He addresses the King as God!

In Psalm 45:7, we find a strangely constructed sentence that underscores the divine nature of this Messiah-King even more clearly. The King is addressed as God, yet the King is also told, "Your God has anointed you." There is only one way that such a statement makes sense: The King must be both God and man!

Here we see that the secret of Jesus' incarnation was recorded in the book of Psalms, a thousand years before He appeared on earth. Here we catch a glimpse of the amazing mystery that caused the shepherds to whisper in wonder on that first Christmas, "Emmanuel—God with us!" Imagine—God became a human being for our sakes. This astounding truth moved the apostle Paul to exclaim: "Without question, this is the great mystery of our faith: Christ appeared in the flesh (1 Timothy 3:16a, NEW LIVING TRANSLATION).

In Jesus, the Messiah-King, human nature and the nature of God unite. His deity was hidden in human flesh. He relied completely on the Father for everything He did and said. Though fully God, He never acted or spoke from His own power. This is a mystery beyond our comprehension.

Because of this great mystery, the psalmist tells us that the Messiah-King is not only God but the One anointed by God. He fulfills all the offices for which an anointing is required: prophet, priest, and king. What are the functions of these three offices? The prophet speaks the words of God. The priest offers the sacrifice for the sins of the people. The king rules.

Jesus the Messiah-Prophet spoke the words of God in a way that has never been equaled. Jesus the Messiah-Priest offered Himself as the perfect sacrifice for human sin. Jesus the Messiah-King rules not only the people but nature itself. Even death must obey Him. "Therefore God," says the psalmist, "your God, has set you above your companions by anointing you with the oil of joy" (v. 7).

Notice that beautiful phrase "the oil of joy." To what does it refer? In the Bible the symbol of oil is used to refer to the Holy Spirit. The physical act of anointing a prophet, priest, or king with oil was symbolic of the anointing of the Holy Spirit. We see this principle clearly demonstrated in Samuel's anointing of King David: "So Samuel took the horn of oil and anointed him in the presence of his brothers, and from that day on the Spirit of the LORD came upon David in power (1 Samuel 16:13).

We see this principle reinforced in the New Testament where

Jesus stands in the synagogue at Nazareth and says: "The Spirit of the Lord is on me, because he has anointed me . . ." (Luke 4:18).

Now in Psalm 45:7, we read the psalmist's words to the Messiah-King: "Therefore God, your God, has set you above your companions by anointing you with the oil of joy." The oil of joy is the Spirit, for truly it is the Holy Spirit who brings lasting joy to the human heart. Here we catch a glimpse of the heritage of all who know the Son of God as their Lord and Savior: They share with Him in the anointing with the oil of joy.

The Wedding of the King

Next the psalmist tells us about the relationship that the Messiah-King wishes to have with us. After all, that is what this psalm has been leading up to. That's why we've been learning about the One who is called "the most excellent of men," whose "lips have been anointed with grace," who is mighty in battle and clothed "with splendor and majesty," and who is anointed "with the oil of joy." That's why we've been learning of the One who wondrously unites the nature of God and the nature of man.

This is not merely a psalm of praise. It is (as the inscription tells us) a *maskil*, a teaching psalm, and it is a wedding song. Psalm 45 teaches us the unique character of the Messiah-King, and it announces that He desires a relationship of marriage. The Messiah-King has come for His bride:

> *All your robes are fragrant with myrrh and aloes and cassia;*
> *from palaces adorned with ivory*
> *the music of the strings makes you glad.*
> *Daughters of kings are among your honored women;*
> *at your right hand is the royal bride in gold of Ophir (45:8–9).*

These verses describe a marriage ceremony. Here we see a series of preparations for the wedding. First, the King has prepared Himself. He is fragrant with the scent of myrrh, aloes, and cassia. Why are these particular spices significant? They are burial spices.

You recall that after Jesus was crucified, the women went to the tomb on Easter morning, carrying with them a quantity of burial spices they would use in order to preserve Jesus' body. We find that the Messiah-King applies these same burial spices to His body at His wedding. The mention of these spices tells us that this marriage is made possible through the death of someone, the death of the One who is fragrant with the scent of burial spices, the Messiah-King.

This scene is beautifully complemented by Paul's words to the Ephesian Christians: "Husbands, love your wives, just as Christ loved the church and *gave himself up for her* to make her holy, cleansing her by the washing with water through the word (5:25–26, emphasis added).

Jesus died for the church, His bride. He passed through the darkness of death for us. Why? So that He might present to Himself a glorious church, a beautiful bride, holy and clean, washed by the waters of baptism and by God's own Word. We catch another glimpse of the marriage relationship between Jesus and the church in this passage from the last book of the Bible:

> *Then I heard what sounded like a great multitude, like the roar*
> *   of rushing waters and like loud peals of thunder, shouting:*
> *"Hallelujah!*
> *For our Lord God Almighty reigns.*
> *Let us rejoice and be glad*
> *and give him glory!*
> *For the wedding of the Lamb has come,*
> *and his bride has made herself ready" (Revelation 19:6–7).*

The psalmist also tells us where this wedding ceremony is to take place: "from palaces adorned with ivory the music of the strings makes you glad" (v. 8). This is a picture of a beautiful place, and it reminds us of Jesus' words to His disciples before He went to the cross:

> *In my Father's house are many rooms; if it were not so, I would*
> *have told you. I am going there to prepare a place for you. And if I*
> *go and prepare a place for you, I will come back and take you to be*
> *with me that you also may be where I am (John 14:2–3).*

Jesus is preparing that place for us right now. It is a place of beauty and glory beyond description. The imagery in these verses in Psalm 45 are mere metaphors designed to give us a glimpse of what this place will be like: ivory palaces filled with music and gladness.

Finally, the bride herself is prepared: "At your right hand is the royal bride in gold of Ophir" (v. 9). In the ancient custom of that culture, the kingly bridegroom himself always presented this golden gown to the queen. He paid for the golden wedding gown.

The wedding pictured in Psalm 45 is a beautiful ceremony that symbolizes for us the wonderful relationship that we have with our Lord Jesus Christ. Who prepares the bride for the day that she and the King will begin sharing their life together? The King Himself! Who prepares us, the church, the bride of Christ, for our life in eternity with Him? Jesus, the Bridegroom, the Messiah-King, our Lord and Savior! He is preparing us. He has clothed us with His own righteousness, our golden robe.

In Scripture gold is always the symbol of deity. What does this suggest to us? It is a hint of what the apostle Peter tells us when he says that we are to "participate in the divine nature" (2 Peter 1:4). It is difficult to grasp what this really means. These are not mere words of poetry and symbolism. This is a deep truth of our life with Christ! He is blending our lives with His, and He is sharing with us His position, power, and privileges. All that belongs to Him belongs to us because we are joint heirs with Him.

Tragically many of us have forgotten the privileges that are ours in Christ. We do not realize how amazing His promises are to us. We do not stand on the power and position that is ours in Christ. We do not recognize that as the bride of Christ we are clothed in gold, a golden gown of royalty that He has provided for us through His death upon the cross. May we learn to live worthy of this amazing truth: We are the bride of the Messiah-King!

The Psalmist Speaks to the Bride

The next section is addressed to the bride. Because we, as Christians, are the bride of Christ, this section holds special significance for us:

> *Listen, O daughter, consider and give ear:*
> *Forget your people and your father's house.*
> *The king is enthralled by your beauty;*
> *honor him, for he is your lord.*

The Daughter of Tyre will come with a gift,
men of wealth will seek your favor (45:10–12).

We find two important statements of exhortation to the bride in this passage. Verse 10 gives the first exhortation to the bride to forget her people and her father's house." What does that mean for us today? What is the psalmist saying to us when he exhorts us as Christians to forget our people and our father's house? Our father's house symbolizes our old nature, the place where we were born. It is the life we inherited in Adam—the sinful flesh, the self-centered life. The psalmist tells us to turn our backs on the flesh and the self. What will result when we turn away from our people and our father's house—the flesh and the self? The king will desire the beauty of the bride!

I believe the New International Version's translation of verse 11 misses the point that the psalmist makes: "The king is enthralled by your beauty; honor him, for he is your lord." In the original Hebrew, the psalmist is not simply making a statement: "The king is enthralled by your beauty." He is making an if-then statement, which logicians call a statement of conditional logic: If a certain condition is met, then there will be a specific consequence. The psalmist is saying, "*If* you forget your people and your father's house, *if* you turn away from the flesh and the self, *then* the King will be enthralled by your beauty." That is how the New American Standard Bible translates this statement: "Then the King will desire your beauty."

This is a powerful and life-changing exhortation to each of us as followers of Jesus Christ. Here, in effect, is what the psalmist says to us in these verses: "Listen Christian, bride of Christ. Consider and listen carefully: Forget your sinful past, your fleshly desires. Turn away from what you were in Adam and embrace what you are becoming in Christ. If you do that, then the Messiah-King will desire your beauty as His lovely bride."

Isn't that a beautiful statement? The psalmist puts this spiritual truth into the intimate language of a marriage relationship: When you live a holy life, honoring to Christ your King, you actually arouse in Him a desire and a hunger in His heart for you because of the beauty of your life!

The second exhortation to the bride is in verse 11, and again it comes in the form of an "if-then" statement of conditional logic. The

New International Version reads: "Honor him, for he is your lord. The Daughter of Tyre will come with a gift, men of wealth will seek your favor." In the original Hebrew, the sense of this exhortation is: "*If* you honor the King as your Lord, *then* the princess of Tyre and other people of great wealth will bring you gifts and seek your favor."

Throughout the Scriptures the Phoenician city of Tyre is used as a picture of the might, power, and riches of the world. Founded around 3000 BC, Tyre was an island city of incredible splendor. At around 1000 BC, when Psalm 45 was written, Tyre experienced a golden age under King Hiram. The city-state of Tyre had amassed great wealth and worldly power through trade with its flourishing colonies around the Mediterranean region and its primary industry, the production of costly purple-dyed cloths.

The psalmist is saying that if we, as Christians, as the bride of Christ, will worship our Lord as we should, then the world in all of its power will come to our door, seeking our counsel and help. If we want to know why the world sees the church as irrelevant, here is the answer: We have not worshiped our Lord as we should. We have ceased making Him the King of our hearts. Instead, we relegate Him to the status of a figurehead to whom we nod occasionally before going on about our business. We do not follow Him. We do not obey Him. We do not worship Him as Lord. When the church begins to worship and honor the Lord again, the world will look to the church for wisdom and light in the darkness.

Our Messiah-King Has Come!

The rest of the psalm describes the beauty of the wedding ceremony. The psalmist writes:

> *All glorious is the princess within her chamber;*
> *her gown is interwoven with gold.*
> *In embroidered garments she is led to the king;*
> *her virgin companions follow her*
> *and are brought to you.*
> *They are led in with joy and gladness;*
> *they enter the palace of the king (45:13–15).*

Here the psalmist speaks in beautiful metaphors and imagery. The apostle Paul described this same event in his letter to the Christians in Rome:

> *The creation waits in eager expectation for the sons of God to be revealed. For the creation was subjected to frustration, not by its own choice, but by the will of the one who subjected it, in hope that the creation itself will be liberated from its bondage to decay and brought into the glorious freedom of the children of God (Romans 8:19–21).*

The marriage of the Messiah-King and His bride in Psalm 45 corresponds to that future moment when God's plan in history is suddenly unveiled, the children of God are revealed, and creation is delivered from the bondage of the fall of Adam. Then the universe will shout and sing and rejoice, as in a great wedding celebration. On that day the King will claim the bride He has purchased at the cost of His own blood.

God is secretly orchestrating events of eternal importance. The battle of all eternity is being fought and decided right now, behind the scenes of history, in the quiet places of your life and mine. Every time our Lord delivers us from a sinful attitude, a trait of selfishness, a habit of sin, He wins a skirmish on the only battlefield that ultimately matters—the battlefield of the human heart.

The psalm concludes with God's promise to the mighty Messiah-King. Although the Messiah will come from the line of David, according to human ancestry, God promises that He will have sons, children who are His not by reason of genetic lineage but through a faith relationship:

> *Your sons will take the place of your fathers;*
> *you will make them princes throughout the land.*
> *I will perpetuate your memory through all generations;*
> *therefore the nations will praise you for ever and ever (vv. 16–17).*

In his letter to the Philippians, Paul expressed this same thought in different words. Referring to Jesus, the Messiah-King, Paul wrote:

> *Therefore God exalted him to the highest place*
> *and gave him the name that is above every name,*

that at the name of Jesus every knee should bow,
in heaven and on earth and under the earth,
and every tongue confess that Jesus Christ is Lord,
to the glory of God the Father (2:9–11).

That is the Messiah-King in all of His majesty and glory. The people of the psalmist's day had to be content with the promise of a coming King. But we do not merely possess a promise. Our Messiah-King has come, and He is our Lord! He was born to us on that first Christmas. He died for us on a Roman cross. He was raised in glorious resurrection power on that first Easter Sunday. He lives forever, and we eagerly await the day when we, as His bride, can take our place at His side forever. May we worship Him as we should, confessing before the entire world that Jesus Christ is Lord!

IO

A Song of Justice

PSALM 50

I f you are acquainted with American folk songs, you know that many express the lament of a prisoner who has been found guilty of a crime. These songs have titles like "The Ballad of Jesse James" (the story of the famed fugitive train robber), "Joe Turner" (about a prisoner who spent six months in jail for killing a man), "The Birmingham Jail" (about a convicted criminal who was "crying for freedom, dying a slave"), and "The Judge and the Jury" (about a lad accused of murder but saved from the gallows when "a maiden fair with golden hair" pleaded for his life).

As we come to Psalm 50, we find one of the earliest folk songs in that tradition. This psalm depicts a courtroom scene. Here we see the psalmist recreating what will take place when God judges His people. If we were to put this in today's street jargon, we might call this psalm "Busted by God."

Psalm 50 is a psalm of Asaph, one of the musicians of King David's court. Though this psalm is from the pen of Asaph, it reflects the experience and emotions of many believers as they contemplate what it means to stand before the Judge of the universe.

The God of Might, Majesty, and Mercy

The psalm opens with a scene of awe and majesty. Every inhabitant of the earth is summoned to appear before the Lord God, the eternal Judge:

> *The Mighty One, God, the LORD,*
> *speaks and summons the earth*
> *from the rising of the sun to the place where it sets (v. 1).*

My doorbell rang one Saturday morning. I opened the door, and there stood a man I had never seen before. Without a word he handed me a piece of paper and then turned and walked away. I looked at the paper and saw that it was a summons to appear in court. A strange feeling came over me, a sense of mingled fear and awe. Even though I knew I had done nothing illegal, I wanted to go back to bed and start the day all over again.

I think my experience was just a faint glimmer of how the human race will feel when this great summons rings out over all the earth. The psalmist pictures an impressive cosmic courtroom. The Judge enters in His solemnity and majesty. There is a reverent hush, and all of humanity is summoned to appear before Him.

> *From Zion, perfect in beauty,*
> *God shines forth.*
> *Our God comes and will not be silent;*
> *a fire devours before him,*
> *and around him a tempest rages.*
> *He summons the heavens above,*
> *and the earth, that he may judge his people:*
> *"Gather to me my consecrated ones,*
> *who made a covenant with me by sacrifice."*
> *And the heavens proclaim his righteousness,*
> *for God himself is judge.* Selah *(vv. 2–6).*

The most awesome words in this passage are these: "God Himself is judge." This is a courtroom in which God sits to judge His people. Who is this great and majestic Judge?

We saw a threefold description of God the Judge in verse 1: He is the Mighty One, God, the LORD. In the original Hebrew, these three names are El, Elohim, and Jehovah. These three names are impressive, for they capture the major characteristics of God. He is first El, the Mighty One, the all-powerful One, the God of authority and strength. Next He is Elohim, the God of majesty and greatness, the Supreme One, sovereign over all. Next He is Jehovah, the God of mercy, the One who graciously condescends to His people's frailty and need. The Judge introduces Himself to us as the God of might, the God of majesty, and the God of mercy. These three attributes of God are in perfect balance.

Future Judgment and Continuing Judgment

Next it's important to note that this Judge does not come down from the top of Mount Sinai, where the Law was given, but from Mount Zion: "From Zion, perfect in beauty, God shines forth" (v. 2).

Why is this an important point? You may recall that at Mount Sinai, when the Law was given to Moses, it was accompanied by thunderous judgment with lightning and the sound of a trumpet so loud that the people could not stand it. They cried out to Moses, "Speak to us yourself and we will listen. But do not have God speak to us or we will die" (Exodus 20:19).

Here in Psalm 50:2, it is no longer Mount Sinai but Mount Zion from which God comes to pronounce judgment. Mount Zion is the mountain around which the holy city of Jerusalem is built. It is the highest point in the city of Jerusalem, slightly higher than the Temple Mount. Mount Zion symbolizes the mercy, grace, and redemptive love of God. Though God is still the Judge when He comes from Zion, He is the Judge who tempers justice with mercy. It is well to remember this truth as we meditate on this psalm. God's judgment is realistic, but it is neither vindictive nor harsh.

Because Zion is associated with Jerusalem, I believe that this psalm describes the second coming of our Lord Jesus Christ, when He shall return to earth in power and glory (see Matthew 25). After His return Jesus will judge the nations. When He came to earth the first time, He came in weakness and humility. When He returns He will come in glory and power to judge the people of the earth as they are summoned before Him. That, I believe, is the scene that Psalm 50 depicts.

But I also believe it would be a mistake to view Psalm 50 as referring only to that event. I'm convinced that this passage, like many prophetic portions of Scripture, applies to more than one event in human history. It not only looks forward to the time when Christ will return to judge His people but it also describes a judgment that is going on right now. This interpretation is indicated in verse 1. Notice that this verse refers to a process that takes place every day: The sun rises every morning and sets every evening.

I believe that God daily judges His people. He sits among them as a Redeemer-Judge. That is why verse 3 says, "Our God comes and will not be silent." It does not say "Our God *is* coming" sometime in the future; it says, "Our God comes." He is continuously arriving and summoning people before Him in His capacity as Judge. We are always living in the presence of the great Judge of all the earth.

The Fire and Wind of God's Judgment

Who is this Judge who comes to judge His people? What is He like? The psalmist goes on to describe His character by employing two symbols of judgment: fire and wind. He writes:

Our God comes and will not be silent;
a fire devours before him,
and around him a tempest rages (v. 3).

These same two symbols, a devouring fire and a tempest wind, are also used in the New Testament to describe God. For example Hebrews 12:29 tells us, "God is a consuming fire." And in John 3:8, Jesus tells Nicodemus, "The wind blows wherever it pleases. You hear its sound, but you cannot tell where it comes from or where it is going. So it is with everyone born of the Spirit."

God is symbolized as fire because fire purifies. As a purifying fire, God will burn the dross, waste, and trash of our lives, the garbage of our souls. And God is symbolized as wind because wind is one of the mightiest forces in nature.

I once saw a photo of a single straw that had been caught by a tornado and driven entirely through a telephone pole. If I gave you a piece of straw and a hammer and said, "Hammer this straw through a telephone pole," you'd think I was crazy. But a straw that is driven by a mighty wind is capable of doing what is seemingly unthinkable.

In Acts the Spirit of God is described as a mighty rushing wind; when that wind blew among the first disciples in Jerusalem, they became caught up in its power. Like straws that could pierce a telephone pole, those disciples began doing things they had never done before—impossible things, unthinkable things. Empowered by the wind of God's Spirit, they startled and astonished the world by the amazing power that blew through their lives.

In comparing God to fire and wind, the psalmist is telling us that God's judgment accomplishes two things in our lives: First, it burns out the trash that clutters our souls; and second, it fills us with unimaginable power, enabling us to do things we could never do before.

Who has the righteous and mighty Judge come to judge? The answer may surprise you! The psalmist writes:

> *He summons the heavens above,*
> *and the earth, that he may judge his people:*
> *"Gather to me my consecrated ones,*
> *who made a covenant with me by sacrifice" (vv. 4–5).*

He judges His people! God Himself says, "My consecrated ones, who made a covenant with me by sacrifice."

In the Old Testament, God's people made a covenant with Him by sacrifice, the animal sacrifices that Israel offered up day by day. Israel made these sacrifices to reflect God's special covenant relationship with His people, a covenant made in blood. A life had to be poured out on behalf of the people. The Old Testament sacrifices were a picture of the sacrifice of the Lord Jesus Christ upon the cross.

Today we also make a covenant with God by sacrifice, the sacrifice of the Lord Jesus Christ. This psalm describes what God is doing at this very moment. It pictures God among His people. He is the God who comes from Zion, the God who loves, and the God who sees us as we are.

That is why this section ends with that little word *selah.* As we have already seen, that word means, "Pause for a moment. Stop and think. Reflect and meditate." The psalmist wants us to pause and think about the fact that God, the righteous Judge, is in our midst, judging His people.

What Is Missing from Our Lives

Next the Judge speaks:

> *"Hear, O my people, and I will speak,*
> *O Israel, and I will testify against you:*
> *I am God, your God.*

I do not rebuke you for your sacrifices
or your burnt offerings, which are ever before me.
I have no need of a bull from your stall
or of goats from your pens,
for every animal of the forest is mine,
and the cattle on a thousand hills.
I know every bird in the mountains,
and the creatures of the field are mine.
If I were hungry I would not tell you,
for the world is mine, and all that is in it.
Do I eat the flesh of bulls
or drink the blood of goats (vv. 7–13)?

There is a sardonic twist to the Lord's words: "I do not rebuke you for your sacrifices or your burnt offerings, which are ever before me." In other words, "There are certain things you are doing right—but for the wrong reasons." The Israelites regularly brought the sacrifices the law prescribed, and God said it was good that the people kept the law. Their actions were right, but their thinking was wrong. The people mistakenly thought that all God wanted from them was the act of sacrificing animals, as if God had some need for the spilling of blood. The people had a distorted concept of their God, seeing Him as a blood-thirsty deity.

So God, the righteous Judge, corrected their mistaken impression of Him. He said, in effect, "How absurd can you be? Do you really think I'm that kind of a God? Do you think I need to feed on flesh or drink the blood of animals? I own the cattle on a thousand hills. I own the wild beasts of the forests and the birds of the air. They're all mine, and I can do with them as I wish. If hunger were my motive, I would hardly need you to feed me! What kind of God do you think I am?"

Perhaps you see a contemporary parallel to this ancient misimpression about God. Today many people come to church and think that God wants them to sing hymns, bow their heads in prayer, utter certain words, and go through certain rituals, as if ceremony and liturgy are all God cares about. How absurd! While there's nothing wrong with ceremony or liturgy, these are not the things God desires from our lives.

A young pastor once asked me, "What's wrong with the evangelical church today? Why doesn't the church seem to have any influence in the world?"

"Well," I said, "there's a lot that's right about the church today. Our doctrines are right. Our emphasis on the authority of Scripture is right. Our concern for holding fast to the truth is good. But I think there are two fundamental flaws in the church today.

"First, many average evangelical churches are dead. We have the form of genuine Christianity and we say all the right words, but we are not living out the character of Christ. We're not loving, forgiving, healing, restoring, celebrating, praying, and worshiping. These are the things Jesus did when He was here in the flesh. Today, we are His body on earth, so why are we not doing all the things He did?

"Second, the average evangelical church is removed from the realities of life. The church has withdrawn from the places where human need, sin, and suffering are great. It has moved out to the suburbs and away from Main Street and Skid Row and Needle Park and the Red Light District—all the places where Jesus went to minister to the downcast and outcast people of society. We in the church don't want the stink of humanity in our nostrils. Instead of following the example of the Good Samaritan, we follow the example of the Levite. We avoid the wounded man in the road by walking on the other side.

"That's what's wrong with the church today, and that's why the church lacks influence. God is judging His people. He is saying to us, 'You observe the form and the right doctrines, but the reality is missing.' "

In the next two verses, God tells us exactly what kind of reality is missing from our lives:

> *"Sacrifice thank offerings to God,*
> *fulfill your vows to the Most High,*
> *and call upon me in the day of trouble;*
> *I will deliver you, and you will honor me" (50:14–15).*

What does God want from us as followers of Christ and members of His body? He doesn't merely want our hymn singing, although it is a good thing to sing hymns. Nor does He merely want only prayer, though that, too, is an important thing to do. What God desires from us, first and foremost, is *a thankful heart*. Or, as God says in verse 14, "Sacrifice thank offerings to God." Each of us should offer Him a sacrifice of thanksgiving, and a sacrifice is something that costs us something.

Have you ever asked yourself, "Why do the Scriptures stress thanksgiving so much?" The theme of gratitude to God runs through both the Old and New Testaments. "Give thanks in all circumstances," says the apostle Paul, "for this is God's will for you in Christ Jesus" (1 Thessalonians 5:18).

You say "thank you" when someone has given you something you didn't already have. Thanksgiving is the proper expression of genuine Christianity because Christianity, at its very essence, is a lifestyle of continually receiving something from God (grace, forgiveness, and salvation) that we are incapable of supplying by ourselves. If you have not received anything from God, you can't be thankful, and if you aren't thankful, then you've probably never received the gift He wants to give you.

God is a realist. He doesn't want phony expressions of thanksgiving. He has no use for insincerity. He does not want people going to church, mouthing the words to hymns, pretending to worship, and putting on a religious show if they really aren't thankful to Him.

There are people in the church (and they are awfully hard to live with) who think that Christianity consists of *pretending* to be thankful. They think it means pasting a smile on their face and going around pretending that troubles don't bother them. But God does not want you to go around shouting, "Hallelujah! I've got cancer!" He accepts our honest emotions, including our sorrow and fear.

But He also wants us to know that there is something about having cancer for which we can be genuinely thankful. No one could ever enjoy having cancer, but God can use the cancer process in our lives to reveal His love and power. God wants us to see this side of thankfulness so that we can, as Paul says, "give thanks in all circumstances." Thanksgiving is the first thing He wants from us in our worship.

The second thing God wants from us is an obedient will. "Fulfill your vows to the Most High," He says in this psalm (v. 14). Notice the nature of the obedience God asks for here: Fulfill your vows to God. A vow can't be forced on you; a vow is something you have willingly chosen to perform. It's a promise you make out of the eagerness of your own heart. God says, "If you have made a willing promise to Me, keep it. Act on it. Follow through on it."

The third thing God wants from us is a prayerful spirit. "And call upon me in the day of trouble," He says. "I will deliver you, and you will honor me." He wants us to recognize where our deliverance and security come from. As the psalmist elsewhere writes:

> *The* LORD *is my light and my salvation—*
> *whom shall I fear?*
> *The* LORD *is the stronghold of my life—*
> *of whom shall I be afraid (27:1)?*

The psalmist could confidently thrust out his chest and say, "God is my light, my salvation, my fortress! I'm not afraid of anyone or anything!" That was the spirit in which David went forth to meet Goliath, the champion of the Philistines. Here was a shepherd boy going out onto the field of battle against a nine-foot-tall warrior. Goliath was clad in armor, waving a spear as big as a telephone pole and shouting threats and insults against God and His people. David's response to Goliath was, "Who is this uncircumcised Philistine that he should defy the armies of the living God" (1 Samuel 17:26)?

The Lord is our light, our salvation, our strength, our fortress. Of whom shall we be afraid? That was David's mindset. May it be ours as well. When David went into battle, he didn't go arrogantly, trusting in his own strength; he went prayerfully and confidently, trusting in the fact that God is light, salvation, and a secure stronghold for all who follow Him. That is why God, through the psalmist Asaph, tells us, "And call upon me in the day of trouble; I will deliver you, and you will honor me" (v. 15).

God Is Judge of the Wicked

We have just seen that God is the judge, first, of His own people, including you and me as followers of Jesus Christ. But there are other people of whom God is also the righteous judge. The psalmist writes:

But to the wicked, God says:
"What right have you to recite my laws
or take my covenant on your lips?
You hate my instruction
and cast my words behind you.
When you see a thief, you join with him;
you throw in your lot with adulterers.
You use your mouth for evil
and harness your tongue to deceit.
You speak continually against your brother
and slander your own mother's son (vv. 16–20).

In almost every church, there are three kinds of people: First, there are honest, pure, sincere followers of Jesus Christ. Second, there are people who genuinely belong to Christ but their lives have become superficial and they no longer sincerely practice what they believe; they need to be challenged to renew their faith and commitment to their Lord. Third, there are people who are false Christians who attend church so that other people will think they are good and religious. While they may use the right words and fool other people, they are hypocrites and ungodly. They are, to use God's own term, "wicked."

To be ungodly is to be wicked. The wicked have ruled God out of their lives. Some wicked people are openly ungodly and proud of their wicked lifestyle. But other wicked people make a great pretense of their religiosity and good deeds so that their wickedness is cloaked by an appearance of self-righteousness.

But God, the righteous Judge, knows the heart. He knows who are the godly, who are the superficial, and who are the genuinely wicked. He knows even those wicked individuals who sit in the front pew of the church who give hours and hours of time to religious activities and who donate thousands of dollars to God's work in order to make themselves look holy and righteous. The Judge, however, cannot be deceived.

In this passage the wicked are identified by three characteristics. First, God says to the wicked, "You hate my instruction and cast my words behind you" (v. 17). The wicked hate the discipline and instruction of the Lord. They reject His truth and only want their own way. They do not accept an absolute morality; they prefer to believe that morality is relative, that people can live as they please without consequences.

Second, God says to the wicked, "When you see a thief, you join with him; you throw in your lot with adulterers" (v. 18). In other words, the wicked admire and enjoy the comraderie of those who do evil. That's the same charge the apostle Paul levels at the wicked:

> They have become filled with every kind of wickedness, evil, greed and depravity. They are full of envy, murder, strife, deceit and malice. They are gossips, slanderers, God-haters, insolent, arrogant and boastful; they invent ways of doing evil; they disobey their parents; they are senseless, faithless, heartless, ruthless. Although they know God's righteous decree that those who do such things deserve death, they not only continue to do these very things but also approve of those who practice them. (Romans 1:29–32).

The wicked don't only do evil but they also approve of other evildoers! That is what God the Judge describes here: If the wicked see a thief, they do not condemn his thievery; they admire his cleverness! They congratulate him for getting away with it! If the wicked see an adulterer, someone who is openly and flagrantly immoral, they admire her because she lives without moral restraints. They envy her, thinking that the adulterer enjoys her life of sin and sexual depravity. They want to be around the adulterer, hear all of her sexual adventures, and copy her lifestyle. The wicked, however, will not escape the judgment of the righteous Judge.

Third, God says to the wicked,

> You use your mouth for evil
> and harness your tongue to deceit.
> You speak continually against your brother
> and slander your own mother's son" (vv. 19–20).

In other words, the wicked possess a reckless tongue that stirs up trouble and condemns others, spreading slander even against their own family. That, God says, reveals that they are wicked and do not have God living within them. Their cloak of religiousness doesn't fool the Judge. He looks at the heart and judges accurately.

The wicked are often self-deceived. The reason they are so quick to lie to others is that they have lied to themselves for so long. God tries to penetrate the haze of denial and self-deception that surrounds the wicked. He pleads with them to come to their senses, saying:

These things you have done and I kept silent;
you thought I was altogether like you.
But I will rebuke you
and accuse you to your face.
Consider this, you who forget God,
or I will tear you to pieces, with none to rescue (vv. 21–22).

God, the righteous Judge, says to the wicked, "Stop fooling yourself. Stop telling yourself that you are not in any danger. Just because you have not already been judged does not mean that you will never be judged. I am patient. I do not always act immediately. I do not always strike people with judgment the moment they sin. I am trying to bring you to repentance, but My patience will not last forever."

Sometimes we wonder why God allows evil people to continue in their sin and especially in their crimes against humanity. History is spattered with the blood of millions who have suffered and died under wicked men such as Nero, Hitler, and Stalin. We wonder, "Why does God allow such evil to continue? Why doesn't He strike these evil men dead and spare the world a lot of suffering?"

It's a reasonable question. But the moment we ask that question, we have to ask, "Why didn't God cause my hand to wither away when I signed that fraudulent tax form?" Or, "Why didn't God cause my tongue to fall out when I swore a blue streak in that traffic jam this morning?" Or, "Why didn't God strike me blind when I lusted after my co-worker?" You see, if God is going to judge the wickedness of one, then He must judge the wickedness of all, including your sins and mine.

God tells us, "I am patient. Remember, friend, that I have let you go on because I want to reach you. I don't want you to continue in sin. I want to change you, redeem you, and turn your life in a new and godly direction. But don't mistake my patience for indifference. Don't make the mistake of thinking I'm like you, that I'm indulgent toward sin. If you do not judge the sin in your life, I will. If you do not choose friendship with Me, I will one day become your enemy. Please, repent now. If not, you will regret it later."

Who can defend themselves against the supreme Judge of the universe? Who can take on God? Who can outwit Him? God is not fooled by anything or anyone. He sees us exactly as we are. He will judge righteously.

The Salvation of God

The subject of judgment makes us all uneasy, and it should. Who among us could stand God's judgment clothed only in our own miserable self-righteousness? Who among us is able to withstand the scrutiny of a righteous and holy Judge?

Thanks be to God, He does not expect us to justify ourselves before Him. He has already justified us through the sacrifice of our Lord Jesus Christ. The righteousness of Jesus is our only defense in the courtroom of God, the omnipotent and omniscient Judge. Fittingly, God closes this psalm with a reassuring promise of salvation:

> *He who sacrifices thank offerings honors me,*
> *and he prepares the way*
> *so that I may show him the salvation of God (v. 23).*

When you worship God, go to Him with an attitude of thanksgiving. If you go to church in a critical, complaining, grumbling mood, you are not honoring God with your thanksgiving. No matter how many hymns you sing or prayers you recite, you are not worshiping God unless you are, first of all, thanking God.

To those who come to God with genuine worship and thankfulness, He will show "the salvation of God." That word *salvation* is a powerful word. *Salvation* means so much more than eternal life in heaven with God, as wonderful as that is. This word *salvation* actually gathers up all that God wants to do for us, in us, through us, and by us. He wants to save us and empower us so that we can live for Him, serve Him, speak for Him, fight for Him, and die for Him.

"The salvation of God" is that wonderful transforming experience of God's reality within the human heart, a reality that enables men and women to stand for the right even though the earth shakes and the heavens reel; a reality that enables people to look a hostile and threatening world in the eye and speak God's truth; a reality that enables people to live humbly yet courageously, soberly yet joyfully, boldly yet wisely. God, our Judge, wants men and women, boys and girls, who know that the only place to find strength, life, and salvation is in Him.

There is an old story about a king from ancient Hungary. One day this king was unhappy, anxious, and depressed, so he sent for his younger brother, the prince. This younger brother was a happy-go-lucky fellow who never had a care in the world. When the young prince came to the king's throne room, the king said, "Little brother, my soul is troubled. My sins are great, and I'm afraid to die and face the judgment of a holy God."

The king expected his younger brother to give him a word of comfort or cheer. Instead, the young prince *laughed*! "Why be so gloomy, big brother?" the younger man said. "Forget tomorrow! Live for today! Throw a party and drink away your fears! Don't give God another thought!"

The king's face turned red with fury. "I asked you for help!" he growled. "Is that all you have to say? Get drunk and forget about God? Get out of my sight!"

The young prince bowed and left the throne room, smirking at his brother, the king.

Late that night the prince was awakened by a loud pounding on his bedchamber door. He rose bleary-eyed, opened the door, and found himself face to face with the royal executioner. The executioner pulled the prince out of his bedchamber, where several strong guards grasped him. The guards dragged the prince through darkened hallways and down a long, steep staircase.

As the prince was pulled along, he sobbed, "What's this about? At least tell me what I'm accused of!" The executioner said nothing.

The prince was brought to the dungeon and flung down on the stone floor. Pale and shivering, the prince said, "You can't treat me this way! I'm the prince, the brother of the king! Tell him—"

"Tell him yourself," said the executioner, pointing.

The young prince looked where the executioner pointed, and there, stepping out of the shadows, was his brother, the king.

"Brother!" the prince wept. "What have I done to offend you?"

"Why be so gloomy?" the king replied sarcastically. "So what if you've been dragged out of your bed by the executioner? Forget about it! Why don't you throw a party and pour yourself a drink?"

"What are you going to do to me?" asked the quaking prince.

"Nothing," the king said. "I just wanted you to understand how I feel. If a mere human executioner can fill you with such terror, consider how awful my own terror when I think of being dragged before the throne of God? I have sinned so greatly, and I can't bear to think of the punishment that awaits me. Perhaps instead of laughing at me, you'll pity me."

Every sinner should fear the judgment of the righteous Judge. But thanks be to God, our righteous Judge is also our merciful Savior. Though the Law was given on Mount Sinai, God's justice and mercy come from Mount Zion. That is the song of the great Judge of our souls.

II

The Song of a Cleansed Conscience

PSALM 51

Sir Arthur Conan Doyle, the creator of the fictional detective Sherlock Holmes, once decided to play a joke on twelve of his prominent friends in London. He wrote twelve notes, all identical. Each read, "All is found out. Flee at once." The notes were unsigned, and Doyle was careful to leave no clue as to who had written them. He then mailed the notes to his twelve friends.

The results astonished Doyle: Within twenty-four hours, all twelve men had fled from England! That's the power of a guilty conscience.

We all have secret sins and shames. We all wrestle with guilt from time to time. We experience regret and remorse. There are so many experiences in our lives that we wish we could take back or do over.

A psychologist in Great Britain once told Billy Graham that seventy percent of the people in mental hospitals could be released if they could find forgiveness. Their problem was a bad conscience, and they could gain no relief from the awful torment and guilt under which they lived.

The Sin Syndrome

We come now to Psalm 51, a psalm of guilt, confession, forgiveness, and a cleansed conscience. It's a psalm that speaks to a universal human need. It was the crying need of King David's heart three thousand years ago, and it is still the crying need of your heart and mine today. David was a victim of a universal human syndrome, a condition that continues to afflict us today. This syndrome consists of three elements that always go together: sin, guilt, and fear.

What is sin? Essentially, sin is self-centeredness. We commit sins because we are thinking of ourselves, indulging ourselves, and taking care that no one else gets ahead of us. We are all perpetrators of sin because we are all partakers in the sin nature we inherited from the first sinner, Adam. There is not a single person who doesn't sin. The curse of sin hangs over our whole race.

God originally made us to be channels of His love to everyone around us. When Adam fell our nature became twisted and inverted, so that instead of reaching out to help others we reach out to help ourselves! When we sin we do not think of the needs of others. We do not think of God. We think only of ourselves. Selfishness is the root of sin.

Sin always produces guilt, which is a dislike of ourselves. We realize that we have hurt others or shamed ourselves or offended God, and we dislike or even hate ourselves because of it. We know we are responsible for the damage and pain another person has suffered, and the awareness of what we have done is almost unbearable.

Psychologists tell us that much of humanity suffers with an intense feeling of self-hatred due to guilt. Dr. Karl Menninger, co-founder of the famed Menninger Clinic in Topeka, Kansas, wrote a book called *Man against Himself,* which documents this very issue. He observed that guilt causes us to hate and sabotage ourselves. We think, "I don't deserve to succeed. I don't deserve to be loved. I don't deserve to be happy."

As a result of our guilt and self-hate, we may (without being aware that we are doing so) sabotage our careers, our relationships, and our own happiness. In extreme cases, guilt and self-hate can even drive people to suicide. The cure for guilt and self-hate, Menninger wrote, is love and forgiveness. That's why he concludes in *Man against Himself* that faith in God and the forgiveness that faith brings have been "the world's psychiatrist throughout the centuries."

Guilt is always accompanied by fear for two reasons. First, at the base of our fear is a distrust of ourselves. Fear is the feeling that we are unable to handle life. It's the feeling that there are forces in our lives that we can't control and that will be our undoing. Some of these forces are outside ourselves, but many are within us. We fear that we will repeat those actions that have made us feel guilty. We fear that we will not be able to resist or control the forces of temptation, lust, laziness, gluttony, or anger that led us to sin in the first place. We fear ourselves and our inability to control our own impulses and behavior.

Second, at the base of our fear is an expectation of punishment. We've sinned, we know we deserve punishment, and we expect God to deal with us as we deserve. So we fear God, and we run from Him. We see this kind of fear at work in the Garden of Eden. As soon as Adam and Eve sinned, they felt guilty and hid from God in fear. That has been the pattern of human behavior ever since. We sin, then we fear God's punishment. It is torment without equal.

Guilt drives some people to become rigid legalists. They respond to their guilt and shame with denial, convincing themselves that they are "good people," while those who fail to measure up to their strict moral standards are "bad people." Though these legalists don't measure up either, they convince themselves that they do. Their strict legalistic lifestyle is a way of paying for the guilt and shame of past sins.

Some people are driven to extremes of self-torture by their feelings of guilt. I once visited the Shrine of Guadalupe in Mexico City, the site of the largest Roman Catholic cathedral in North America. According to legend, the Virgin Mary appeared to a believer named Juan Diego in December 1531, and in time, the site became a shrine of healing. There is one feature of the Shrine of Guadalupe that I think is sad and disturbing. You can go there any day and find people walking on their bare knees. They have crawled for blocks over dirty, rough pavement, enduring pain and humiliation to reach the shrine. Their lacerated knees leave bloodstains on the pavement as they crawl along.

Why do people physically torture themselves in this way? It's because they are inwardly tormented by guilt and fear. By suffering the pain of crawling on their knees, they hope to purge the pain of their guilt. They hope that their physical suffering will ward off God's anger over their sin. For them, the physical torture of bleeding knees is nothing compared with the spiritual and emotional torture of guilt and fear.

We may pity these people for their superstitious notions, but don't we respond to our own guilt in parallel ways? Some Christians try to purge their guilt by giving money to charity. Perhaps they think that by depriving themselves financially and doing a good deed with their money, they can somehow "pay" or "atone" for their sins. There are many churches and organizations today that have benefited richly from the donations of wealthy people with guilty consciences.

We cannot atone for our own sins. If we want to live free of sin and guilt, there is only way to do so: the way that King David sets forth in Psalm 51.

"You Are the Man!"

This is one of the few psalms that is introduced with the historical background. The inscription reads, "A psalm of David. When the prophet Nathan came to him after David had committed adultery with Bathsheba." The inscription tells us that David wrote this psalm during his reign after committing both adultery and murder (see 2 Samuel 11–12). It's amazing that David records his own sin for us, because it must have been a humiliating experience for him. According to David, the following incidents occurred.

King David was on his palace roof one day when the army had gone out to war. From the roof he saw a beautiful woman bathing. His passion was aroused, and he sent messengers with orders to bring the woman to him. The king entered into an adulterous relationship with the woman, Bathsheba, who was married to a high-ranking soldier in David's army. The soldier, Uriah, was out on the battlefield, fighting for his king.

Later, when David learned that Bathsheba was pregnant with his child, he panicked and tried to cover up his sin. He ordered Uriah home from the battlefield, hoping the soldier would sleep with his wife so that the child of the adulterous relationship would be presumed to be Uriah's own. But loyal Uriah felt that duty came before pleasure, so instead of going to his own house, he bunked with the other soldiers before returning to the battlefield.

Knowing his sin would be exposed, David did what those in a sinful state often do: He tried to cover up one sin with another. From adultery David progressed to murder. He ordered Uriah, Bathsheba's unsuspecting husband, to be put in the forefront of the battle, where he would inevitably be killed. When David first lusted for Bathsheba, it never entered his mind that lust would lead to murder, but it did.

When news of Uriah's death reached King David, he thought he had covered his sin. But though his plan succeeded, David was not relieved. In fact he had only compounded the guilt of adultery with the guilt of murder. He was haunted by what he had done to Uriah. In Psalm 32 David records how he felt while covering up his sin. "When I kept silent," he wrote, "my bones wasted away through my groaning all day long" (v. 3).

David's sin took place after he had walked with God for many years. He was widely known as "Israel's singer of songs" (2 Samuel 23:1) and had gained a reputation as a prophet, a man who understood the deep things of God. He was the established political and spiritual leader of Israel. But somehow King David indulged in the unthinkable. How could a great man of God do something as loathsome as commit adultery with the wife of a loyal soldier, followed by cold-blooded murder?

For a year the king tried to live with his guilty conscience. But God loved David too much to let him continue destroying himself and his kingdom because of hidden sin. So God sent the prophet Nathan to David. Because David was the king, Nathan had to approach him with care. If he blatantly accused King David, he might lose his own life. So Nathan told King David a story.

The prophet told the king about a certain rich man who owned a flock of sheep. This rich man, said Nathan, wanted to show hospitality to a prominent visitor. But instead of taking a sheep from his own flock, he went to his poor neighbor, who owned just one little ewe lamb. The rich man seized the lamb and slaughtered it, leaving the poor man without anything.

When David heard Nathan's story, he was indignant. "As surely as the Lord lives," David said, "the man who did this deserves to die! He must pay for that lamb four times over, because he did such a thing and had no pity" (2 Samuel 12:5–6).

Then the prophet triggered the trap he had set for the king. Pointing an accusing finger at David, Nathan said,

"You are the man! This is what the LORD*, the God of Israel, says: 'I anointed you king over Israel, and I delivered you from the hand of Saul. I gave your master's house to you, and your master's wives into your arms. I gave you the house of Israel and Judah. And if all this had been too little, I would have given you even more. Why did you despise the word of the* LORD *by doing what is evil in his eyes? You struck down Uriah the Hittite with the sword and took his wife to be your own'"* (2 Samuel 12:7–9a).

Instantly David knew his sin was exposed. He fell on his face before God and confessed his sin. Out of that confession came this beautiful psalm, the psalm of a conscience cleansed by God.

The Fullness of God's Forgiveness

King Frederick II of Prussia (1712–1786) was known as Frederick the Great. One of Europe's more enlightened monarchs, he granted widespread religious freedom to his people and abolished the torture of prisoners.

Once while inspecting a prison, he walked along a row of cells. Prisoners called out to him, "I'm innocent! I was falsely accused! Please set me free!"

As the king reached the end of the row, he saw one prisoner sitting quietly in his cell saying nothing. "You there," said King Frederick. "Have you nothing to say? All of these other prisoners tell me they are innocent."

"Your Majesty," said the prisoner, "I deserve to be here. I'm guilty of theft."

"Guards!" King Frederick shouted. "Seize this man! Take him out of that cell and toss him in the streets! I won't have this criminal staying here and corrupting all the innocent men in this prison!" So the guilty man was set free because he confessed his sin.

Psalm 51 opens with a confession of guilt and a plea for cleansing and forgiveness. The psalmist writes:

Have mercy on me, O God,
according to your unfailing love;
according to your great compassion
blot out my transgressions.

Wash away all my iniquity
and cleanse me from my sin.

In these opening verses, David asks for three things. First, he asks for mercy. David understands that every sin is a crime against God and that he stands before the Almighty Judge as a condemned criminal. When a condemned criminal stands before a judge, he doesn't want justice—he wants mercy! So David, knowing there is no defense for his crimes, comes before the Judge, confesses to God, and throws himself on the mercy of the court.

Second, David asks God to wipe his slate clean by blotting out his transgressions. David understands that sin is a debt that can never be repaid. In spite of all his kingly riches, David is morally bankrupt before God.

Third, David asks God to cleanse him. David knows that sin is an ugly stain upon his soul. Even though an act of sin may occur in the past, the stain remains.

In Shakespeare's *Macbeth*, there is a scene where Lady Macbeth is walking and talking in her sleep. At her insistence her husband has murdered the king of Scotland, and now Lady Macbeth is going slowly insane with guilt. As she sleepwalks Lady Macbeth looks at her hands and curses the spots of blood she sees in her dreams. Though her hands are physically clean, her soul is stained with blood. Her sin is an ugly, indelible spot that cannot be washed away with water.

That's how David feels about his own sin: it's a stain that defiles him. Only the love and mercy of Almighty God can remove that stain. Nothing else will ever make David clean again.

David understands the basis for all forgiveness: God's love and His compassion. He understands that he deserves nothing from God and that God has no obligation to forgive him. Some people act is if they are entitled to God's forgiveness, as if God *owes* them mercy! But David knows better. He realizes that the only reason he has any right to ask forgiveness is because of God's unfailing love and great compassion. So in effect David says, "I come to you sinful and unworthy, pleading for mercy because you are a merciful and loving God."

Notice that David refers to God's "great compassion," His abundant and overflowing mercy. God does not dole out mercy in dribs and drabs; He pours it out in overflowing buckets! Psalm 103 contains a beautiful description of God's forgiveness: "As far as the east is from the west, so far has he removed our transgressions from us" (v. 12). How far is the east from the west? It's a question without an answer! There is no absolute east or west, no point where you can say, "I have arrived at the easternmost (or westernmost) point in the world." No matter how far east or west you go, you can always go further. When God removes our sin, He sends it an infinite distance away.

God has also promised through the prophet Micah that He will "hurl all our iniquities into the depths of the sea" (7:19). I once heard a Bible teacher add, "And God also puts up a sign that reads, 'No Fishing!' So don't go down there and try to fish old sins out once God has tossed them in the sea!" What a relief it is to understand the fullness of God's forgiveness!

Drop Your Defenses

Next David goes on to point out by his own example how all of us can lay hold of God's forgiveness:

> *For I know my transgressions,*
> *and my sin is always before me.*
> *Against you, you only, have I sinned*
> *and done what is evil in your sight,*
> *so that you are proved right when you speak*
> *and justified when you judge (vv. 3–4).*

Here King David makes a frank and full acknowledgment of his sin. He says, "I know my sins, and I can't escape them or cover them up. I have no excuse or defense. I can't shift the blame. I'm guilty."

In these verses we glimpse another reason many people fail to experience forgiveness. They suffer for years with a guilty conscience because they are not willing to acknowledge their sin honestly. They will not call it what God calls it. They make excuses. They defend themselves or blame others. They try to call sin by some other name, such as a "mistake" or an "indiscretion."

It's interesting, isn't it, how we have one list of terms to describe our sins but a different list for the sins of others. We have convictions; other people have prejudices. We have righteous indignation; other people have nasty tempers. We share valuable information; other people gossip. We're candidly outspoken; other people are obnoxiously opinionated. We're leaders; other people are bossy.

While trying to rationalize and excuse our own sins by switching the labels, we add another sin to our list: hypocrisy. We can never be forgiven until we confess that we have sinned. As long as we pretend that our sin was not really sin, we cannot receive God's forgiveness.

The apostle John tells us, "If anybody does sin, we have one who speaks to the Father in our defense—Jesus Christ, the Righteous One" (1 John 2:1b). If we defend ourselves, then our heavenly Advocate can no longer defend us. If we would have our Advocate speak in our defense, then we must drop our own defenses and let Him speak on our behalf. He will defend us, and His defense is perfectly acceptable to God.

Many people today are quick to blame God for their sin. They say, "God, you put me in these circumstances. It's not my fault! You allowed me to be married to this person, and that's why I did what I did. You allowed me to work for this company, and that's why I committed this sin. God, why did You put this temptation in my path? Why did You make it so hard for me to resist temptation?" But David refuses to blame God. Instead he says, "Against you, you only, have I sinned and done what is evil in your sight" (v. 4).

That's an amazing statement: David says his sin is against God and God alone. Why does he say that? Certainly he knows that other people have been harmed. Bathsheba has been harmed, her reputation ruined, her marriage broken, her husband murdered. And there is Uriah, that loyal servant who was not a Jew but a Hittite who had adopted Israel as his nation. Uriah gave full allegiance to King David, and David repaid him with betrayal and murder.

Clearly other people were harmed by David's sin. Indeed, the whole nation of Israel was harmed. So how can David say to God, "Against you, you only, have I sinned"?

David can say this because he knows that sin is an insult to God. It is God's love that is wounded by sin. This does not mean that the wounds done to others are unimportant. But we must be aware of the fact that the greatest harm that comes from our sin is the affront to God and His grace. When we acknowledge that our sins are violations, first and foremost, of our love relationship with God, then His forgiveness becomes available to us.

Conquering the Sin Problem

David's sin problem is not over yet. Notice how he continues to move even more deeply into confession and repentance in the next few verses. Why does he go deeper? Because he fears that he will repeat his sin. He recognizes that he is weak and prone to sin. So he writes: "Surely I was sinful at birth, sinful from the time my mother conceived me" (v. 5).

David expresses a deep understanding of his fallen sin nature. To paraphrase, he says, "I now realize that I was born with the inclination to sin. I have been a fallen and sinful creature from the moment of my conception." Please don't misunderstand this passage. David is *not* saying there is anything sinful about the act of sexual intercourse in marriage that results in the conception of a child. Throughout the Bible married sex is treated with honor and reverence as a gift from God, not an act of sin.

David is saying that when he was conceived, the tendency to sin was embedded in his human flesh. No one had to teach David how to sin, nor did anyone have to teach you and me how to lie, cheat, steal, or behave selfishly. It's in our flesh. It's in our genetic code. As children of Adam and Eve, we are natural-born sinners.

Sin, says David, is not a superficial matter. It is the deepest of all human problems. David is saying that unless he finds some solution for his polluted nature, passed down to him by his own parents, he can't keep from falling back into sin again."

Next the psalmist outlines an eight-step approach that protects us from falling back into sin. Let's take careful note of each step.

Eight Steps to Conquering Sin

Step one: David prays for wisdom and understanding in the deepest places of his heart. He writes: "Surely you desire truth in the inner parts; you teach me wisdom in the inmost place" (v. 6).

In other words, "Give me an understanding of the way life truly is. One reason I fall into sin is self-deception. I fool myself whenever I say, 'This is just a little sin,' or, 'I'm not really hurting anyone,' or, 'God doesn't really care if I sin now and then.' Lord, teach me to understand reality so that I won't sin against you again."

Step two: David prays for the purging of his guilt by means of a sacrifice. That is the deep meaning of these words: "Cleanse me with hyssop, and I will be clean; wash me, and I will be whiter than snow" (v. 7).

Hyssop is a sponge-like plant that was always associated with blood sacrifices in the Old Testament. For example, at the first Passover in Egypt, God told Israel He would send the angel of death to kill all of the first-born throughout the land. There was only one way a household could be spared: by slaying a sacrificial lamb (symbolizing the sacrifice of Jesus) and collecting the lamb's blood in a basin. Regarding the hyssop God said: "Take a bunch of hyssop, dip it into the blood in the basin and put some of the blood on the top and on both sides of the doorframe. Not one of you shall go out the door of his house until morning" (Exodus 12:22).

We find hyssop used again to apply the sacrificial blood as a part of the ceremonial cleansings of Leviticus (see 14:6 and 14:51–52). To be cleansed with hyssop is an expression that acknowledges our need for a blood sacrifice.

People are sometimes troubled by these blood sacrifices. They wonder why a river of blood flows through the history of Israel—the blood of millions of slain lambs, bulls, goats, and other animals. Some have even called Judaism a "slaughterhouse" religion because of these sacrifices.

But all the Old Testament sacrifices were designed to point toward the one perfect New Testament sacrifice, the death of the Lord Jesus on the cross. The blood of all those animals was a picture of His blood poured out and streaming down the cross for your sake and mine.

Still, people wonder: Why did Jesus have to die in order for our sins to be forgiven? The answer: Sin is so deeply embedded in us that it cannot be cured by anything but death. The old life has to die. God cannot make us acceptable and clean by simply improving our old lives. The old has to die, and the new must take its place. When Christ died our old humanity died too. When He rose again, we received His new life.

David understands this principle. He says to God, "If you are going to deal with my sin problem, there must be a blood sacrifice. So cleanse me, God. Apply the blood of the perfect Sacrifice to my life with hyssop. Then—and only then—will I be truly clean."

Step three: David prays for that sense of joy that always accompanies the forgiveness of sin. "Let me hear joy and gladness; let the bones you have crushed rejoice" (v. 8).

When David writes, "Make me hear joy and gladness," he is pleading with God: "Speak to me, Lord. Tell me what the blood sacrifice means in my life so that my bones, crushed by the weight of my sin, can rejoice. If *You* tell me the truth, then I know it's true."

Step four: David prays that his sin would be blotted out of God's sight. "Hide your face from my sins and blot out all my iniquity" (v. 9).

He prays, "Lord, in order for me to keep from falling into future sin, I have to resolve the issue of the past. If I continue to be reminded of my old sins, I'll become depressed and defeated. So God I ask You, please hide Your face from my sins and blot out my iniquity." God is ready and willing to do that; David is only asking for what God has said He would do.

Step five: David asks God for renewal in his heart and spirit. "Create in me a pure heart, O God, and renew a steadfast spirit within me" (v. 10).

Do you see the progress he is making? David sees that his old life, his old heart, and his past must all be put to death. His old self is naturally inclined toward sin and evil. When he sinned his old heart was simply doing what came naturally. So David asks God for a new and pure heart. He asks God to renew his spirit, a steadfast spirit that will stand firm against temptation and the inclination to sin.

Step six: David asks for assurance that the Holy Spirit of God will be present to guide and comfort him. "Do not cast me from your presence or take your Holy Spirit from me" (v. 11).

Some people have interpreted this to mean that the Old Testament saints could lose their salvation once they possessed it. I don't think that's what the psalmist is saying. He is praying for the assurance of the Holy Spirit's guiding and comforting presence to be with him. It's the same assurance we read of in the New Testament letter to the Hebrews: "God has said, 'Never will I leave you; never will I forsake you'" (13:5b). That is the assurance David desperately wants to hear.

Step seven: David prays that God would give him a renewed sense of what it means to belong to Him. "Restore to me the joy of your salvation" (51:12a).

What is salvation? Does salvation mean living eternally in heaven with God? Yes—but it means more than that. Does it mean we have been saved from sin so we can live a righteous lifestyle in the here and now? Yes—but it means even more! It means that we have been accepted by God because of the sacrifice of Jesus the Messiah on the cross. There is a special joy that comes from knowing we are accepted and forgiven by God.

Step eight: David asks for a willing spirit—a spirit that *wants* to do God's will. "And grant me a willing spirit, to sustain me" (v. 12b).

In order to avoid falling back into old sins, we must replace our old sinful heart with a spirit that actively, eagerly wants to do God's will. We will struggle, we will be tempted, and we will fail from time to time. But we will be sustained and empowered to resist temptation if we are actively engaged in doing God's will: worshipping, praising, praying, witnessing, and seeking opportunities for ministry to others.

We must follow all eight of these steps to avoid returning to the sins of the past. David followed these eight steps to freedom from guilt three thousand years ago, and these eight steps are just as necessary in our lives today. As we read the words of Psalm 51 and pray David's prayer along with him, we have so much to be grateful for: Our sins are forgiven, and we can live free from the guilt, shame, and fear that sin produces in our lives. Best of all God has given us a new start, a new heart, and the power to leave our old sins behind us and to live a new life for Him.

Once when I was preparing to preach on Psalm 51, I received an anonymous letter. The writer said he was a Christian, but he was involved in a serious and ongoing pattern of sin. Though he couldn't bring himself to reveal his identity, he wanted me to know that he was struggling in this area and didn't know how to overcome his sinful habits.

This letter weighed heavily on me. I decided to read from the letter in my sermon because I wanted to help this man if I could. Speaking to the entire congregation was the only way I could reach out to him. So I read a portion of the letter to the congregation, ending with these words: "I've accepted the fact that this habit is sinful, but I don't think God will judge me for my sin because He hasn't given me the power to break this habit."

After reading from the letter, I said, "This man is self-deceived. God *has* given us the power to live victoriously over sin. As Peter tells us: 'His divine power has given us everything we need for life and godliness through our knowledge of him who called us by his own glory and goodness' (2 Peter 1:3). The life of Jesus Christ in us gives us the power to break old habits. In Psalm 51:12, David said, 'And grant me a willing spirit, to sustain me.' If that is our sincere prayer, God *will* grant us a willing spirit."

A few days later, I received a second anonymous letter from the same person. He told me that God had used that message to convict him of his sin and to deliver him from the grip of a habit he had never been able to break. "Pastor Stedman," he wrote, "I didn't believe it was possible, but you were right. God *does* grant us a willing spirit if we sincerely ask Him. Psalm 51 is now the daily prayer of my heart."

God wants to give us the power to put our sins in the past and live willing and righteous lives for Him. He gave this power to the psalmist, King David. He gave this power to my anonymous friend. And He will give this power to you if you sincerely ask Him.

Saved to Teach and Lead Others

If we go to God and seek His forgiveness after the pattern of Psalm 51, God promises to give us a profound new ministry for Him, a ministry of teaching others and leading others back to God. David writes: "Then I will teach transgressors your ways, and sinners will turn back to you" (v. 13).

Too many Christians talk about God's forgiveness in an academic, theological sense. David says that we should talk about our own experience of God's forgiveness, about how God has forgiven us and what a joy it is to be free from the burden of sin. If we want to see sinners turn to God, then we must show others how to follow the path of forgiveness that we ourselves have traveled.

Next David concludes with a hymn of praise to God, His Redeemer:

> Save me from bloodguilt, O God,
> the God who saves me,
> and my tongue will sing of your righteousness.
> O Lord, open my lips,
> and my mouth will declare your praise.
> You do not delight in sacrifice, or I would bring it;
> you do not take pleasure in burnt offerings.
> The sacrifices of God are a broken spirit;
> a broken and contrite heart,
> O God, you will not despise (vv. 14–17).

What a deep understanding the Old Testament saints had of the nature and character of God! They knew that God was not interested in burnt offerings and animals. They saw beyond the symbolism of the offerings to the reality of life. David praises God for two things: First, God has taken his guilt away. Second, God has broken his willful spirit. That broken spirit, that contrite heart, is the true sacrifice God is looking for. So David praises God because He has broken his stubborn will and brought him to the end of himself.

Finally David, as king of Israel, recognizes the fact that his sin has hurt the entire kingdom. So he concludes with these words:

> In your good pleasure make Zion prosper;
> build up the walls of Jerusalem.
> Then there will be righteous sacrifices,
> whole burnt offerings to delight you;
> then bulls will be offered on your altar (vv. 18–19).

King David has stupidly and recklessly jeopardized his entire kingdom because of his sin. The very walls of the city—which symbolize security—are said to have crumbled because of David's sin. Now he prays, "Lord, please heal the harm I have done to the kingdom. Make Zion, the nation of Israel, prosperous again. Rebuild the walls of safety that have been broken down by my foolish sin."

The result will be that the worship that is done in Israel will be based on righteousness and reality. It will not be mere ritual and form but a genuine, sincere worship that comes from the heart. Every song that is sung and every prayer that is uttered will be an overflowing, joyful expression of a heart that is cleansed and set free.

At first glance you may think that this section of Psalm 51 doesn't apply to you. After all, you're not a king—or are you?

In a real sense, each of us is a ruler over a kingdom. Each of us has a certain realm of influence. The sins we commit, even the "secret sins" that we have so carefully kept hidden from the world, have an impact on the people around us: on family members, neighbors, friends, peers, students, co-workers, employees, fellow Christians, and fellow citizens of our nation and our world. All of our "kingdoms," our various spheres of influence, are harmed when sin reigns unchallenged in our lives.

God stands ready to restore the "kingdoms" of your life. He stands ready to heal your damaged and broken relationships and to rebuild them on a righteous foundation. He stands ready to heal your society, which has been torn apart by sins of adultery, pornography, sexual immorality, child abuse, lying, theft, idolatry and witchcraft, violence, alcoholism, drug abuse, corporate greed, indifference, and neglect of the poor. Each of us must confess, "I have been part of the moral and spiritual problem in our nation—not part of the solution." Yet God has made this promise to us:

> *If my people, who are called by my name, will humble themselves and pray and seek my face and turn from their wicked ways, then will I hear from heaven and will forgive their sin and will heal their land (2 Chronicles 7:14).*

Our prayer should be the same as David's: "In your good pleasure make Zion prosper; build up the walls of Jerusalem" (v. 18). May God rebuild the walls of our society, walls that we have destroyed by our own selfishness and sin. If we will pray the prayer of Psalm 51 and seek God's face and turn from our wicked ways, then He will hear, He will forgive, and He will heal our land.

12

A Song from the Sanctuary

PSALM 73

Writer Samuel Beckett was widely praised throughout the world for his novels and plays, such as *Waiting for Godot*. There was one person, however, who was not favorably impressed with Beckett's success: his wife, Suzanne.

Suzanne Dechevaux-Dumesnil Beckett was an accomplished pianist who admired her husband's ability as a writer but envied his fame. In 1969 Samuel and Suzanne Beckett were in Tunisia when a telegram arrived from a friend. Suzanne opened the telegram, read it—and turned pale. "This," she said, "is a catastrophe!"

"What does it say?" asked the writer.

"It says," his wife replied, frowning, "you've just won the Nobel Prize for Literature!"

Suzanne's envy turned good news into a catastrophe. Envy is a problem for us all. It was even a problem for one of the writers of the Psalms.

Envying the Wicked

The writer of Psalm 73 was Asaph, a Levite and a leader of King David's choir. He states the problem for us in the opening verses:

Surely God is good to Israel,
to those who are pure in heart.
But as for me, my feet had almost slipped;
I had nearly lost my foothold.
For I envied the arrogant
when I saw the prosperity of the wicked (vv. 1–3).

Asaph is troubled. He has believed that God is good to the upright and the pure in heart, yet he looks around him and sees that the wicked and arrogant seem to prosper. So he became envious of their success. In fact, these feelings of envy troubled him so deeply that they threatened to destroy his faith.

You may identify with Asaph and his struggle. When you first became a Christian, you may have assumed that becoming a child of God would make life easier for you. In time you discovered that becoming a Christian made some things worse, not better. You experienced personal setbacks, frustration, and even depression. You saw ungodly people seemingly enjoying life to the full. You may have envied them, and you might have even been tempted to give up on your Christian faith.

Here we see how these wonderful folk songs of our faith reflect a range of experience that is common to us all. The Psalms echo what we all go through in the walk of faith. Many Christians today ponder the very issues reflected in these verses. The atheist and the agnostic confront us and say, "How can your God be a God of love? How can He be called fair? He allows the innocent to suffer. He allows the wicked to prosper. Doesn't He care at all about justice? If He cares, why doesn't He do something? If He's a God of power, then He must not be a God of love. If He's a God of love, then He must not have any power."

How do we answer such arguments? That's the problem the psalmist addresses in this passage.

The Man of the World

Psalm 73 introduces the third division in the book of Psalms. This third division, Psalms 73 through 89, corresponds to the book of Leviticus—a book of laws and symbolism, a book that describes the building of the tabernacle and a detailed program of sacrifices. Many people see the ceremonial regulations of Leviticus and fail to understand that these rules are symbols designed to teach important truths. The underlying theme of Leviticus and of the third division of the Psalms is God is pleased to dwell among His people.

When we look at Leviticus, we see that it is largely about the tabernacle, God's dwelling place in Israel. The key to understanding all of the rules and regulations regarding the tabernacle is to understand that the tabernacle is a symbolic picture of Jesus Christ and His work on our behalf. The tabernacle is also a picture of human beings as God intended us to be.

The tabernacle is the turning point of Psalm 73. The theme of this psalm is that everything hinges on the tabernacle: the psalmist's faith, the issue of God's fairness, and the question of His love and power.

In verses 4 through 9, the psalmist gives us more detail regarding how the arrogant and ungodly seem to prosper:

They [the ungodly] have no struggles;
their bodies are healthy and strong.
They are free from the burdens common to man;
they are not plagued by human ills.
Therefore pride is their necklace;
they clothe themselves with violence.
From their callous hearts comes iniquity;
the evil conceits of their minds know no limits.
They scoff, and speak with malice;
in their arrogance they threaten oppression.
Their mouths lay claim to heaven,
and their tongues take possession of the earth.

This is a detailed description of what is commonly called "a man of the world"—a man of worldly success and power, a man who never seems to have any troubles. He is well fed, well clothed, and expensively dressed; pride is like an ornament to his life. He carries himself with an arrogant swagger. If crossed, he's quick to retaliate. He indulges in every luxury. He takes pride in his power, and he squashes anyone who gets in his way.

How do other people respond to the worldly and ungodly? The psalmist writes:

Therefore their people turn to them
and drink up waters in abundance.
They say, "How can God know?
Does the Most High have knowledge?"
This is what the wicked are like—

always carefree, they increase in wealth.
Surely in vain have I kept my heart pure;
in vain have I washed my hands in innocence.
All day long I have been plagued;
I have been punished every morning (vv. 10–14).

The psalmist observes how people bow and scrape and kowtow to the ungodly. This is true whether the ungodly person is a powerful politician, a famous movie star, or a notorious gangster. There are always people who will fawn over the ungodly because of their wealth and power.

People defend the wrongdoing and arrogance of the ungodly saying, "Look at how the ungodly live! They have everything, and God doesn't do anything about it! There's no divine judgment, no punishment! If the ungodly get their way in everything, then that's the way to live! That's for me!" When people see the ungodly "get away with murder" because of their power and influence, they begin to believe that God either doesn't care or doesn't exist.

The psalmist Asaph compares his life with the life of the ungodly, and he begins to think he's wasted his life! The wicked give no thought to God, yet everything goes well with them. They have no problems, no worries, no woes. By contrast Asaph laments, "I have kept my heart pure—*in vain*! I have kept my hands clean and innocent—*in vain*! While the ungodly are living it up, I'm plagued with problems and punished all day long! How unfair! What an idiot I've been!"

Have you ever felt that way? I certainly have! So has the psalmist. And so have many Christians through the years.

The New Testament tells us of a young man named Demas who accompanied the apostle Paul. Demas let the seeming injustice of the world get to him. Whereas the psalmist almost slipped, Demas fell headlong. He gave up, left the ministry, and joined the ranks of those whose god was money and power. As Paul sadly records, "Demas, because he loved this world, has deserted me and has gone to Thessalonica" (2 Timothy 4:10).

Many people have gone the way of Demas. After a strong start in the faith, they look at the world and say, "What's the use of being a Christian? You read the Bible, go to church, and try to obey the Lord—and what happens? Everything goes wrong. The wicked prosper while I suffer. Why bother trudging on when life just gets harder?" And they fall away.

The Seven-Step Solution

But there is a solution to the problem Asaph describes. That's why Psalm 73 was written: to show us how to keep from being discouraged by the seeming unfairness of life. The psalmist gives us a seven-step solution, and each step is vitally important.

Step One: Consider the faith of others. The psalmist writes:

If I had said, "I will speak thus,"
I would have betrayed your children.
When I tried to understand all this,
it was oppressive to me (vv. 15–16).

The psalmist is full of doubt and self-pity. He's almost ready to give up, but something stops him. "Lord, If I speak these doubts," he says, "I'll betray Your children. I'm going to put a stumbling block in somebody else's path. I don't want to spread my doubts to other people."

Admittedly this is a very thin motivation for persevering in his faith, but it's a start. This man paused to consider the effect his doubts would have on others. He was not willing to undermine the faith of other people. That may be all you can hold onto in times of doubt and unbelief, but be grateful for anything that halts your downward slide.

The psalmist adds, "When I tried to understand all this, it was oppressive to me." In other words, he might be wrong. He might be missing some piece of the puzzle. He was beginning to doubt his doubts, and he knew it would be wrong to express doubts in the midst of his confusion. This was a wise decision on the part of the psalmist.

Step Two: Go to the sanctuary of God. Asaph describes the point at which he gained understanding: "Till I entered the sanctuary of God; then I understood their final destiny" (v. 17).

What does the psalmist mean when he says he "entered the sanctuary of God"? He says he came before the presence of God. He actually went into the place where God meets with His people. When the psalmist entered the sanctuary of God, he began to see life from God's point of view.

Now we see why this is the turning point of Psalm 73. This is where the psalmist's viewpoint changes. This is where he begins to shift from natural thinking to spiritual thinking. The problem was that he had been thinking like a natural man, looking at life from a natural viewpoint. But now, in the sanctuary, he is able to gain God's perspective on life.

Notice this all-important phrase: "then I understood." It is a wonderful thing to go from confusion to understanding. The psalmist had an "Aha!" moment. That's what happens when we come into the presence of God.

Of course there are many ways in which we can come into His presence. Yes, we can often feel His presence more intimately when we are in church, but we don't have to go into a church building to experience His presence. When we read His Word, we hear His voice; we come into His presence when we meditate on the Scriptures. When we pray—not just by talking to Him but by listening to Him as well—we come into His presence.

When we are in the presence of God, our eyes are opened to the way life really is. We understand reality more fully than we did before. God didn't give us the gift of His Word and the gift of prayer merely to soothe our emotions. He gave us these channels of access to Him so that we could have our eyes opened and understand reality.

That's what happened to the psalmist. He came into the sanctuary of God's presence. Perhaps he heard God's Word. Undoubtedly he prayed. As a result he began to view life from God's point of view. He began to think in spiritual rather than natural terms.

The trouble with so-called "natural" thinking is that it is always centered on the self. Natural thinking is governed by feelings and moods, and it is limited by our experience, perception, and prejudice.

Spiritual thinking is centered on God. It's governed by the reality of God's Word and guided by the Holy Spirit. It's infinite and eternal in scope because God is unlimited in His perspective. Spiritual thinking shakes us out of our prejudices so that we can see the world with new eyes. We can only experience spiritual thinking when we enter the sanctuary of God.

But what does that mean for us now? How do we enter the sanctuary today? According to the New Testament, we are the sanctuary of God because He lives in us. To draw near to God through prayer and His Word is to enter the sanctuary. As we expose ourselves to His truth in Scripture or by prayer or through fellowship with other Christians, we enter the sanctuary. That is how we move from natural thinking to spiritual thinking.

Forgotten Like a Dream

Step Three: Recognize the ultimate destiny of the ungodly.

> *Then I understood their final destiny.*
> *Surely you place them on slippery ground;*
> *you cast them down to ruin.*
> *How suddenly are they destroyed,*
> *completely swept away by terrors!*
> *As a dream when one awakes,*
> *so when you arise, O Lord,*
> *you will despise them as fantasies (vv. 17b–20).*

The psalmist begins to see new truths he couldn't see before. He had forgotten the fate of the ungodly, and that phrase "their final destiny" does not refer merely to death, judgment, and eternal punishment. It also refers to the spiritual deterioration that takes place in this life.

All the time that he envied these people he writes about, the psalmist had failed to consider what was happening within them—the destruction of their souls. When he considered the final destiny of the ungodly from God's point of view, his thinking changed. He discovered that without God, human beings cannot have inner strength. God has set them, he says, "on slippery ground," and He casts them down to ruin. Outwardly, ungodly people seem to have few problems; inwardly it's a different story. This explains why we often read of a prominent person—someone who seems to have everything, including wealth and fame—who commits suicide or dies of a drug overdose.

Why do so many wealthy film, TV, and rock stars have drug and alcohol addictions? They are the "beautiful people." They have wealth, power, and fame. Why should such people have to numb their brains with drugs or alcohol? It's because they have no inner strength. They are empty inside. They are on slippery ground with nothing to hold onto. They may have everything they want, but they don't want anything they have. What they really want, but don't know it, is the peace and forgiveness that comes only from knowing God.

Long before they physically die, the ungodly come to their final destiny. Their lives fall apart. They become full of self-loathing. Their riches and power no longer satisfy. They can't stand living, yet they're afraid to die. At this point we see the fulfillment of the psalmist's words: "How suddenly are they destroyed, completely swept away by terrors!" (v. 19).

The ungodly reach a point of despair. Their lives become a living hell of fear and hopelessness. I have counseled many non-Christians who told me that while they seemed happy and calm on the outside, inside they were tormented by fear, especially the fear of death.

William Randolph Hearst, the newspaper baron who built the fabulous Hearst Castle on a mountaintop in coastal California, was one of the most powerful businessmen who ever lived. His life is said to be the inspiration for Orson Welles' motion picture *Citizen Kane.* Despite all of Hearst's wealth and power, he was tormented by the fear of death. He had a standing rule that anyone who mentioned the word *death* in his presence would be instantly ejected.

There is nothing wrong with wealth or influence per se; there are many godly people who have both. But those whose god is wealth or fame or power are destined for a terrible fate. Their gods cannot give them peace in this life or a place in the life to come. They will be destroyed and swept away by terrors.

The ungodly will also be forgotten. Those who pin their hope of some sort of permanence on fame or achievements will find their legacies have one day crumbled to dust. The psalmist comments that the ungodly and their works will vanish as a dream vanishes when the sleeper awakes.

Once we look closely at the destiny of the ungodly, we see that they are not to be envied after all. Some years ago I was teaching a

Sunday school class, and I read our Lord's parable of the rich man and Lazarus. My young listeners hung on the story of how poor Lazarus lay at the gate while the dogs licked his sores. Meanwhile the rich man ate fine foods as he was surrounded by the splendor of his mansion. I paused in the story and said, "Which of these two people would you rather be—the rich man or Lazarus?"

They all said, "The rich man!"

Then I read them the part of the story where both men died. The rich man was in torment, but Lazarus was carried to the bosom of Abraham. Then I said, "Now which man would you rather be?"

They all said, "Lazarus!"

What made the difference? These young people saw the lives of these two men from God's perspective. They saw the ultimate destiny of both men. They realized it is far better to be godly and poor than ungodly and rich, because the fate of the ungodly is destruction.

Like an Animal

Step Four: Honestly admit your flawed perspective.

> *When my heart was grieved*
> *and my spirit embittered,*
> *I was senseless and ignorant;*
> *I was a brute beast before you (vv. 21–22).*

It's not easy to face our own shortcomings. In fact, it's painful! That's why we avoid looking at the truth about ourselves. But if we do not take stock of ourselves and our flawed thinking, we'll never make the changes that lead to godly thinking and behavior. We'll doom ourselves to repeating the same mistakes over again. The psalmist honestly confronted his failed patterns of thinking, and he was able to change his approach to the problems in his life.

The psalmist realizes that when he looked at life from a natural viewpoint instead of God's viewpoint, he was thinking as ignorantly as a brute beast. He was behaving like an animal, reacting instinctively, enjoying life when he was being fed and cared for but stupidly charging and butting and roaring in frustration when life didn't go his way. When he finally gains God's perspective, he no longer behaves like a dumb animal but like a true human being made in God's image.

A woman who had taught school for twenty-five years applied for an administrative position. She was bitterly disappointed when the job went to a teacher with fewer years on the job. The woman went to the principal and said, "That job should be mine! I've had twenty-five years' experience!"

"No," the principal corrected. "You haven't had twenty-five years of experience. You've had one year's experience twenty-five times."

There's a big difference! Experience only counts if we learn and grow from our experiences. If we keep repeating the same mistakes, we are *wasting* those experiences. Here the psalmist reflects, learns, and grows.

Step Five: Recognize God's love for you.

Yet I am always with you;
you hold me by my right hand.
You guide me with your counsel,
and afterward you will take me into glory (vv. 23–24).

After recognizing how wrong he has been, the psalmist experiences instant reassurance. He realizes that God still loves him and holds him by his right hand. All the wonders of God's grace are distilled into that one word "yet." This word expresses the psalmist's profound realization that even though he has behaved as stupidly as an animal, God still holds him by the hand and guides him with divine counsel.

I once counseled a young woman who struggled with guilt feelings because of an immoral past. She said, "I feel so dirty, guilty, and impure. Though God has forgiven me, I can't forgive myself. But one thing I've noticed: Since I gave my life to Jesus Christ, God has been good to me. I've seen Him lead me and help me make good decisions. He's shown me so much grace in the past few years that I can't help feeling amazed."

"Doesn't that tell you something?" I said. "Doesn't that tell you that God loves you yet and that He has forgiven you? Even while you've had trouble forgiving yourself, God has been showing you that He cares about you. He's active and involved in your life.

Remember what the Lord said to Peter in Acts 10:15: 'Do not call anything impure that God has made clean.' God has made you clean; it's time to accept His evaluation of your life."

Her face brightened. "That's right! God has cleansed me! It would be an *insult* to God to keep calling myself impure!" It was a moment of liberating insight for her.

The psalmist experienced this same liberating insight. He found that God had forgiven him and was holding him by the right hand. He realized that God would guide him for the rest of his life and take him to glory at the end of his earthly existence. That's the destiny of the believer.

Step Six: Place total reliance on God. The psalmist realizes that the only thing in the world worthy of his desiring is God Himself.

> *Whom have I in heaven but you?*
> *And earth has nothing I desire besides you.*
> *My flesh and my heart may fail,*
> *but God is the strength of my heart*
> *and my portion forever (vv. 25–26).*

Can you say what the psalmist says? This is a startling statement: "God is the strength of my heart and my portion forever. There is nothing I desire besides Him." The psalmist Asaph has seen the utter adequacy of God. The Lord is all we need to meet us in our loneliness, despair, disappointment, and sorrow. He is all we need, whether in life or in death.

What was the psalmist's problem at the beginning of Psalm 73? In verse 3 he wrote, "I envied the arrogant when I saw the prosperity of the wicked." He had compared himself to other people and envied their prosperity. They had riches he didn't have. They had luxury he coveted. He thought material things would make him happy. After all, the ungodly had everything they wanted, and they seemed happy!

But then the psalmist came to a different perspective: Material things do not bring satisfaction. Only God can bring joy, peace, and life. All he needs is God Himself. So the psalmist concludes with a final step.

Step Seven: Trust God to keep His word.

Those who are far from you will perish;
you destroy all who are unfaithful to you.
But as for me, it is good to be near God.
I have made the Sovereign LORD *my refuge;*
I will tell of all your deeds (vv. 27–28).

God keeps His word. He does what He says He will do. He destroys the unfaithful. He is good to the upright and pure of heart. If we take refuge in God, we'll have a great story to tell of the wonderful things He has done for us. As the apostle James writes, "Come near to God and he will come near to you" (4:8). When we live for Him, pray to Him, and study His Word, we take a step toward Him. And God promises that when we step closer to Him, He will rush closer to us.

God will see us through any difficulty in life. We can endure trials and injustice, secure in the knowledge that God is with us and His promises are sure. This "Song from the Sanctuary of God" reminds us that we have no reason to envy the ungodly. He, and He alone, is all we need.

13

In Times of Doubt

PSALM 77:1-12

Someone once said, "You know you have a problem with doubting when your prayer goes like this: 'O God (if there is a God), save my soul (if I have a soul) so I can go to heaven when I die (if there is a heaven)." We chuckle at this prayer, but when it's three a.m. and we are unable to sleep, doubt is nothing to laugh about.

Doubt is painful and disturbing. It robs us of our joy and peace. It creates distance in our relationship with God.

Sometimes doubt comes from our emotions. When the doctor says "It's cancer," when we lose someone we love, or when our hearts are broken, we sometimes ask God, "Why? You could have stopped this from happening but You didn't! If You are all-powerful and all-loving, how could You allow this to happen?" At such times we may feel disappointed with God. Our painful emotions will trigger an attack of doubt.

At other times doubt comes from intellectual questioning. Bible teacher G. Campbell Morgan (1863–1945) preached his first sermon when he was thirteen years old. Though he had no formal training, he was deeply devoted to Bible study. While still in his teens, he was greatly sought after as a Bible teacher. But at age nineteen, he experienced a crisis of doubt that nearly drove him from the ministry.

Morgan had begun reading the works of various scientists and agnostics, such as Thomas Huxley and Herbert Spencer, and some of their arguments against the existence of God began to make sense to him. As his doubts deepened, he cancelled all of his speaking engagements and shut himself in a room with his Bible. For days he did nothing but read the Bible from cover to cover. He told himself,

"If the Bible is the Word of God, and if I come to it with an open mind, it will be all I need to bring assurance to my soul."

Days later Morgan left his room and announced, "The Bible has found me!" He went back to his preaching ministry convinced of the reality of God in his life and the reliability of God's Word. Those who heard him preach said he spoke with a new sense of power and conviction.

Psalm 77 was written to help people who struggle with doubt. It is the story of a man who is driven nearly to despair because God seems to refuse to respond to his prayers. This psalm shows how we as believers—and yes, sometimes as doubters—can move from despair to a durable faith in God.

Distressing Problems, Perplexing Doubts

This psalm opens with a cry of pain. The psalmist Asaph writes:

> *I cried out to God for help;*
> *I cried out to God to hear me.*
> *When I was in distress, I sought the Lord;*
> *at night I stretched out untiring hands*
> *and my soul refused to be comforted.*
> *I remembered you, O God, and I groaned;*
> *I mused, and my spirit grew faint. Selah (vv. 1–3).*

Asaph doesn't tell us what his affliction is. It may have been a terrible loss in his life, extreme illness, the rebellion of a son or daughter, or a friend's betrayal. We don't know the source of his distress, but we know his emotions are twisted in knots. He has cried out to God, and his spirit has withered within him. He feels crushed by sorrow and disappointment. Though he tries to focus on the Lord's goodness, the psalmist's soul refuses to be comforted. He can't take his mind off his pain.

The writer continues: "You kept my eyes from closing; I was too troubled to speak" (v. 4).

He tries to sleep, but his eyelids won't close. His emotions are so disturbed that he cannot even describe his problem to others. The psalmist Asaph speaks authentically to human affliction. He holds nothing back but describes exactly how he feels.

Sometimes we church members don't like to admit that such intense affliction and doubting are a normal part of the Christian experience, but they are! Charles Haddon Spurgeon once visited a seminary where he was approached by one of the students. "Sir," said the young seminarian, "could we meet privately? I need to talk to you about a problem."

Spurgeon met privately with the young man, who said, "Sir, I'm afraid I may be losing my faith." And he began talking about the problems he'd been having. He had experienced situations where he had prayed but God had not answered. He concluded by saying, "Sir, how did you manage to reach a place where you don't have doubts anymore?"

At this Spurgeon had to laugh. "Son, I've never reached that place," he said. "I have all kinds of doubts. When you've been a Christian as long as I have, you'll deal with such doubts that those little problems you told me about won't seem like anything at all!"

Spurgeon gave an honest response—as honest as the response of the psalmist Asaph. Doubts are a normal part of the Christian life. Part of our growth and maturity as Christians is learning how to persevere through our doubts so that God can bring us to a place of unshakable faith.

Many Christians think, "Now that I'm a believer, my faith will answer every problem, every doubt." But the book of Psalms is testimony to the contrary. Life is full of problems and doubts, and no one understood this better than Jesus Himself.

Think of His agony in the garden in Gethsemane. There we see Him perplexed and troubled by what lies ahead of Him. He cries out to the Father, saying, in effect, "I don't understand what is happening. If at all possible, let this horror, this awful cup, pass from me. Yet, let it not be as I will, but let Your will be done" (see Luke 22:42). Later, on the cross, He is left alone to wonder, "My God, my God, why have You forsaken Me?" (Matthew 27:46). If Jesus knew such intense inner struggle over God's will for His life, then He certainly understands how perplexed we often feel.

In 2 Corinthians 4:8 the apostle Paul speaks of being hard pressed and perplexed, so we should not feel that we are unspiritual if we face similar struggles in our lives. In fact it is superficial and unrealistic to imagine that the Christian life can be lived without trials of pain and doubt. The history of God's people is a lengthy record of tragedies, catastrophes, problems, pain, and, yes, doubt.

But thank God that's not the end of the story! The psalmist cites two things he does in response to trials of pain and doubt: He prays and he meditates on God. It's clear that the psalmist is not a mere beginner in the faith. He knows how to approach God in times of affliction, and he uses those approaches of prayer and meditation. Even so, his pain continues unabated. In fact the pain of his affliction is compounded by God's apparent failure to answer his prayers.

It's hard enough to endure affliction, but what really troubles us is the possibility that our faith may collapse under the pressure. If that happens we not only lose *this* battle but we lose *all* of our battles because faith in God is all that makes life worth living. Whenever we are in pain, we are tempted to disbelieve.

That's the temptation the psalmist faces. He has tried prayer, but prayer doesn't seem to work. He has tried meditating on God's Word, but that too leaves him empty. Why? Because he is relying on prayer and meditation as techniques, and his problems cannot be solved by techniques.

A Disturbing Conclusion

This psalm unmasks the glib and superficial advice we Christians often give one another in times of trial and discouragement. We see a person whose heart has been ripped out, and what is our response? "Pray about it," we say, "and meditate in the Word."

I'm not saying that such advice is wrong. I'm saying it's useless advice as far as it goes. Prayer (as we will see later in the psalm) is not the first thing to do when you are in trouble. Does that surprise you? Does it seem almost blasphemous? Yet Psalm 77 assures us that it is so. When we are afflicted, there's something we should do *before* we pray—but what?

The problem that the writer of this psalm expresses is a common one: He thought that prayer would solve his problems. He used prayer as a problem-solving technique. Prayer was never designed for that purpose. God designed prayer as an instrument of intimacy between Him and us. We make a serious mistake when we reduce prayer to a technique.

If we advise a fellow Christian in distress to "pray about it" and that person has prayed and received no answer from God, then we have not helped in any way. That person will end up even more discouraged and defeated and will be all the more tempted to give up on the Christian faith thinking, "Faith doesn't work. God doesn't respond to my prayer."

It's not good enough simply to "muddle through" a time of doubt. These are times that God can use to help us grow stronger in Him. He allows these painful experiences in our lives because they are designed to teach us something. If we do not find God's solution to our trial of doubt, then our faith may not survive the testing.

The psalmist in Psalm 77 comes perilously close to that point of collapse in his own faith. Desperately hoping to shore up his faith, the psalmist tries an approach that was probably suggested by a well-meaning friend or counselor. He reflects on the past:

I thought about the former days,
the years of long ago;
I remembered my songs in the night.
My heart mused and my spirit inquired (vv. 5–6).

In other words, "I'm looking for answers so I go back over the past. I recall the times when I've been troubled at night and unable to sleep, but God put a song in my heart. I meditate, and my spirit asks questions and ponders the past." The psalmist remembers past blessings and God's goodness. He remembers the songs and psalms that God has given him to sing in previous nights of pain and affliction.

Does it help to go back over the past? No. Even as he remembers the former days and the songs in the night, his spirit insistently inquires, asks questions, and doubts. In fact doubts continue to assail him from every direction. In one way or another, these doubts are all about the *same* question: "Why doesn't God answer me?" This questioning drags him to the depths of despair in the next few verses:

"Will the Lord reject forever?
Will he never show his favor again?

Has his unfailing love vanished forever?
Has his promise failed for all time?
Has God forgotten to be merciful?
Has he in anger withheld his compassion?" Selah *(vv. 7–9).*

These are logical questions: "If God has blessed me in the past, then why doesn't He bless me now? Why do I seem to be forgotten and abandoned? Has His mercy come to an end? Is He angry with me?"

Finally the psalmist states the terrible conclusion to which he has come. It is an honest conclusion—and a painful one. The New American Standard translation offers a clearer rendering of verse 10 than the New International Version: "Then I said, 'It is my grief, that the right hand of the Most High has changed.'"

In other words, "I've analyzed my situation. I've prayed all night long. In the past God answered my prayers, but this time He's given me no help. I've searched my heart, and I can't answer these questions.

"There is only one conclusion I can draw: I was mistaken about God in the past. I thought that He was changeless, that He would always respond every time I came to Him, but He hasn't. So I'm forced to conclude that God has changed. You can't count on Him, and that's the most disturbing conclusion of all."

This man faces the loss of his faith. He sees this possibility as the tragedy that it is. All that he once rested in, all that was a comfort to him, is now crumbling beneath his feet. What can he do? How can he be delivered from his crisis of doubt?

The Unthinkable Thought

Psalm 77 takes a sudden turn at verse 11. Asaph writes:

I will remember the deeds of the LORD;
yes, I will remember your miracles of long ago.
I will meditate on all your works
and consider all your mighty deeds (vv. 11–12).

The psalmist has undergone a radical re-thinking of his crisis of doubt. He voices a new sense of confidence and peace, which he expresses to God in prayer. What has changed? What happened between verse 10 and verse 11 to move the psalmist from doubt to faith? Just this: He suddenly saw where his thoughts were leading him!

The psalmist had reached the brink of unbelief. He had concluded that God can change, and the next step in his thinking would be to believe something horrible, something unthinkable: God is not really God.

After all, if God can change, then He is nothing more than a manlike being with godlike powers. The steadfastness and unchanging character of God is essential to the psalmist's understanding of who God is. If God can change, if He can be unloving and unjust, then God is not really God.

That is the brink where the psalmist stands in verse 10. One more step, and he will go over the brink and tumble into the abyss of unbelief. Seeing where his thinking is leading, the psalmist draws back from the brink. At verse 11 we see him moving in a completely different direction.

The psalmist understood that one of the most fundamental truths of Scripture is that God cannot change. As the apostle James puts it in his New Testament letter, God is the "Father of the heavenly lights, who does not change like shifting shadows" (1:17). He is absolutely reliable and dependable. His love for us never changes. His mercy towards us never changes. These truths are fundamental to the biblical concept of God.

It's important to understand that the psalmist's doubts were not answered at this point. His decision to believe God was not an emotional decision or an intellectual decision. It was a determination he made purely in his will. He made a volitional choice to step back from the brink of unbelief, and that choice saved him.

This is a good thing to do when you struggle with doubt. Look to the end of the road you are on. See where your steps are taking you. When you see the destination of that road, you will probably be appalled, but taking that hard look will force you to proceed with care. What's at stake here is nothing less than your fundamental philosophy of God and meaning. The conclusion you reach will affect every aspect of your life. So take a good, hard, honest look.

Don't be afraid to face your doubts squarely. The Bible is true, God is alive, and the Christian faith is strong enough to withstand your honest inquiry.

If you examine the Scriptures, I believe you'll come to the same conclusion the apostle Peter reached. In John 6, Jesus made some demanding statements to His disciples. At that point many of them turned away and left Him. When Jesus saw the crowds leaving Him, He turned to the Twelve and said, "You do not want to leave too, do you?" And Peter responded: "Lord, to whom shall we go? You have the words of eternal life" (John 6:68).

In a sense he was saying, "Lord, the things You've said are disturbing, and we have a hard time understanding it all. Just when we think we have You figured out, You make a statement that shocks and baffles us. But we've examined the alternatives, and we've asked ourselves, 'Who else speaks the truth as Jesus does? Where else can we go? We've decided to follow You, because You have the words that lead to eternal life.'"

So it is with the psalmist. His doubts drove him to think unthinkable thoughts. He stood at the brink of unbelief and stared into the abyss, then he resolved in his mind and will to continue believing that God is God.

The Place to Begin

And what about the psalmist's unresolved doubts? We cannot live our lives in a state of tension between faith and doubt. Ultimately we must come down on one side or the other. When we doubt we need to take action to resolve our doubts. If we fail to settle the questions of our faith, if we try to live in a state of unresolved doubt, then those doubts will pull on us until we finally tumble into the abyss of unbelief and become enemies of faith.

How did the psalmist avoid this fate? He began by thinking about God. Let's look again at these two verses:

> *I will remember the deeds of the* LORD*;*
> *yes, I will remember your miracles of long ago.*
> *I will meditate on all your works*
> *and consider all your mighty deeds (vv. 11–12).*

Notice that the psalmist begins by saying, "I will." Those two words show us that he has made a decision to act. He has chosen to stop being a victim of his feelings. His mind and his will now enter the picture. The control of his life shifts from his heart to his head. The moment he makes this decision, the psalmist stops focusing on himself and his circumstances, and he starts focusing on God.

You'll recall that earlier in this chapter I said that prayer is not the first thing to do when you are in trouble. Did you find that surprising? I'm sure you're wondering what we should do before we pray. Here is the answer: Before you pray, meditate on God. Before you pray, make sure you understand who God is. Focus on God Himself before you focus on your petitions, your hurts, your needs, and your feelings through prayer.

Our tendency is to pray first, then meditate (if we meditate at all). When we pray before we meditate, we pray about our problems, our suffering, our anxiety, and our worries. When we pray before meditating, we put ourselves at the center of our prayers: "I'm in trouble! I'm in pain! I'm depressed! I need you to save me from my problems, God!"

We need to learn to put God at the center of our prayers. We need to meditate in the Scriptures that speak to us about God. We need to meditate on the nature of God, the person of God, the wonder of God, the activity of God in human history and in our own lives. Then when we pray, we can put God in the center of our prayers instead of ourselves. "God, You are the Lord of my life and my problems. You are holy and merciful. You are unchanging and dependable. You are all I want and all I ever need in life."

Do you see how meditating on God completely changes the way we pray? Do you see how it shifts our focus away from ourselves, our problems, and our feelings? Do you see how it causes us to focus on who God is, what He is like, and what He can do? Do you see how meditating on God moves us out of our natural thinking and lifts us to a spiritual way of thinking?

Now perhaps you begin to see what Psalm 77 is all about. The psalmist begins by describing a natural view of his problems. He prays from a natural and self-centered mindset. He begins with the thought, "See how afflicted I am! See how I cry out and nothing happens!" When self is at the center, the heart takes over and the mind is governed by feelings.

But when the psalmist's perspective changes at verse 11, his prayer changes as well. Instead of being focused on his own pain and self-pity, he focuses entirely on God. There is profound psychological insight contained in this account. Psalm 77 begins with a man who is a slave to his emotions. His anxiety and despair color his outlook on his problems as well as his outlook on God. His emotions have actually brought him to the brink of a total collapse of his faith. When the psalmist takes himself out of the center of his prayers and puts God there instead, his perspective is changed.

You and I are limited beings. If we begin by praying about ourselves, our problems, and our feelings, we are starting out with limited thinking. When we start with God, we start with the fact that God knows no limits. He is the Creator of the universe, the Author of life. All knowledge and all truth are His. By focusing on Him instead of ourselves, we remove all limitations from our thinking and our prayers. All things become possible when you begin with God.

Explaining the Silence of God

Before we leave this section of Psalm 77, there is one more question that demands an answer: "Why was God so unresponsive to the psalmist's cries? Why was God silent?"

This is a question that we often ask ourselves. In one sense the answer is obvious and perhaps shocking: God is silent because He chooses to be. His silence is deliberate.

We don't like to think that God would deliberately ignore our pleas for help, especially in our times of physical, emotional, or spiritual suffering. We know that God is loving and merciful, and it seems a violation of His nature for Him to treat us with silence just when we need Him most.

Why then would God deliberately allow the psalmist to go through such a time of trial, doubt, and despair? There is only one answer: God wants the psalmist to move to a deeper level of faith. This time of trial and doubting is part of the process that makes us grow spiritually strong and wise.

Here's a spiritual principle that we can't deny: If God always responded instantly to our cries for help, we would remain spiritually immature forever. We would always be mastered by feelings and moods. Our prayers would always be self-centered rather than God-centered. Our outlook would remain natural, not spiritual.

One sure mark of maturity in a Christian's life is that he or she is no longer controlled by circumstances, emotions, and moods. Yes, mature Christians still have feelings, but their feelings no longer rule their lives and govern their relationship with God. Their lives are no longer a roller-coaster ride of mood swings, of soaring highs and depressing lows. They are stable and strong in their faith, regardless of circumstances, just as Jesus our Lord was.

We would never reach that place of spiritual maturity if God always responded to us the instant we called upon Him. We will never achieve Christlike faith and character as long as our trust in God is subject to our moods, emotions, and circumstances. So God deliberately hides Himself at times so that we will grow to become like Christ.

If you are going through a trial and God seems silent, I want you to know that He is there with you, hurting and weeping with you, but He is also helping you to grow in your character and your faith. Through this painful experience, you are learning lessons that you could never learn any other way.

God may seem silent right now, but He is alongside you in a deeper way than you have ever known before. He is leading you into a richer, more rewarding, more exciting experience of faith than you ever dreamed possible. The momentary trial you are going through is designed to build in you a Christlike character, a steadfast soul, and a believing spirit.

Soon you'll be able to rejoice with the psalmist and say, "I will remember the deeds of the Lord!" You have God's Word on that.

14

Through the Deep Waters

PSALM 77:13–20

If there is one moment that defined Israel as a nation blessed by God, it was the time God led the people of Israel out of their bondage in Egypt. This Old Testament event established Israel's national identity for all time. The book of Psalms continually refers to this event when God brought the plagues upon Egypt then miraculously opened the Red Sea and led the people to safety from the Egyptian army. God fed them in the wilderness and went before them in a pillar of fire by night and a pillar of cloud by day.

Thousands of people witnessed these events, including the people of other nations. The details of these events were well known throughout the ancient world. When the people of Israel came to the edge of the Jordan River and were about to enter the Promised Land, they found that word had gone before them. Israel's enemies were already frightened of them, and that paved the way for Israel's conquest of the land. The Gentile nations had heard the stories of the plagues in Egypt and the parting of the Red Sea, and these nations could not deny that Israel served a great God.

These are the events that the psalmist Asaph recalled when he wrote:

> *I will remember the deeds of the LORD;*
> *yes, I will remember your miracles of long ago.*
> *I will meditate on all your works*
> *and consider all your mighty deeds (vv. 11–12).*

As Christians we have a similar heritage of New Testament history on which to reflect. We can remember the mighty deeds of the Lord Jesus and His miracles of long ago. We can meditate on His works of teaching, healing, and raising the dead as well as His work of dying on the cross and rising from the tomb. These events are historical facts.

The apostle Paul testified to this same historical heritage before King Agrippa when he said of the death and resurrection of Jesus, "None of this has escaped [the king's] notice, because it was not done in a corner" (Acts 26:26). In other words, the historic fact of the death and resurrection of Jesus was a well-attested event that took place before many witnesses. The risen Lord didn't appear to only one or two people but to dozens, and to over five hundred people at once on one occasion. These people all bore witness to the resurrection.

When we read the words of the psalmist, "I will remember the deeds of the LORD," we can say, "Yes! Amen! God has done great things! He has led Israel out of Egypt through the depths of the Red Sea, and He has taken our Lord Jesus through the darkness of death itself and has raised Him up to live and reign forever!"

One of the most moving experiences of my life was when I visited the Holy Land and walked on the very ground where Jesus, the patriarchs, and the prophets walked. The reality of biblical history was evident all around me. I went down to Hebron and into the building that stands over the Cave of Machpelah, the tomb of Abraham. I stood on the very place where Solomon's temple once stood. I touched the Wailing Wall, which is constructed from the stones that were once part of that great temple.

I walked along the shores of Galilee and saw the synagogue where Jesus once taught. I walked in the courtyard where Jesus stood before Pilate and saw where Roman soldiers had scratched games to play into the paving stones as they waited for judgments to be rendered. I visited the hill where Jesus was crucified—Golgotha, the place of the skull.

It is a fact that God has acted in history. The story of Jesus is not a myth. The Word became flesh and lived among us, was crucified, and rose again. The Bible is grounded in history. The church could never have survived those early years of persecution if so many people had not witnessed the resurrection of Jesus. The early Christians would never have withstood such fiery, bloody persecution for the sake of a lie. The resurrection is the central fact of human history.

That is why we can say along with the psalmist, "I will remember the deeds of the LORD."

The Greatness of God

The psalmist has shown us the present-day value of remembering what God has done in the past. He goes on to tell us what will result when we meditate upon who God is and what He has done:

> *Your ways, O God, are holy.*
> *What god is so great as our God?*
> *You are the God who performs miracles;*
> *you display your power among the peoples.*
> *With your mighty arm you redeemed your people,*
> *the descendants of Jacob and Joseph.* Selah *(vv. 13–15).*

As we saw in the first half of Psalm 77, the psalmist had experienced a period of doubting that brought him to the brink of unbelief. But then he arrived at the conclusion about God that is so wonderfully expressed in these verses. His conclusion is that God is holy and great.

Our faith will stand firm as long as we are convinced of the two towering truths the psalmist expresses here: God is holy and God is great. The psalmist is filled with a sense of awe regarding the moral perfection and utter majesty of God.

We human beings like to applaud our own greatness. We think we are powerful beings because of technological terrors such as the hydrogen bomb. This device, which releases energy by fusing the nuclei of hydrogen atoms, is capable of destroying a city of several million people in a single flash. But how does the power of an entire arsenal of hydrogen bombs compare with the power of God?

Our sun works on the same principle as a hydrogen bomb, generating energy by fusing the nuclei of hydrogen atoms. But did you know that our sun unleashes the equivalent of 100 billion hydrogen bombs every second? What's more, the sun, which is more than 300,000 times the size of planet Earth, is just one of 100 billion stars in the Milky Way Galaxy, which is just one of 100 billion galaxies in the known universe! In other words, at any given split-instant of time, God's universe is unleashing trillions and trillions of times the energy of humans' most powerful invention!

The next time you hear someone boasting of human greatness, remind that person of the greatness of a God who could create such a universe as ours! It helps to keep things in perspective.

The Reality of Miracles

The psalmist writes: "You are the God who performs miracles; you display your power among the peoples" (v. 14). This was a profound statement when it was written, a thousand years before the birth of Jesus. It is still a profound statement today.

The miracles of God reveal a power beyond human comprehension. I know many people today would consider a belief in miracles to be superstitious. Yet these events we call miracles have convinced men and women of faith for centuries that God is at work. It is precisely because these events are supernatural that people find them convincing evidence of the reality of God.

Take, for example, the crossing of the Red Sea. Here is an amazing event that shaped the course of history. Nations exist today as a result of that supernatural occurrence. The waters were rolled back so that the Israelites could walk across the seabed on dry land, but when the Egyptians followed, the waters collapsed on them and they were drowned.

Humans have never done such a thing. It is humanly impossible. People can't duplicate such a feat; they can only belittle it. As one agnostic put it, "Miracles cannot happen; therefore miracles have not happened." Some skeptics manage to argue in a complete circle: "There is no God, so there can be no miracles. Since there are no miracles, there is no God."

Such arguments prove nothing. Logicians call such thinking "begging the question." It's the fallacy of basing a conclusion on an unproven assumption. You can't logically say, "Miracles can't happen; therefore miracles have not happened." You first have to prove that miracles can't happen. If you can't prove your assumption, then any conclusion you base on that assumption is unproven as well.

It's amazing to see how otherwise intelligent people simply dismiss with a wave of the hand the evidence that miracles do happen. If we look at the events of the Bible as a record of eyewitness accounts made by honest, sincere men and women, then the Bible becomes a compilation of strong and convincing evidence for miracles.

Another foolish thing that otherwise intelligent people do is that they reserve all of their skepticism and cynicism for the Bible alone. They accept as trustworthy the accounts of Suetonius, Philo, Justin Martyr, Tertullian, Tacitus, Eusebius, Herodotus, Xenophon, Polybius, Livy, and Flavius Josephus, but they regard the accounts of the Old and New Testaments as highly suspect, if not downright dishonest. On what basis do they draw this distinction? Purely on the basis that the Bible records miracles, and "everybody knows that miracles can't happen."

On the basis of prejudice alone, many historians and scholars simply dismiss the miracles of the Exodus, the miracles of the prophets, and the miracles of Jesus. Yet in the days when these events occurred, even hostile witnesses had to admit that they were real.

We see an example of this in Matthew 28. After the resurrection of Jesus, the guards from the tomb ran to the chief priests and told them that the stone had been rolled away from the opening and the body of Jesus was gone. The chief priests bribed the guards and told them to say, "His disciples came during the night and stole him away while we were asleep" (v. 13). So the guards went out and circulated the false story.

Why did the priests and the guards have to fabricate such a story? Because the empty tomb demanded an explanation! The location of the tomb was no secret. Anyone could go out to the tomb, look inside it, and see that Jesus wasn't there. Hundreds, perhaps thousands, of people did just that. There was no question that the tomb of Jesus was empty. The only question was why it was empty—and what did the empty tomb mean? To an unbiased mind, the most reasonable explanation was that Jesus truly was alive again.

The God of the psalmist is a God who creates a universe out of nothing, a God who leads a nation out of bondage by taking them through the depths of a parted sea. This same God opened a sealed tomb and breathed life back into the dead body of our crucified

Lord. He is a God who displays His awesome power among the peoples.

The God of Redemption

The psalmist goes on to make another profound observation about the deeds of God. His deeds are not merely great but they are redemptive as well. God did great works that saved His people and restored them to a central place in His eternal plan. The psalmist writes: "With your mighty arm you redeemed your people, the descendants of Jacob and Joseph. *Selah*" (v. 15).

As we have previously noted, the psalmist always placed the word *Selah* at a crucial point in the psalm. The word means, "Stop and think. Pause and reflect on what this means."

So what does the psalmist mean by "You redeemed your people"? The word *redeem* means to restore to usefulness something that has been rendered useless. Let me give you a practical example.

When I was a seminary student, I spent three years as a summer intern in two different churches in Pasadena. Each spring I arrived in town completely broke, with nothing to hold me over until my first paycheck. How did I get by? I picked up the most valuable thing I owned—my typewriter—and took it to the pawnshop and hocked it. The money the pawnbroker lent me was just enough to carry me through the next two weeks. When my paycheck arrived, I'd hurry down to the pawnshop and redeem the typewriter.

While my typewriter was in the pawnshop, it was absolutely idle. I couldn't use it. The pawnbroker couldn't use it. The typewriter was useless to anybody until I returned to the pawnshop and paid the price of redemption. Once the typewriter was redeemed, I put it back into service.

That's what redemption does. Redemption is a special work that only God can do. I can't redeem you from your sins. I can't even redeem myself. Redemption is God's special work, and everything He does in our lives is focused on our redemption, on restoring us to usefulness for Him.

The miracles of the Bible are redemptive in nature. The miracles that God did in Egypt redeemed the people of Israel from bondage and moved them to a place of usefulness for God in the Land of

Promise. The miracles that Jesus did in the gospels—the transformation of water into wine, the healings, and the feedings—were all designed to impress people with truths that would transform their hearts and redeem their lives.

The miracle of the resurrection was, of course, the most redemptive miracle of all, for it was the supernatural event that made it possible for us to be saved from sin and death. In the crucifixion and resurrection, God paid the price of our redemption. He bought us back from the pawnshop of sin and death, and He restored us to usefulness for Him.

In the New Testament we are told that everything about the life of our Lord Jesus was focused on our redemption. The apostle Paul wrote, "For you know the grace of our Lord Jesus Christ, that though he was rich, yet *for your sakes* he became poor, so that you through his poverty might become rich" (2 Corinthians 8:9, emphasis added). Note that phrase: "for your sakes." That is an expression of our Lord's redemptive love. For our sakes He left heaven and became poor. For our sakes He was beaten and crucified.

"God made him who had no sin to be sin *for us,* so that in him we might become the righteousness of God" (2 Corinthians 5:21, emphasis added). God the Father made the Sinless One, Jesus, become sin in our place so that we could be redeemed to live for Him. Jesus was crucified and raised so that we might be set free from sin. Scripture tells us that at this very moment Jesus is interceding for us in heaven—again, for our sakes! As we read in Hebrews, Jesus "is able to save completely those who come to God through him, because he always lives to intercede for them" (7:25).

Notice that the psalmist writes, "With your mighty arm you redeemed your people" (v. 15). He didn't say that God redeemed the entire human race. Those who are God's people are redeemed; those who are not God's people are not redeemed. Redemption is not just for anyone. No people are ever redeemed without their knowledge or against their will. Redemption is for God's people, for those who respond to His invitation and act upon His Word.

The proclamation of God's redemptive love demands a response. The book of Hebrews tells us, "And without faith it is impossible to please God, because anyone who comes to him must believe that he exists and that he rewards those who earnestly seek him" (11:6). You might say, "But I don't know if God exists. I can't find Him. How can I believe in Him if I don't know if He is real or not?" Answer: Draw near to God, and He will draw near to you. That is always the promise of Scripture. If you sincerely and earnestly seek Him, you will find Him. Those who truly want to find Him will find Him.

I can testify to the reality of God's redemptive love. When I was a college-age youth, I had many bad habits, I was confused in my thinking, and I blamed others for my own problems. I didn't know how to free myself of the habits and attitudes that held me back. Over the years as I have grown in my relationship with Christ, His redemptive love has patiently stripped away many of those bad habits and bad attitudes, one by one. I'm a long way from where God wants me to be, but I've come a long way from where I started. God's redemptive work is an ongoing process in my life.

Are you responding to God's redemptive call upon your life? Or are you sitting in sullenness, waiting for God to do something to you in spite of yourself? With His mighty arm, He has redeemed His people, and He is still redeeming His people today. I urge you to seek Him, draw near to Him, and respond to His invitation so that you can say with the psalmist, "What god is so great as our God?" (v. 13).

The Thing You Fear

This psalm opened with a cry of doubt and despair. But the psalmist has traced his way to faith and triumph. Now in the closing lines of Psalm 77 he writes:

> *The waters saw you, O God,*
> *the waters saw you and writhed;*
> *the very depths were convulsed.*
> *The clouds poured down water,*
> *the skies resounded with thunder;*
> *your arrows flashed back and forth.*
> *Your thunder was heard in the whirlwind,*
> *your lightning lit up the world;*
> *the earth trembled and quaked.*
> *Your path led through the sea,*
> *your way through the mighty waters,*

though your footprints were not seen.
You led your people like a flock
by the hand of Moses and Aaron (vv. 16–20).

The psalmist returns to that pivotal event in Israel's history when God led His people out of Egypt by parting the Red Sea. What truths does the psalmist discover in that event?

First, he recognizes God's sovereign control over all human events and over nature itself. He observes that the waters of the Red Sea saw God and trembled in fear before His might. This is a powerful poetic image of how the waters responded to the mighty power of God.

You can imagine the fear of the Israelites when they reached the edge of the sea. The Egyptians were behind them, and the impassable sea was before them. Their plight seemed hopeless. Yet the very thing that terrified the Israelites—the water of the sea—was afraid of God! In the psalmist's poetic imagery, the water saw God, and it writhed and convulsed in fear.

God commanded Moses to stretch forth his rod. Moses obeyed and the sea parted. The waters stacked up on either side, held back by the hand of God. The Israelites went down into the dry channel between the waters. They were afraid of the waters, but the waters were afraid of God. The sea didn't dare touch those whom God protected with His hand.

There is a parallel incident in the New Testament. On one occasion, Jesus was in a boat with His disciples on the Sea of Galilee. A storm arose and the waves beat against the boat so that it began to fill with water. Yet Jesus was so calm in the midst of the storm that He slept on a pillow in the back of the boat. The disciples, afraid that they were about to drown in the storm, woke Him and said, "Don't you care that we're about to die?"

Jesus arose and spoke to the wind and sea, saying, "Peace! Be still!" And the wind ceased, and the sea instantly became calm. Though the disciples feared the wind and sea, the wind and sea feared Jesus even more.

This is a lesson you and I need to learn for the times of peril and fear in our own lives: The very powers and forces that frighten us are themselves under the command of God. The thing you fear fears Him.

Through the Depths of the Sea

Next the psalmist tells us that the forces of nature are nothing but instruments in God's hands. He writes:

The clouds poured down water,
the skies resounded with thunder;
your arrows flashed back and forth.
Your thunder was heard in the whirlwind,
your lightning lit up the world;
the earth trembled and quaked (vv. 17–18).

If you have ever been through an electric storm, you know what the psalmist is describing: the soul-shaking roar of thunder, lightning flashing across the heavens like fiery arrows, the earth trembling in response. All of these forces are under God's command. No power, natural or human, can operate except by permission of the Almighty. That's the great truth the psalmist reflects on as he thinks back to the crossing of the Red Sea.

We see this truth illustrated in the last hours before Jesus went to the cross. Forsaken by His friends, betrayed by Judas, and denied by Peter, Jesus stood alone and seemingly powerless before Pontius Pilate, the Roman governor. When Pilate tried to question Jesus, the Lord gave him no answer. Exasperated, Pilate asked Him, "Do you refuse to speak to me? . . . Don't you realize I have power either to free you or to crucify you?"

Jesus answered, "You would have no power over me if it were not given to you from above" (John 19:10–11).

How our lives would change if we truly lived by that great truth: All of the world's forces, systems, and authorities are under God's control. All power belongs to God. Nothing can touch us without the express permission of God Himself.

The psalmist goes on to say,

Your path led through the sea,
your way through the mighty waters,
though your footprints were not seen" (v. 19).

God led the steps of the Israelites through the depths of the sea. The people of Israel didn't know where God was leading them, but

God had prepared the way. He knew what He was doing. As the psalmist ponders this miraculous event, he discovers a second great truth: The fact that we can't understand what God is doing does not mean He isn't at work in our lives.

This is a difficult concept for us to wrap our minds around. We are impatient beings, and we want God to explain all of His plans and purposes to us now. Unless God constantly reassures us, we fret and panic, just as the Israelites did when they reached the edge of the Red Sea.

In Exodus 14 we read that the Israelites were camped in the desert near the sea when they saw a cloud of dust and heard the thunder of horses' hooves and chariot wheels. Pharaoh's army was coming after them. The people cried out to the Lord; then they panicked and blamed Moses for their peril. "Why did you bring us out into the desert to die?" they said accusingly. "When we were slaves in Egypt, didn't we tell you, 'Just leave us alone and let us continue serving the Egyptians.' Better to live as slaves than to die out here!"

The people of Israel lost faith in Moses and in God. Moses had to give them a pep talk: "Don't be afraid! Stand firm and watch how the Lord delivers you today! He will fight for you."

It's hard for me to criticize the Israelites very harshly. If we had been in their sandals, would we have reacted differently? Whenever things go wrong and we can't see the solution to our problems, aren't we just as quick to hit the panic button? In desperate situations haven't you often prayed, "Lord, there's no way out! I'm trapped! Why don't You do something?" I confess that I have prayed that way many times, and that is not a prayer of faith. That's a prayer of panic.

What the people of Israel didn't understand and couldn't imagine is that God had planned all along to lead them through the Red Sea. His path led through the sea; His way led through the mighty waters. God's plan of deliverance never even entered their minds! But though His footprints were unseen and His people were unable to understand His plan, God knew exactly what He was doing. His plan, though inscrutable, was perfect.

This is a principle we all need to rely on in those times when our back is against the wall, when our enemies are closing in or the obstacles in our lives seem insurmountable, when hope is fading fast and there is no way out of total disaster. We need to place our confidence in Him, trusting that He has a plan that, though inscrutable, is perfect. We can't imagine what God will do, but we can trust that whatever He does will be the best thing for us, and it will be amazing!

A Red Sea Experience

Psalm 77 began on a heartbreaking note of crisis and despair. Early in this psalm, the writer Asaph wrote:

> *I remembered you, O God, and I groaned;*
> *I mused, and my spirit grew faint.* Selah.
> *You kept my eyes from closing;*
> *I was too troubled to speak (vv. 3–4).*

He groaned, his spirit failed, he was too depressed and anxious to sleep or even speak. He was haunted by questions about God that he couldn't answer:

> *"Will the Lord reject forever?*
> *Will he never show his favor again?*
> *Has his unfailing love vanished forever?*
> *Has his promise failed for all time?*
> *Has God forgotten to be merciful?*
> *Has he in anger withheld his compassion?" (vv. 7–9).*

The psalmist looked at his desperate circumstances, took stock of his anxious and depressed emotions, and concluded that God was doing nothing. He told himself, "Here I am in deep trouble, and God is silent and remote. He won't act for me."

But by the closing verses of Psalm 77, the writer comes to a different conclusion. Why? Because he remembers a parallel experience in the history of Israel, a time when God seemed for a while to be doing nothing. The Israelites found themselves trapped between Pharaoh's army and the waters of the Red Sea. There was no way out of their deadly predicament, and God seemed to be silent. His footprints were unseen. Yet God had a plan that led through the sea, an unseen path through the great waters. He led them out of certain death and brought them to safety on the far shore.

Can you identify with the psalmist and the ancient Israelites? Have you ever been in a situation so desperate you could see no way out, and you prayed and prayed and God seemed silent—until He provided an answer from a completely unexpected source? I think most Christians have had that experience at one time or another.

Annie Johnson Flint was born in 1866. She and her sister were orphaned at an early age and raised by Christian foster parents who led them to know Jesus Christ as Lord and Savior. When Annie was a teenager, both of her foster parents died, leaving Annie and her sister orphaned once again. Only two years after she completed high school, Annie was diagnosed with painful, crippling arthritis. By her early twenties, the arthritis was so advanced that she could no longer walk.

Annie supported herself by writing inspirational poetry. Her meager earnings barely covered her living expenses, much less her medical bills. Some friends told her that her suffering was due to a lack of faith or hidden sin in her life. Annie wondered if those friends were right. After weeks of prayer and searching the Scriptures, she concluded that problems and afflictions are a normal part of life, even for the Christian. Sometimes we pray and God lifts us *out* of our afflictions. Other times God leads us *through* our afflictions.

One of the Bible stories that comforted her in her suffering was the story of how God led Israel out of Egypt. She saw the way God led the people through the deep waters of the Red Sea as a metaphor of her own life. Out of that realization, Annie wrote a poem called "A Red Sea Place":

> *Have you come to the Red Sea place in your life,*
> *Where in spite of all you can do,*
> *There is no way out, there is no way back,*
> *There is no other way but through?*
> *Then wait on the Lord with a trust serene*
> *Till the night of your fear is gone;*
> *He will send the wind, He will heap the floods,*
> *When He says to your soul "Go on."*
>
> *And His hand will lead you through—clear through—*
> *Ere the watery walls roll down,*

No foe can reach you, no wave can touch,
No mightiest sea can drown;
The tossing billows may rear their crests,
Their foam at your feet may break,
But over their bed you shall walk dry-shod
In the path that your Lord will make.

In the morning watch, 'neath the lifted cloud,
You shall see but the Lord alone,
When He leads you on from the place of the sea,
To a land that you have not known;
And your fears shall pass as your foes have passed,
You shall no more be afraid;
You shall sing His praise in a better place,
A place that His hand hath made.

That is what a Red Sea experience is like. It's a lesson that all men and women of mature faith must learn. God's path leads through the sea, through trouble and trial. His plan does not take us around trouble but through the depths of it. You may not be able to see His answer before it comes, but when it arrives you'll rejoice and praise Him for the marvelous way He has delivered you.

The Shepherd of His People

The final truth the psalmist discovered was this: The Lord is the Shepherd of His people. He writes: "You led your people like a flock by the hand of Moses and Aaron" (v. 20).

I don't think there is any figure of speech so beautifully descriptive of the relationship of God to His people than that of a Shepherd with His flock. The closing verse of Psalm 77 reminds us of the opening verse of Psalm 23: "The LORD is my shepherd, I shall not be in want." Because the Lord is our Shepherd, we lack nothing. He leads us as His own flock, and He supplies everything that we lack in ourselves.

What does the Lord supply to His sheep?

First, He supplies a sense of meaning and purpose for our lives. A shepherd always has a goal in mind for the flock. If he leads his sheep to the mountain pastures, it's because he has something he wants to accomplish there. If he leads them beside the still water, he has a reason for doing so. If he leads the sheep out in the midst of wolves, it's because he wants them there. It's the shepherd who supplies the purpose.

Meaning is an essential ingredient of life. Why are so many people depressed and suicidal today? Their lives lack meaning and purpose. Why are alcohol abuse and drug abuse rates skyrocketing, even among people who are wealthy and successful? They have no reason for living. They use chemicals to numb the pain of their meaningless existence.

A man once came to me for counseling. He said, "I have everything I want, but I don't want anything I have." He was suffering from "destination sickness," the sickness of having achieved all of his life goals only to find that none of his achievements brought him peace and satisfaction.

God, our Good Shepherd, supplies us with meaning, purpose, and a reason for living. He makes life worthwhile.

Second, the Shepherd supplies love, another desperate need in our lives. Our Lord loves the sheep. He gives us everything that love entails: caring, protection, and provision. As the apostle Peter writes, "Cast all your anxiety on him because he cares for you" (1 Peter 5:7). We matter to Him. He cares about our needs. That is the heart of a shepherd.

Jesus called Himself the Good Shepherd, and He said that what defined Him in that role was His self-sacrificing love for the sheep:

"I am the good shepherd. The good shepherd lays down his life for the sheep. The hired hand is not the shepherd who owns the sheep. So when he sees the wolf coming, he abandons the sheep and runs away. Then the wolf attacks the flock and scatters it. The man runs away because he is a hired hand and cares nothing for the sheep.

"I am the good shepherd; I know my sheep and my sheep know me—just as the Father knows me and I know the Father—and I lay down my life for the sheep (John 10:11–15).

Our Lord portrayed Himself as a loving Shepherd who gathers His lambs to His bosom and leads straying and faltering sheep back to the right path—always gently and tenderly—because of His love for them. This is the essence of God's relationship to His people.

Whenever we feel abandoned or neglected by God, we need to remember that He is our Shepherd. We are always in His protective care, even when we are not aware of it. God always shepherds His own.

That's the conclusion that the psalmist comes to. Have you come to that same conclusion? Are you able to trust God, even through times of doubt and pressure, trial and temptation? Have faith in God! He will lead you through the deep waters and bring you safely to the other shore. Once there you'll be able to say with the psalmist, "Your ways, O God, are holy. What god is so great as our God?" (v. 13).

15

A Psalm for Our Great God

PSALM 84

King Louis XIV of France is remembered as the monarch who declared, *"L'état, c'est moi"*—"I am the state." He was not exactly known for his humility; after all, he did name himself "Louis the Great." He believed himself to be an absolute monarch, appointed by God to rule France. He levied high taxes on the working class yet he exempted rich nobles from having to pay any taxes at all. He kept numerous mistresses, built the palace at Versailles as a monument to his own ego, persecuted Protestant Christians, annexed lands and cities, and launched several bloody wars that left France militarily and economically depleted. In 1715, after a seventy-two-year reign, King Louis XIV died.

The king had left instructions for a spectacular funeral. In accordance with his wishes, his body was placed in a golden coffin and put on display in a great cathedral so that the people of France could file by and pay their respects. The cathedral was kept dark, with only one candle lit above the coffin, casting a dramatic glow to symbolize the king's greatness.

At the funeral service, the bishop rose to give the eulogy for the king. As he walked up to the altar, he paused by the casket, reached out, and snuffed the candle flame. Then he told the audience, "Only God is great."

The bishop spoke truly. Only God is great. He is the Lord Almighty, our King and our God. Every other king who ever ruled was just a man.

The Dwelling Place of God

Psalm 84 is a psalm of our great God. It opens with an inscription that reads "According to *gittith*." As we saw when we looked at Psalm 8, the *gittith* is an eight-stringed instrument much like our modern guitar. In fact the word *gittith* passed through several cultures until it became our modern word *guitar*. This psalm, like Psalm 8, was written to be accompanied by the music of a guitar-like instrument.

In recent years the words of Psalm 84 have been set to music by songwriter Matt Redman. The song he wrote is called "Better Is One Day," and it is usually performed with guitars. So in our own day we have come full circle. In many of our churches today, we are singing the words of this psalm and many other great folk songs of faith, and we are singing to the accompaniment of an instrument David would have loved: the amplified electric *gittith*, or guitar.

Psalm 84 was written by the Sons of Korah, a family that was in charge of worship music for the nation of Israel. The theme of this psalm is the blessings and advantages that come to those who know, love, and serve our great and living God. It is a folk song about a life of fellowship with God. This psalm divides into three parts. Each part is marked off by the word *selah*, which in Hebrew means "pause and think."

In the first four verses, the psalmist sets before us the blessings of a life spent in fellowship with God:

How lovely is your dwelling place,
O Lord Almighty!
My soul yearns, even faints,
for the courts of the Lord;
my heart and my flesh cry out
for the living God.
Even the sparrow has found a home,
and the swallow a nest for herself,
where she may have her young—
a place near your altar,
O Lord Almighty, my King and my God.
Blessed are those who dwell in your house;
they are ever praising you. Selah *(vv. 1–4).*

This is a powerful, soul-lifting expression of the excitement and exhilaration believers feel when they are in the presence of God. When this psalm was written, the dwelling place of God to which this psalm referred was the temple, the building where God's *shekinah* glory was manifested. The *shekinah* glory was a strange and mysterious light that resided in the Holy of Holies within the temple, demonstrating that God was present with Israel. No Israelite was permitted to enter the holy place except the high priest, and he could enter only once a year under the most rigorous of rituals.

Though average Israelites could never enter the Holy of Holies and see the *shekinah* glory, they could worship in the temple. The people of Israel were grateful that the living God was present among them. They appreciated the profound truths about God that were pictured in the sacrifices and ceremonies of the temple. This spirit of gratitude for God's fellowship among the people is reflected in the psalmist's opening statement about the dwelling place of the LORD Almighty, the courts of the LORD.

When the psalmist wrote those words, the dwelling place of God was a building. This is not to say that the Israelites believed that God could be contained in a building. Far from it! They understood that the temple was merely a repository for a special measure of God's presence and glory on earth. When Solomon had finished building the great temple in Jerusalem, he said, "But will God really dwell on earth? The heavens, even the highest heaven, cannot contain you. How much less this temple I have built!" (1 Kings 8:27).

Today when we as Christians talk about the dwelling place of God—the place where God's glory and presence are manifested on earth—we are talking about our bodies. As the apostle Paul writes, "Do you not know that your body is a temple of the Holy Spirit, who is in you, whom you have received from God? You are not your own; you were bought at a price. Therefore honor God with your body" (1 Corinthians 6:19–20).

Once we realize that our own bodies are God's dwelling place, Psalm 84 takes on a new meaning. We can read the words of this psalm as an expression of the excitement and exhilaration we feel because of the presence of God within us. There are three things the psalmist identifies as marks of true fellowship with God: (1) an inner beauty that God creates by His presence; (2) an eagerness and a compelling hunger for God; and (3) the joyful vitality that the presence of God gives.

You may be a genuine Christian but not see these three marks of fellowship with God in your own life. If so, the reason may be that you need to grow deeper in your intimacy with Him. This psalm was written to urge us on to a deeper relationship with God. Let's take a closer look at each of these three marks of close fellowship with the Lord.

The Three Marks of Fellowship with God

The first thing the psalmist sees is an inner beauty that God creates by His presence: His dwelling place is lovely. The psalmist is thrilled to be in the presence of God because He creates beauty and loveliness wherever He dwells, whether in a temple made of hands or a human temple.

The apostle Paul in Ephesians prays "that Christ may dwell in your hearts through faith" (3:17), because the heart where Christ dwells will always be a lovely place. The character of that heart is changed by His presence by becoming conformed to the heart of Christ. It is a heart that is agreeable and gracious, characterized by the qualities Paul calls "the fruit of the Spirit, . . . love, joy, peace, patience, kindness, goodness, faithfulness, gentleness and self-control" (Galatians 5:22–23). Isn't that a description of a beautiful person in the truest sense?

The second mark of true fellowship with God is a hunger for God. The psalmist yearns desperately to be in the courts of the Lord. Have you ever felt this way? Have you known a deep-seated longing to have more of a sense of His presence in your life? Have you fed upon His Word and been satisfied and yet as you went away felt a hunger for more? We sing of this profound hunger for God in the ancient hymn "Jesus, Thou Joy of Loving Hearts":

We taste Thee, O Thou living Bread,
And long to feast upon Thee still;
We drink of Thee, the Fountainhead,
And thirst our souls from Thee to fill.

It's a strange paradox, this wonderful ability God has to satisfy us and make us hunger at the same time.

The third mark of true fellowship with God is the joyful vitality that the presence of God gives. The psalmist writes, "My heart and my flesh cry out for the living God" (v. 2b). This is an exciting experience, and it's exactly what God has meant for life to be. You may have been a Christian for many years, but if you haven't yet found this kind of excitement, then you haven't tapped the rich possibilities and resources of the Christian life.

There is nothing artificial about this excitement over God's presence. It's not an act or a mask. It's a genuine vitality that bubbles up within us as we live in the energizing presence of the living God. Mere words are inadequate to convey what this excitement is like, but it's a thrill that runs deeper and higher than the emotions, reaching to the depths of the soul and the heights of the spirit.

A young man once wrote me, "My work is boring. It's just the same old thing over and over. What can you suggest that will help me with this problem of boredom?" I answered him by pointing out that the secret to experiencing an exciting and satisfying life can be found in John 4. The Lord Jesus was at a well in Samaria where He encountered a jaded, worldly woman who was bored with her life. She had been married five times and was living with yet another man.

Jesus said to her, "If you knew the gift of God and who it is that asks you for a drink, you would have asked him and he would have given you living water . . . Whoever drinks the water I give him will never thirst. Indeed, the water I give him will become in him a spring of water welling up to eternal life" (John 4:10, 14).

What was this "spring of water" Jesus described? Himself, of course! Jesus told this woman that He would enter her heart and become to her a living, bubbling spring from which she could drink at any time.

Whenever life seems boring, drink from the spring within. Take a good, long drink of the living God within you. Remind yourself of whom He is, of your relationship with Him, and that He is continually there. Whenever you do so, your spirit will be refreshed and re-energized.

The Sparrow and the Swallow

The next two verses describe the contentment that the presence of God brings:

Even the sparrow has found a home,
and the swallow a nest for herself,
where she may have her young—
a place near your altar,
O LORD Almighty, my King and my God.
Blessed are those who dwell in your house;
they are ever praising you. Selah *(vv. 3–4).*

The two birds mentioned here—the sparrow and the swallow—are frequently found in Scripture. In the book of Matthew, the Lord Jesus spoke of sparrows to his disciples:

Are not two sparrows sold for a penny? Yet not one of them will fall to the ground apart from the will of your Father . . . So don't be afraid; you are worth more than many sparrows (10:29, 31).

With this statement, Jesus acknowledged that the sparrow was a symbol of insignificance in the Jewish culture of His day. Sparrows represent those who feel they have no worth or value. The psalmist says that even those who feel insignificant can draw near to God and find a home, a place of warmth and security, a place of belonging and fulfillment. No matter how useless and insignificant you feel, when you come to God, you'll find a wonderful sense of purpose.

I am impressed as I read the Scriptures how many times God passes over the proud, the haughty, and the powerful, and He selects some obscure individual to accomplish His purposes. He often chooses the humble over the proud.

Gideon was a humble, obscure man—the kind of man God uses. He lived in Old Testament times when Israel had been undergoing seven years of oppression at the hands of an enemy nation, Midian. The Midianites would attack the Israelites, ruining the crops and stealing the livestock, forcing the Israelites to hide in mountain clefts and caves. During these harsh days, God called upon Gideon and told him to go deliver Israel from the Midianites. Gideon was so sure he didn't amount to anything that he demanded proof that God had actually called him to deliver Israel. Gideon thought God had called him by mistake!

Gideon set a wool fleece upon the floor one night and told God, in effect, "If there's dew on top of this fleece when I wake up in the morning, I'll know you called me." The next morning Gideon got up and wrung the dew out of the fleece, and there was a whole bowl-full of water! Even so, Gideon was not sure. He asked God to confirm it once more the next night, only this time he asked for the dew to appear underneath the fleece and let the top side remain dry. Again God confirmed that He had chosen this humble man.

So Gideon began assembling an army to attack the enemies of Israel. He started with thirty-two thousand men. Then, at God's direction, he whittled that force down just to the men who showed no sign of fear—ten thousand men. God directed him to whittle that force down just to the men who drank water from a stream in such a way that they were always alert—a mere three hundred men. With that seemingly insignificant force of soldiers, led by a humble and self-effacing leader named Gideon, the tiny Israelite army defeated the Midianite army—a force of 135,000 well-armed soldiers.

We see the same principle in the New Testament. God uses the humble, not the proud; the small, not the great. As the apostle Paul wrote, "But God chose the foolish things of the world to shame the wise; God chose the weak things of the world to shame the strong" (1 Corinthians 1:27).

It is instructive to us all that Jesus was unable to use the apostle Peter in a great way until Peter had failed Him in a major way. Throughout the time Peter walked with Jesus, he was proud, boastful, and impetuous. He would compare himself to the other disciples and say, "Lord, look at these other fellows; you can't count on them. But you can always count on me. I'll never let you down!"

Later this same proud, boastful Peter denied Jesus three times, then went out into the streets of Jerusalem, weeping bitterly because he had failed his Lord. Humiliated, defeated, no longer sure of himself, Peter felt unworthy to call himself a follower of Jesus. Only then could Jesus say to him, "Feed my lambs" (John 21:15).

God rarely uses anyone in a great way until He has taken that person through failure, an experience that leaves a person feeling insignificant and worthless. Why? I believe the answer is that God wants to make sure that His servants are emptied of pride and ego and are able to empathize with the least and the last and the lost, the ones He seeks to save.

This is the significance of the psalmist's mention of the sparrow. Though the sparrow may be humble, small, and insignificant, it has found a home, a place of belonging and significance in the heart of God. And the psalmist mentions not only the sparrow but also the swallow too. Even the swallow will find a home in God.

Where I lived in northern Minnesota, we had many swallows. Every evening we could see them darting about the skies. They are among the swiftest of birds, and in Scripture they are used to symbolize restless activity. The swallow represents people who are restless, who are forever looking for something new. They try this and that, look here and there, but they can never settle down.

But even the restless, fast-darting swallow, says the psalmist, can find a home with God—a place to nest, a place of belonging and peace. They will find in Him the rest of which Jesus spoke when He said, "Come to me, all you who are weary and burdened, and I will give you rest. Take my yoke upon you and learn from me, for I am gentle and humble in heart, and you will find rest for your souls" (Matthew 11:28–29).

If you are restless, God is speaking to you. He wants to give you rest. You won't find rest over the next hill chasing some new adventure. You will find rest only in God—as the psalmist puts it, at "a place near your altar, O Lord Almighty, my King and my God" (v. 3).

When we find our home and rest in God, what else can we do but praise Him? And so the psalmist says, "Blessed are those who dwell in your house; they are ever praising you" (v. 4).

Power All Around!

In the next section, the psalmist sets before us a description of what happens when God is at work in our hearts.

> *Blessed are those whose strength is in you,*
> *who have set their hearts on pilgrimage.*
> *As they pass through the Valley of Baca,*

they make it a place of springs;
the autumn rains also cover it with pools.
They go from strength to strength,
till each appears before God in Zion.
Hear my prayer, O LORD *God Almighty;*
listen to me, O God of Jacob. Selah *(vv. 5–8).*

The psalmist reveals the secret of our usefulness to God when he writes that those whose strength is in God are blessed. When troubles and trials come your way, where is your strength? Is your strength in God?

I returned home one Saturday night after a day away from my church responsibilities. I was very tired. When I came in the door, my wife told me of some of the problems that had arisen at home while I was away, problems relating to the church and to my family. Normally I would immediately lay those problems before the Lord in prayer, but on this evening I was tired, and I just wanted to go to bed. I thought, "What's the use of praying, anyway? I'm so tired that my prayers wouldn't have any power."

Then it struck me: What a ridiculous thing to say! What difference does it make how I feel? My reliance isn't upon my prayers but upon God's power. (We sometimes hear people talking about "the power of prayer." But that's a mistaken notion. There isn't any power in prayer. There is power in God, who answers prayer.)

I was rebuked in my own spirit when I remembered that it makes no difference how tired I happen to be. So I prayed a very short prayer. (The power of prayer doesn't lie in the length of it, either!) I had learned the lesson of Psalm 84:5: "Blessed are those whose strength is in you."

Some time ago I was trying to sell my car. Intending to put an ad in the paper, I read through several car ads to learn how to phrase it. I noticed a phrase that appeared frequently throughout the ads. It said, "Power all around." At first I didn't know what that meant, and then I realized it meant power steering, power brakes, automatic transmission, power windows, and power seats. Power all around! All this power is designed to take the strain out of driving so that all you need to do is sit and drive. What a tremendous description of the Christian life! Power all around!

The apostle Paul put it this way: "For God did not give us a spirit of timidity, but a spirit of power, of love and of self-discipline" (2 Timothy 1:7). Power all around!

Someone once suggested that when you get into difficult places where it is hard to know what decision to make, try "power steering." Let God and His power take control of the steering wheel of your life. As the prophet Isaiah wrote, "Whether you turn to the right or to the left, your ears will hear a voice behind you saying, 'This is the way; walk in it'" (30:21).

Do you wrestle with a sinful habit? Try your "power brakes." Paul said, "No, in all these things we are more than conquerors through him who loved us" (Romans 8:37).

Are you bothered by moodiness and discouragement? Try your "power windows." Again Paul writes, "And the peace of God, which transcends all understanding, will guard your hearts and your minds in Christ Jesus" (Philippians 4:7).

For a satisfying life, try your "power transmission." In the book of Acts, we see the transmission of God's power to His people in the early church, just as Jesus said it would happen: "But you will receive power when the Holy Spirit comes on you; and you will be my witnesses in Jerusalem, and in all Judea and Samaria, and to the ends of the earth" (1:8).

The Valley of Weeping

In verse 5 the psalmist writes about those whose hearts are "on pilgrimage." A pilgrimage to where? The psalmist continues: "As they pass through the Valley of Baca, they make it a place of springs; the autumn rains also cover it with pools" (v. 6).

The pilgrimage is to a place called the Valley of Baca. This can literally be translated from the Hebrew as "the Valley of Tears" or "the Valley of Weeping." The term does not refer to any actual geographical valley but to any piece of land that has been spoiled by sorrow and sin.

The Valley of Baca refers to the ministry that all believers can have. Whenever we find ourselves in a place of sorrow, discouragement, and tears, we can respond with radiant faith and a cheerful outlook. We can turn our "Valley of Baca" into a place of refreshing fountains and joy. But we can only do so by the power of the Holy Spirit.

The psalmist writes, "The autumn rains also cover [the valley of Baca] with pools." Rains normally come in the spring. An autumn rain is an early rain, and early rain is a picture of the Holy Spirit. This beautiful, picturesque language of Scripture lends itself to exact interpretation if you understand how these symbols are used in other parts of the Bible. For example, we see these same symbols used by the prophet Joel:

> *Be glad, O people of Zion,*
> *rejoice in the* LORD *your God,*
> *for he has given you*
> *the autumn rains in righteousness.*
> *He sends you abundant showers,*
> *both autumn and spring rains, as before (2:23).*

The autumn rain and the spring rain are sometimes referred to as the "early rain" and the "latter rain." The early and latter rains are symbols of the outpouring of the Holy Spirit. Pentecost was such an event: the outpouring of the Holy Spirit upon the early church as recorded in Acts 2. And that is what the psalmist refers to in Psalm 84: People will enter the Valley of Tears, and they will turn sorrow into joy by means of the indwelling Holy Spirit. The Spirit will transform God's people into pools of blessing and fountains of joy, giving life and refreshment in a parched land, the Valley of Weeping.

Do you know people like those described by the psalmist? Do you know people who spread joy and blessing just by their mere presence, their uplifting words, and their cheerful attitude? Isn't it wonderful to be around people like that? All of us as Christians need to be such people, pilgrims through the Valley of Baca, spreading joy and refreshment wherever we go.

I remember one event that burned this truth into my heart and soul. It happened in November 1969, when my dear friend Dr. Jack Mitchell came to our church as a guest speaker. Jack was the kind of man described in Psalm 84—a sincere Christian whose heart was set on living as a pilgrim through the Valley of Weeping, transforming it

as he went into a place of refreshing springs. He was always opening the windows of heaven and helping people to see the love, forgiveness, and glory of the Lord Jesus.

On this weekend when Jack came to speak, there was a young
man who came to church struggling with some painful problems in
his life. This young man was depressed and defeated, lost in the
Valley of Baca.

But as Jack spoke on that Sunday morning, this young man was
captivated by what he heard: a beautiful message of God's forgiving, liberating grace. The young man sat in the second row, his eyes
fastened on Jack, his ears taking in every word. At the end of the
service he said to a friend, "Now I understand what Jesus Christ did
for me! What a burden of guilt has been lifted from my life!" He was
so hungry to hear more about the forgiving grace of God that he
came back for the evening service, when Jack spoke again.

The following Tuesday the young man met with one of our asso-
ciate pastors, Dave Roper. This fellow wanted to learn all he could
about the Lord and how God wanted to lead him through this time
of trial. As they drove to the restaurant in Dave's Volkswagen, they
stopped at a red light. They were talking together when a huge truck
came through the intersection, clipped the front of Dave's car, and
ripped open the right-hand side of the car. The young man was
tossed out of the car and instantly killed.

Though Dave was unhurt, he was in shock. He came back to the
church office where our entire church staff had just prayed for that
young man that morning. Ashen-faced, Dave told us, "The young
man we all prayed for this morning—he's dead."

Our staff was stunned and shaken. It was impossible to imagine
such a thing. My first thought was, "How could God allow this to
happen? This young man had just discovered the joy of God's forgiveness! Now he's dead!"

Then I remembered how much comfort this young man had
received when Jack passed through his Valley of Baca and turned
his weeping into a spring of joy. If the young man hadn't come and
heard that message of forgiveness, he might have lived a life of misery and guilt, never knowing that God loved him and forgave him.
Instead he had experienced two-and-a-half days of joy in knowing
God, and then the Lord received him into His glorious presence.

What a ministry Dr. Jack Mitchell had in this young man's life! Isn't that the kind of ministry you want to have in the lives of those around you? Don't you want to become a pilgrim in the Valley of Baca so that you can bring a cool, refreshing spring of joy and life to those who are burdened with sin, sorrow, and grief?

Next the psalmist notes that those who have set their hearts on a pilgrimage through the Valley of Baca do not merely bring joy and blessing to others; they experience a profound blessing from God in their own lives. They receive more and more strength from God, more and more refreshment and blessing in their own lives, more and more victorious power, and a deeper and richer daily experience of God's grace. Ultimately the beautiful lives they lead bring them into the presence of God Himself in the promised land of Zion.

In verse 8 the psalmist prays a prayer that has become the urgent prayer of my own heart: "Hear my prayer, O Lord God Almighty; listen to me, O God of Jacob. *Selah.*"

In other words the psalmist asks, "O Lord, make me this kind of man. Help me make Your strength my strength. Make me a pilgrim in the Valley of Baca. Let springs of living water well up like fountains from my own life so that I can bring joy and refreshment to people who are burdened with guilt and sorrow. Let me go from strength to strength, from victory to victory, until I can see you, the invisible God, in all Your glory!"

That is what I want with all my heart! Don't you?

Better Is One Day in God's Courts

If the prayer of verse 8 is the prayer of your heart, then pay close attention to the final section of this psalm. The psalmist writes:

Look upon our shield, O God;
look with favor on your anointed one.
Better is one day in your courts
than a thousand elsewhere;
I would rather be a doorkeeper in the house of my God
than dwell in the tents of the wicked.
For the Lord God is a sun and shield;
the Lord bestows favor and honor;

no good thing does he withhold
from those whose walk is blameless.
O Lᴏʀᴅ Almighty,
blessed is the man who trusts in you (vv. 9–12).

The psalmist calls to his Lord to look upon his shield. A shield is a broad piece of armor that a soldier straps to his arm and carries into battle for protection. The psalmist is saying, "Look, Lord! Look at what I have chosen to carry into battle against my enemies! Look at what I have chosen to hold before me as a shield!"

What is the psalmist's shield? It is God Himself. The psalmist is saying, "You are my shield, O God. You are my strength and protection in battle. Because I carry You before me in the war against my enemies, please look on me with favor. Please give me the victory! Please let me go from strength to strength in Your power!"

The psalmist cries out to God, asking Him to apply the great truths of this psalm to his own life. That is as it should be. Another way the psalmist could say this is, "Lord, I see your blessing and power in the lives of others, and I want this same blessing and power in my life! Give it to me as well!" It is perfectly right to pray that way. It is never wrong to ask God to do for you what He wants to do.

Next the psalmist gives us two reasons he wants to live this kind of life. The first reason the psalmist desires this life that he has prayed for is this: Life with God is incomparably better than any other kind of life. One day lived in fellowship with God is more desirable, more joyful, more satisfying than a thousand days away from Him. This man has discovered how rich and rewarding the presence of God can be. He would rather be a lowly doorkeeper in God's house than to live in the tents of the wicked.

Notice the contrasting phrases the psalmist uses here: the *house* of the Lord; the *tents* of the wicked. A house is strong, permanent, and durable; a tent is temporary. In the culture of Bible times, a tent might be perfectly comfortable and luxurious; many of the richest people of the ancient Middle East lived in tents. But even the tents of the wealthy and powerful could be torn apart and flung to the winds by the violent sandstorms of the deserts. In the same way, the most opulent tents of the wicked are no match for the storms of life—for illness, loss, disaster, and sorrow. It is far better to be a servant, a doorkeeper, in the everlasting house of the Lord than to dwell in the fleeting luxury of the tent of an ungodly man.

There is no way of living that compares with life in the presence of God. If we could see life as it truly is, we would much prefer a single day in His presence to a thousand days anywhere else.

The second reason the psalmist desires God's presence is this: Life with God is inexhaustibly complete. If I am in darkness, if I can't find my way, then God Himself can be the sun in my world so that my steps will be confident and sure. If I am under attack, if I need protection from my enemies, then God can be my shield, guarding me in the battles of life. Whatever I need, God is. There is nothing good in life that He would withhold from us. From Genesis to Revelation, that's the good news of the Bible.

I love the acrostic of the name Jesus: Just Exactly Suits Us Sinners. Everything we sinners need, God is. He is our sun and our shield. He gives us grace for our times of trouble and pressure. He gives us His strength to go on when our own strength has failed. He doesn't take us out of our problems but gives us grace in the midst of them so that we might experience glory, a deep sense of thanksgiving, joy, and gladness.

The psalmist sums up the three sections of this psalm in the final verse. He writes, "O LORD Almighty, blessed is the man who trusts in you" (v. 12).

Life with God is a life of blessing, of tremendous advantages and spiritual riches. This is the secret of a rich, rewarding, satisfying life, a life of blessing beyond our wildest dreams.

How lovely it is when our lives become the dwelling place of God, when He inhabits our innermost being, when we find our home and our rest with Him. How blessed are those who have set their hearts on a pilgrimage through the Valley of Tears so that they can bring the refreshing good news of Jesus Christ to those who are suffering and sorrowing. How rich and wondrous is the life of those whose sun and shield is God Himself.

Truly blessed are the men, women, or children who put all their trust in Him.

16

A Song of Realities

PSALM 90

Dr. Jay Kesler, president emeritus of Taylor University and former president of Youth for Christ, tells the story of an automobile accident he had when he was a teenager. He had just gotten his driver's license and was driving down the road. Hugging the centerline a little too closely, he sideswiped an oncoming car. The crash ripped the front fender, two doors, and the rear fender off of his car—or, to be precise, his father's car.

Shaken but unhurt, young Kesler pulled off the road and ran back to the other car. Fortunately no one in that car was injured either. Then Kesler stood in the ditch beside the road, closed his eyes, and said aloud, "Dear God, I pray that this accident didn't happen!"

He opened his eyes and looked around. He saw his father's car with the entire driver's side ripped away. He saw the car he had hit, also badly damaged. He closed his eyes again and prayed even more earnestly, "Dear God, *this did not happen!*"

He opened his eyes once more. Everything was still as it was: two wrecked cars. The accident couldn't be undone. That day young Jay Kesler learned a lesson in dealing with reality.

That is the theme of Psalm 90, "A Song of Realities."

The Reality of God

We come now to the earliest written psalm. According to the inscription, Moses wrote Psalm 90, and it is one of two psalms believed to have come from his pen. (Many Bible scholars also ascribe Psalm 91 to Moses.) This psalm undoubtedly set the pattern for all the psalms written later by David, Asaph, and other writers.

Psalm 90 introduces the fourth division of the book of Psalms. You recall that the 150 psalms in the book of Psalms are really five books in one. The entire book divides into five sections, each with its own theme corresponding to a book of the Pentateuch. The fourth section consists of Psalms 90 through 106, and the theme of this section corresponds to the theme of the book of Numbers.

Numbers is the book of wilderness wandering, of testing and failure, and that is what this fourth section of the Psalms is about. Here we find victory alternating with defeat. Moses probably composed Psalm 90 at the end of the wilderness wanderings shortly before he died. This is, in my judgment, one of the greatest of the psalms. In its scope, range, and depth, it is a marvelous expression of the glory of God, and it gives us a profound insight into the nature of reality.

Psalm 90 opens with a powerful declaration of the greatness of God written by Moses, a man who truly walked with God and knew Him:

> *Lord, you have been our dwelling place*
> *throughout all generations.*
> *Before the mountains were born*
> *or you brought forth the earth and the world,*
> *from everlasting to everlasting you are God (vv. 1–2).*

The psalmist begins by declaring that God has been the dwelling place of humanity in all generations. A dwelling place is where one lives; it is one's home. Moses declares that God has been humanity's home ever since the beginning of the human race. In all the generations of humanity, God has been our dwelling place.

This is the same truth Paul declared when he addressed the philosophers of Athens on Mars Hill: "God . . . is not far from each one of us. 'For in him we live and move and have our being.' As some of your own poets have said, 'We are his offspring'" (Acts 17:27–28). God exists as a home for humans. That is a tremendous thought!

Moses was uniquely qualified to make such a statement. He was able to look back over the course of human history and declare that God is the great Lord of history. Moses had seen the pharaohs of

Egypt live and die, and he may well have visited the Valley of the Kings where the tombs of the pharaohs are located. Some of those tombs were over a thousand years old when Moses lived. So Moses had a great sense of history. He understood that no matter how many centuries passed, the relationship of God to humanity did not change. God has been our dwelling place through all generations.

Next Moses points out that God is the God of creation. He writes:

Before the mountains were born
or you brought forth the earth and the world,
from everlasting to everlasting you are God (v. 2).

Notice the order of events. He begins by saying that God was God before the mountains were formed. This event in earth's geological record—the formation of the mountains—seems ancient when compared to a human lifespan.

But Moses goes even further back into history and says that God was God even before "the earth and the world" were formed. To our minds, "earth" and "world" are synonymous, but this phrase in the original Hebrew language actually referred to the earth and the land. This is in accordance with the Genesis account of creation in which God formed the earth, which was originally covered with water, and later brought the land up out of the waters. So Moses moved back in time from the formation of the mountains to the emergence of the land from the waters and even back to the creation of the earth itself. Before all of this happened, God was God.

Then in verse 2, Moses takes a leap backward to a state of absolute timelessness—before time and space even existed. He writes: "From everlasting to everlasting you are God." Here we see the greatness of God. He is the Lord of history, and the Lord of creation. Even more, He is the Lord of eternity, the creator of time and space. As splendid and awesome as the universe is, God is even greater. Before anything existed, God was.

The phrase "from everlasting to everlasting" is fascinating in the original Hebrew. It could well be translated, "from the vanishing point in the past to the vanishing point in the future." From eternity and infinity past to eternity and infinity future, God exists. That is how great He is.

This is vastly different from any pagan concept of God. Plato, the Greek philosopher, was the only ancient writer who wrote of a god who is timeless like the God of the Bible. In the eyes of the other pagan writers, the gods of myth all had a beginning; they were born much as people are born. But the God of the Bible had no beginning and has no end. He is a timeless God who is above and beyond His creation. That is the reality of God.

The Reality of God's Sovereign Will

Moses goes on to focus on the relationship of God to humanity. The question at issue here is, "How do we relate to the greatness of God?" The psalmist begins by underscoring God's sovereignty over man:

> *You turn men back to dust,*
> *saying, "Return to dust, O sons of men."*
> *For a thousand years in your sight*
> *are like a day that has just gone by,*
> *or like a watch in the night.*
> *You sweep men away in the sleep of death;*
> *they are like the new grass of the morning—*
> *though in the morning it springs up new,*
> *by evening it is dry and withered (vv. 3–6).*

Here the psalmist describes one of the most basic facts of human existence, yet it is a fact we often ignore: We live under the absolute sovereignty of God. He controls human life, not we. He turns humans back to dust as he wills.

God sets various limits to human life. There are certain things God will not let human beings do. Some ask, "Is it right for humanity to explore space? Is it right for humanity to manipulate the genetic code? Is it right for human beings to unleash the energies of the atom?" It may be that there is a limit to such endeavors, a point where God will say, "Turn back, children of men." It may be that when humanity reaches a point where we threaten our existence, God will say, "This is the end of human history."

But we have not reached that point yet. We are exploring our solar system with both manned and unmanned machines. We are tinkering with the genetic makeup of plants, animals, and even people. We are using the power of the atom to generate electricity, to cure cancer, and also to build the most horrible weapons ever imagined. Where will it end? We don't know, but God does. He is sovereign. We will never explore where God does not permit us to explore.

The Bible clearly tells us that there are some things human beings are not meant to know. One of these things is the understanding of the times and seasons of God's plan. After Jesus was crucified and rose again, He appeared to the disciples. "They asked Him, 'Lord, are you at this time going to restore the kingdom to Israel?'

"He said to them, 'It is not for you to know the times or dates the Father has set by his own authority'" (Acts 1:6–7).

Another area that God has forbidden us to explore is the realm of the occult. As God warned Israel, "Let no one be found among you who sacrifices his son or daughter in the fire, who practices divination or sorcery, interprets omens, engages in witchcraft, or casts spells, or who is a medium or spiritist or who consults the dead. Anyone who does these things is detestable to the Lord" (Deuteronomy 18:10–12a).

So God sets certain limits for humans. One of the most obvious limits is our lifespan. There comes a point for each of us when God says, "Return to dust." A little girl once learned in Sunday school that human beings come from the dust and return to the dust. She looked under her bed then shouted, "Mother, mother! Come look! There's someone under my bed, but I don't know whether he's coming or going!" Human beings come from the dust, and to dust they must return. God sets limits to human life.

Yet the next verse suggests that the limits of life were once much less restrictive than they are today. Moses writes: "For a thousand years in your sight are like a day that has just gone by, or like a watch in the night" (v. 4). God may have originally intended a greater span of life for humanity. We know that early human beings, as recorded in Genesis, lived to be almost a thousand years old. The oldest man, Methuselah, lived 969 years.

Before sin began to spread through the earth, resulting in God's flood of judgment in the day of Noah, it is likely that God intended that humans should live a thousand years. But even a thousand years, the longest possible lifetime of a human being, is "like a day that has just gone by, or like a watch in the night" compared to eternity.

Human life is brief and uncertain. "You sweep men away in the sleep of death," writes the psalmist. "They are like the new grass of the morning" (v. 5). Even the greatest men and women who ever lived are powerless to determine the length of their own lives.

Think of all the rich, powerful, and famous people who died in the prime of life: Political leaders John F. Kennedy and his brother, Robert F. Kennedy; civil rights leader Martin Luther King, Jr.; rock stars John Lennon, Buddy Holly, Elvis Presley, Jimi Hendrix, Jim Morrison, and Janis Joplin; film stars James Dean, Marilyn Monroe, and John Belushi.

Life is an uncertain proposition even for the young. Many young children die every day of leukemia, lymphoma, brain tumors, and sickle cell disease or are killed by accidents. Many teens are killed by drunk drivers or die in school shootings. It breaks our hearts to think of it, but it's true: Some people die almost before their lives have begun.

Life is full of uncertainties even for those who love the Lord and faithfully serve Him. Death could come at any time. For Christians, of course, death should be nothing to fear. As the apostle Paul wrote, "For to me, to live is Christ and to die is gain" (Philippians 1:21). Still, few of us are eager to leave this life because we want to spend as much precious time as we can with our loved ones, and we want to complete our God-given mission in life. There are few of us who could say, if we were to die right now, that death had come at a convenient time.

Dawson Trotman founded the Navigators, an international evangelism and discipling organization, when he was in his late twenties. For over two decades, the Navigators flourished and grew under his leadership.

On the night of June 17, 1956, when Dawson Trotman was in his early fifties, he and his wife Lila were driving on a country road in the Adirondack Mountains of upstate New York. "Daws" abruptly pulled the car to the side of the road and said, "Lila, would you take some notes for me? I believe the Lord is going to call me home soon. There are some things the Navs ought to do during the next five years if I'm not around."

So Lila took notes as Daws Trotman dictated. When he was satisfied that she had gotten it all down, he pulled the car back onto the road and proceeded on his way.

The next day, June 18, Dawson and a number of friends were boating on Schroon Lake during a break from a Navigators conference. Dawson was at the controls of a speedboat, and the water on the lake was a little choppy, but the conditions were not particularly dangerous. As he cruised around the lake with several passengers in his boat, he ran into trouble. The boat bumped over the wake of another boat, and a jolt caused two girls in the back of the boat to fall overboard.

Dawson knew that one of the girls couldn't swim. He pulled the boat around, killed the engine, and dove into the water. A strong and confident swimmer, Daws Trotman had no concern that he was in any danger.

He swam to the first girl and got her back into the boat. Then he swam to the second girl and brought her back. She too managed to climb into the boat without trouble. Once she was safely aboard, the others in the boat looked around. Someone said, "Where's Daws?"

Dawson Trotman had a reputation as a joker and a strong swimmer. Someone said, "Oh, he swam under the boat. He's going to surprise us and come up on the other side." But he didn't come up. In fact, it would be three days before a dragnet would pull his body out of the lake.

Soon after it became clear that Daws had drowned, one of his friends went ashore and found Lila Trotman. "Oh, Lila," the man said, weeping, "I'm so sorry. Dawson's gone! He's gone!"

Lila took the news quietly and with an amazing acceptance of God's will. After all, Daws had just told her the night before that this was coming. She responded to the news by quoting the words of Psalm 115:3: "Our God is in heaven; he does whatever pleases him." Though to others Daws Trotman's death seemed untimely and senseless, Lila Trotman saw her husband's death as a controlled event, the timing of which was determined by God's sovereign will.

From the long perspective of time and eternity, a human life is like a blade of grass. It is new and green in the morning, but it may be gone before the sun sets.

The Reality of God's Wrath

Next Moses takes up another reality of life: the difficult issue of God's wrath. He writes:

> *We are consumed by your anger*
> *and terrified by your indignation.*
> *You have set our iniquities before you,*
> *our secret sins in the light of your presence.*
> *All our days pass away under your wrath;*
> *we finish our years with a moan.*
> *The length of our days is seventy years—*
> *or eighty, if we have the strength;*
> *yet their span is but trouble and sorrow,*
> *for they quickly pass, and we fly away.*
> *Who knows the power of your anger?*
> *For your wrath is as great as the fear that is due you.*
> *Teach us to number our days aright,*
> *that we may gain a heart of wisdom (vv. 7–12).*

Here the psalmist, with penetrating honesty, faces a reality that most of us try to avoid: what I would call "the tragic sense of life." It is the fact that every moment of enjoyment is tinged with the reality of sorrow and tragedy in the world. There is a bittersweet quality about life, and this psalm faces squarely the bitter side of that equation. Why is human life tinged with a dark side? Why do tragedy, catastrophe, and injustice plague the innocent as well as the guilty?

A Christian attorney and businessman named Horatio Spafford was well acquainted with the tragic sense of life. Spafford and his wife Anna were prominent members of Chicago society in the mid-nineteenth century. They were also close friends and supporters of evangelist Dwight L. Moody.

In 1870 the Spaffords' only son died at age four, stricken by scarlet fever. The following year Horatio Spafford's extensive real estate holdings on the Lake Michigan shore were burned to the ground, along with most of the city of Chicago, in the Great Chicago Fire. Devastated, but trusting in God, Horatio and Anna Spafford decided to start over.

Dwight L. Moody asked for their help as he was planning an evangelistic campaign in England. So in 1873, the Spaffords agreed to go to England. Anna and the four Spafford daughters would leave first, crossing the Atlantic aboard the steamship *Ville de Havre*. Horatio would follow later after wrapping up his business affairs.

On November 2, 1873, the *Ville de Havre* collided with another ship and sank in just twelve minutes. Over two hundred people died. Unable to get to a lifeboat, Anna Spafford stood on the deck with three of her daughters clinging to her skirt and the fourth, a baby, clutched in her arms.

As the deck slipped under the waters, the children were flung away from her, and the baby was torn from her arms. Anna was knocked unconscious by debris. She was later found unconscious, floating on a broken plank. All of her children were gone. The rescue ship that plucked her from the sea took her to Wales. From there she sent her husband a two-word telegram: "Saved alone."

Grief-stricken and devastated, Horatio Spafford hurried to New York and boarded the next ship to the British Isles. During the voyage the captain of the ship called Spafford to the bridge. "You asked me to tell you when we reached the place where the *de Havre* went down," the captain said. "We believe this is the place. The water is three miles deep here."

Spafford stood on the bridge in silence, thinking and praying. Then he went to his cabin and composed the lines of a song. He completed the song by the time the ship docked. That song has become one of the most beloved hymns of all time. It begins:

When peace, like a river, attendeth my way,
When sorrows like sea billows roll;
Whatever my lot, Thou hast taught me to say,
It is well, it is well, with my soul.

That beautiful hymn comes straight from the pain of a man who has known great sorrow, tragedy, and loss. Yes, he maintained his faith and trust in God, but Horatio Spafford knew full well what "the tragic sense of life" was all about. That is the side of life the psalmist writes about in Psalm 90:

> *The length of our days is seventy years—*
> *or eighty, if we have the strength;*
> *yet their span is but trouble and sorrow,*
> *for they quickly pass, and we fly away (v. 10).*

Why do we experience so much suffering, sorrow, tragedy, and loss in a span of life that is all too brief? The psalmist says it is because of something called "the wrath of God." The reality of God's wrath is woven throughout this passage: "We are consumed by your anger and terrified by your indignation," he says (v. 7).

> *All our days pass away under your wrath;*
> *we finish our years with a moan . . .*
> *Who knows the power of your anger?*
> *For your wrath is as great as the fear that is due you (vv. 9, 11).*

Before we go any further, I must point out that many people greatly misunderstand this phrase "the wrath of God." For some the phrase "the wrath of God" suggests that God is a cranky, vengeful deity who is given to uncontrolled outbursts of violent temper. But such a view of God's wrath only reveals the limitations of our understanding. The Bible never speaks of the wrath of God that way.

According to the Scriptures the wrath of God is actually the outworking of God's moral integrity. God has created the universe with certain moral laws, which operate much like the physical law of gravity. When human beings refuse to yield themselves to God, they run up against the moral laws of His universe. When people violate God's moral laws, the result is pain, sorrow, and wounding. It is God's way of saying to humanity, "Look, you must face reality. You were made for Me. If you use the gift of free will I have given you to violate My will, I won't stop you, but you will have to bear the consequences of your actions."

In His moral integrity, God has ordained that certain things will occur as a consequence of sinful human choices. The psalmist shows us the linkage between human sin and God's wrath when he writes:

We are consumed by your anger
and terrified by your indignation.
You have set our iniquities before you,
our secret sins in the light of your presence (vv. 7–8).

God's wrath then is always caused by human sin, both our open iniquities and our secret, hidden sins that we think no one will ever know about.

God knows our inner sins, our secret inner thoughts. Understand, the Scriptures do not teach that a passing thought is a sin. A thought that comes to your mind unbidden and remains there for a moment is not sin; it is temptation. Even the Lord Jesus experienced temptation, yet without sin.

What then is the "secret sin" to which the psalmist refers? It's that sinful thought that we mull over, hang onto, toy with, take pleasure in, and return to from time to time. God is aware of these inner defilements of our lives. We think these sins are hidden safely away where no one can see, but they still harm us. They are violations of the moral order of the universe—the wrath of God—and they gradually poison our spirits from within.

The psalmist continues on about the universality of death and suffering as an inevitable part of the human condition. He writes that people may live seventy or even eighty years, and even those brief years are full of trouble and sorrow. Job, that great biblical paragon of patient suffering, put it this way: "Yet man is born to trouble as surely as sparks fly upward" (Job 5:7).

Why is life this way for the entire human race? Because the entire human race sinned and incurred God's wrath when Adam sinned. As the apostle Paul explained, "Sin entered the world through one man, and death through sin, and in this way death came to all men, because all sinned . . . Death reigned from the time of Adam . . ." (Romans 5:12, 14).

Death and sorrow came into the world as the result of sin. As Paul put it, "Creation was subjected to frustration" (Romans 8:20). The entire created realm was wounded and made subject to death because of Adam's sin. Creation groans under God's wrath against sin, a wrath that is not an expression of God's ill temper but the outworking of the moral laws that God put in place when He created the world. As a result of Adam's sin and God's wrath, the human life span is short, and what time we have is full of trouble and tragedy.

The unjust and tragic events in our lives do not take place because God wants to get even with us or because He has a grudge against us. As Paul writes, those who place their trust in Christ— though they are still subject to death and sorrow—have nothing to fear from the wrath of God's coming judgment against sin. His grace, expressed to us through the death of Jesus Christ, has removed our sins from us and saved us from the wrath to come. "For God did not appoint us to suffer wrath," Paul wrote, "but to receive salvation through our Lord Jesus Christ" (1 Thessalonians 5:9).

The psalmist then asks a question that should challenge and motivate each of us to go deeper in our relationship with God:

> *Who knows the power of your anger?*
> *For your wrath is as great as the fear that is due you.*
> *Teach us to number our days aright,*
> *that we may gain a heart of wisdom (vv. 11–12).*

Here the psalmist faces humanity's strange indifference toward God. He asks, "Why do we ignore the fact of the wrath of God? Why do we try to pretend it does not exist? Why do we not face up to the reality of God's sovereignty over us and the moral consequences of God's ever-present justice working in human society?"

It's a rhetorical question, yet it demands a response. The psalmist tells us the right response is this: We should be aware of the limitations of life. We should remember that life is short, and we have only a finite number of days in which to know God, serve Him, and serve the people around us.

If we learn to number our days and live with an awareness of our limitations, then, the psalmist says, we will gain a heart of wisdom. What is a heart of wisdom? It's a realistic outlook on life.

The Reality of God's Unfailing Love

The psalmist writes about our relationship to God in the closing verses of this psalm:

Relent, O LORD! How long will it be?
Have compassion on your servants.
Satisfy us in the morning with your unfailing love,
that we may sing for joy and be glad all our days (vv. 13–14).

You cannot experience the love of God unless you are ready to cry out, as Moses does here, for a personal relationship with God. This is no remote and unknowable God that Moses prays to. He cries out for God's compassion, for the satisfying joy of God's unfailing love. Moses desires nothing less than for the God of the universe to enter his heart and fill his life with joy and gladness.

When Moses writes here about God's unfailing love, he is laying down for the first time a theme that will run all through the psalms that will later be written:

Save me because of your unfailing love (6:4).

But I trust in your unfailing love;
my heart rejoices in your salvation (13:5).

Many are the woes of the wicked,
but the LORD's unfailing love
surrounds the man who trusts in him (32:10).

The LORD loves righteousness and justice;
the earth is full of his unfailing love (33:5).

How priceless is your unfailing love! (36:7).

Have mercy on me, O God, according to your unfailing love;
according to your great compassion blot out my transgressions (51:1).

The LORD delights in those who fear him,
who put their hope in his unfailing love (147:11).

Another translation of the phrase "unfailing love" is "loving kindness." I like that! It reminds me of the little boy whose Sunday school teacher asked him to describe loving kindness. The boy answered, "If I ask my mother for a piece of bread and butter and she gives it to me, that's kindness. But if she puts jam on it too, that's *loving* kindness."

That's the kind of love the psalmist Moses writes of—God's unfailing love, His everlasting loving kindness. It's the love we sing of in the hymn "O Love That Will Not Let Me Go." It's a love that never changes, that always satisfies. It's a love that doesn't depend on whether we are good or bad. It receives us even in the worst of our sins, it forgives us, and it restores us to a whole and healthy relationship with God.

The Reality of a "Recompensing Joy"

In the next section, the psalmist Moses speaks of a miraculous reality, the reality of life that has been wasted but that God can miraculously restore to us:

> *Make us glad for as many days as you have afflicted us,*
> *for as many years as we have seen trouble.*
> *May your deeds be shown to your servants,*
> *your splendor to their children.*
> *May the favor of the Lord our God rest upon us;*
> *establish the work of our hands for us—*
> *yes, establish the work of our hands (vv. 15–17).*

There is a joy and gladness that comes when God enables us to make up for the past, for the days when we have gone through trouble and loss. The prophet Joel quotes God as saying, "I will repay you for the years the locusts have eaten" (Joel 2:25a). The imagery Joel uses compares life to a field of grain that locusts have eaten. A locust is a variety of grasshopper that migrates in huge swarms, consuming crops as it goes. A valuable wheat field that a farmer has carefully cultivated for months could be rendered worthless in minutes by a swarm of locusts.

God says, "Your life is like a field devoured by locusts. There were years of your life that have been wasted and lost because of sin, ignorance, laziness, or misfortune. I'm going to come into your life, plant a new crop, and bring about a harvest in your life, a harvest so bountiful that it will more than compensate you for what the locusts have eaten.

One of the great joys of my Christian life is to look back upon the wasted years of my past and to see how fruitful and rewarding God is making my life today. Again and again, I've seen God correct what once looked like a hopeless situation, restoring to me the years that the locusts have eaten. I call this work of God in my life a "recompensing joy," in that God is compensating me for the losses I sustained earlier in life due to my own immaturity, foolishness, or sin.

The psalmist makes an amazing request in verse 16: "May your deeds be shown to your servants, your splendor to their children." We are inclined to see ourselves as isolated individuals without any connection to the past or future. But the Bible recognizes that each generation is tied to the generations before and generations to come. Though you or I may experience God's healing touch in our lives, we will never experience the full effect of that healing in our lifetime, but our children will!

That is what the psalmist says here. He is asking God to manifest His healing work to his own generation ("your servants") and to the next ("their children"). I see this principle at work in families all the time. I see a father or a mother who has come from a deprived childhood, having had ungodly or abusive parents. This person becomes a Christian and marries a godly spouse, then begins raising a family. Healing takes place over time in this person's life. Even while this "first-generation" Christian is still recovering from a difficult childhood, he or she is raising Christian children, teaching them about the God of the Bible, loving them as God intended. In the process God makes His healing work known to these children. God's healing power is handed down, generation by generation.

"May the favor of the Lord our God rest upon us," the psalmist adds (v. 17). The King James Version puts it even better: "Let the beauty of the LORD our God be upon us." This is a prayer for the visible manifestation of God's beauty. It's what the New Testament calls "godlikeness," or godliness.

What is the beauty of God? God is beautiful because He is two things: truth and love. Truth is always necessary to beauty. Nothing is beautiful unless it is also true. And love provides warmth, graciousness, and attractiveness; add love to truth and you have beauty. A man, woman, boy, or girl whose life is characterized by truth and love is a beautiful person.

Finally the psalmist prays, "Establish the work of our hands for us—yes, establish the work of our hands" (v. 17b). What does this mean? It is a prayer that God in His love would make the work we do meaningful, valuable, and enduring. We do not want our work to be wasted motion. We want our work to endure and affect the lives of others.

Who does not long for this in their own lives? That, in essence, is what it means to live with purpose and meaning. God promises us that if we join our lives to His, then He will work through us to accomplish deeds of eternal value. That is why the apostle Paul tells us, "He who began a good work in you will carry it on to completion until the day of Christ Jesus . . . For it is God who works in you to will and to act according to his good purpose" (Phillipians 1:6, 2:13).

This is the reality of our lives, the reality Moses expresses in the first psalm ever written, Psalm 90: God is sovereign over us, and we live within the limits He has set for us. Because we live in a world that was wounded by Adam's sin, we are subject to God's wrath, the consequences of human sin. But in the midst of this fallen and suffering world, we see the glory and wonder of God's love, restoring to us the years the locust has eaten, surrounding us with the beauty of His love.

That is the "Song of God's Reality." That is the realistic message of Psalm 90 for our lives.

17

How to Worship

PSALM 95

In the late 1930s, an American jazz musician was invited to give a command performance for King George VI of England. As his band tuned up on stage and prepared to play, the jazzman looked up at the royal box where King George sat. With a bow and a wave, he called, "This song's for you, Rex!"

Some of us, unfortunately, are just as flippant as this musician was when we are in the presence of God, the King of the universe. But as we come to Psalm 95, one of a series of so-called Royal Psalms (Psalms 93 through 100), we will learn about the royal nature of God and how we are to enter His presence.

The Glory Due His Name

The Israelites sang the Royal Psalms as they went up to the temple in Jerusalem to worship. These psalms are not only magnificent examples of poetry but they also instruct us in the reverent attitude we should have toward God our King. Psalm 95 opens with an exhortation for all believers to join together in worshiping the Lord: "Come, let us sing for joy to the LORD; let us shout aloud to the Rock of our salvation" (v. 1).

This is the first of two appeals to worship in this psalm. The second is found a few verses later: "Come, let us bow down in worship, let us kneel before the LORD our Maker" (v. 6).

Here we see two invitations to two separate expressions of worship. The first is an invitation to sing; the second is an invitation to prayer. So in the opening passage of this psalm, we are told that congregational worship consists largely of singing and prayer. There is a reason worship involves singing together, as we see in verse 2: "Let us come before him with thanksgiving and extol him with music and song."

The psalmist tells us that congregational singing should be an expression of thanksgiving and praise (*extol* is synonymous with *praise*). Thanksgiving and praise are essential elements of worshipful singing. Through the ages believers of both Old Testament times and New Testament times have sung praises and thanksgiving to God.

Moreover we should be aware that we do not truly worship God if our singing is half-hearted, if we do not sing with enthusiasm. Our songs should be full of joy, sung at the top of our lungs! As the psalmist tells us at the outset, "Come, let us *sing for joy* to the LORD; let us *shout aloud* to the Rock of our salvation" (v. 1, emphasis added).

And what does that last phrase mean—"the Rock of our salvation"? A rock is a large stone, strong and immovable, a source of strength and stability. We sing for joy and shout aloud to God because He is the strong and stable source of our salvation. He cannot be moved, and that is why our salvation is firm and secure.

What is our relationship to God? We are His creation, and He is our Maker and our King. The psalmist writes:

For the LORD is the great God,
the great King above all gods.
In his hand are the depths of the earth,
and the mountain peaks belong to him.
The sea is his, for he made it,
and his hands formed the dry land (vv. 3–5).

Do you see what the psalmist is doing in this passage? He is giving us the essential reasons everyone should give thanksgiving and praise to God. In truth all human beings should praise Him, not just we who are believers. We are all responsible for giving Him praise and worship because we are all creatures of His hands.

In his letter to the Romans, the apostle Paul brings a serious charge against godless people. He writes:

The wrath of God is being revealed from heaven against all the
godlessness and wickedness of men who suppress the truth by their
wickedness, since what may be known about God is plain to them,

because God has made it plain to them. For since the creation of the world God's invisible qualities—his eternal power and divine nature—have been clearly seen, being understood from what has been made, so that men are without excuse. For although they knew God, they neither glorified him as God nor gave thanks to him, but their thinking became futile and their foolish hearts were darkened (1:18– 21).

Even godless people have a duty to worship God. Their unbelief is no excuse because God's eternal power and divinity can be clearly seen in nature. So those who do not praise Him and thank Him are condemned for their disrespect and disregard for their Creator.

It is amazing how much we human beings take for granted. We accept as perfectly natural the forces that keep us alive. We boastfully talk of being self-made men. We strut through life as if we are not accountable to anyone but ourselves.

My mentor, Dr. H. A. Ironside, told of an experience he once had at a restaurant. He ordered his meal, and just as he was about to eat, a man walked up to his table and said, "Do you mind if I sit down with you?"

"I don't mind at all," Dr. Ironside said. "Please sit down."

After the stranger had seated himself across the table, Dr. Ironside bowed his head and said a silent word of thanks to the Lord. When he raised his head, the other man said, "Do you have a headache?"

"No," said Dr. Ironside, "I don't."

"Well, is there anything wrong with your food?"

"No, why?"

"Well," the man said, "I saw you sitting there with your head down and I thought there must be something wrong."

"No, I was simply returning thanks to God before I eat."

"Oh," the stranger said, "you're one of *those,* are you? Well I never give thanks. I earn my money by the sweat of my brow, and I don't have to give thanks to anybody when I eat. I just start right in!"

"Ah," Dr. Ironside said, "you're just like my dog. That's what he does too!"

When human beings—rational creatures of God who are made in His image—will not give thanks to God, they are like irrational animals. They become bestial and lose a bit of their humanity. That is the basis of this appeal by the psalmist: No matter what our attitude toward God may be, we owe God thanks for His grace to us as our Creator.

Another psalm instructs us, "Ascribe to the Lord the glory due his name" (96:8a). God is worthy of praise and glory. We should not glorify God merely when we feel like it. He is *always* worthy of glory, praise, and thanksgiving.

We tend to praise God whenever we feel emotionally moved, usually in response to some event or circumstance in our lives. If a baby is born, if we receive an unexpected check in the mail, if we see a rainbow after a storm, we are likely to say, "Praise God!" But praise should not merely reflect our transitory emotions. Praise is something we should do regularly and continually because God made us, and we cannot live a moment without him. That is the glory due His name.

The Great King above All Gods

The psalmist reminds us that we are related to God not only as creature to Creator but as subject to King. "For the Lord is the great God," he writes, "the great King above all gods" (v. 3).

The psalmist is not suggesting that there are other gods besides the God of the Bible. The statement that God is the "great King above all gods" refers to the fact that pagan people believed in other gods. The pagans erected idols, called them "gods," and worshiped them. In doing so they invoked evil forces beyond their understanding.

Behind the pagan idols were demonic powers—genuine spirit beings that perform deceptive feats of godlike power. Demons are not gods. They are created beings, fallen angels, capable of deceiving people and using the corrupted remnants of power they once had as angels of the living God. In our own day, we see a dramatic upswing in such occult practices as astrology, sorcery, channeling dead spirits, and casting spells through witchcraft. Those who engage in such practices are denying the fatherhood of God over their lives. When you live as if the stars and planets rule your life, you separate yourself from God's fatherly care.

That is why the Bible strongly warns against such practices as witchcraft and astrology. God is the King over all gods. Even the rebellious devil is under God's authority. Some people see God and Satan as equal opposites, as if Satan is a bad god, a mirror image of God. But that is not true. God and Satan are not equal opposites. God is the King. Satan is subject to God the King. We should never forget that.

Next the psalmist reminds us that God created the grandeur of the world: the canyon and cavern depths, the mountain peaks, and the seas. His hands made all the extreme and remote places of nature that make our lives exciting and fill us with wonder. The psalmist writes:

> *In his hand are the depths of the earth,*
> *and the mountain peaks belong to him.*
> *The sea is his, for he made it,*
> *and his hands formed the dry land (vv. 4–5).*

These are the places that hold forth promise of adventure, fascination, and mystery. We are still searching out the depths of the earth; we are still scaling the heights of the mountains; we are still exploring the mysteries of the sea. We are still trying to solve the problems of the dry land and to discover its resources. The psalmist reminds us that all these things come from the hand of God the Creator.

Life is filled with mystery, excitement, and wonder because God designed life to be enjoyable and worth living. Let us thank God not only for His provision of the things that sustain our existence (food, shelter, and clothing) but also for the things that transform our existence into an adventure.

The Sheep of the Great Shepherd

The next section opens with the second invitation to congregational worship, which involves congregational prayer:

> *Come, let us bow down in worship,*
> *let us kneel before the LORD our Maker;*
> *for he is our God*
> *and we are the people of his pasture,*
> *the flock under his care (vv. 6–7a).*

Notice the dramatic change in the way the psalmist describes our relationship to God. Before, the psalmist has exhorted us to worship God as our Creator. Here he encourages us to view God as our Savior, Redeemer, and Shepherd. We are the sheep of His hand and the people of His pasture.

What changed? Simply this: We have entered into a *personal relationship* with Him. The proper expression of such a relationship is awe and humility: "Come, let us bow down in worship."

Think of what is revealed to us here: Our God is a God of amazing love, a love that has pursued us, rescued us, redeemed us, and won us. Despite all the obstacles we raised against Him, despite our resistance, His love has captured our hearts.

There is not one human being on this earth who has not at one time or another fought against God. We have all resisted His love. We have nothing to boast about in ourselves. We have not added anything to our salvation. We're like stubborn, stupid sheep that wander around lost. As the prophet Isaiah tells us, "We all, like sheep, have gone astray, each of us has turned to his own way" (53:6).

But God, the Good Shepherd, has pursued us, found us, and brought us back. That is why we kneel in worship before the One who is not only our Creator-King but our Redeemer-Savior-Shepherd. We have moved from a distant relationship to a personal relationship with God, and this amazing truth awakens our hearts to love and worship Him.

"Do Not Harden Your Hearts"

Moreover, this amazing truth should awaken us to listen to Him as well. The psalmist writes:

> *Today, if you hear his voice,*
> *do not harden your hearts as you did at Meribah,*
> *as you did that day at Massah in the desert (95:7b–8).*

True worship demands that we listen to God's voice and heed what He says. Worship is not just singing and praising. It is also listening. That's why the exposition of Scripture is so central to public worship. Churches that depart from the Scriptures make a travesty of true worship. If we do not have a chance to hear what God says to us, we will never learn how to correct the errors in our attitudes, habits, and ways of living.

As a pastor I have often stood in front of a congregation seeing all the freshly scrubbed faces looking back at me with rapt attention. From all appearances it seems that everyone in the congregation is totally focused on what God has to say through His Word. But having sat in the pews myself from time to time, I know that's not always true.

Some in the congregation are mentally playing golf. Or planning a vacation. Or recalling a conversation from the day before. Or stewing over hurt feelings. Or anticipating the upcoming Super Bowl game. Or planning a business deal. If our thoughts are far from God, if we are not listening to what He has to say to us, then we are not worshiping. When we come to worship, we don't come to kill time. We come to be changed.

If we do not hear His voice, what happens to us? Our hearts become hardened. We eventually become unable to listen, to learn, to grow, and to change. We turn to stone as we become spiritually deadened. So the psalmist pleads with us in verse 8, "Do not harden your hearts as you did at Meribah, as you did that day at Massah in the desert."

What event does the psalmist speak of here? He is writing of an incident in Exodus 17. It occurred shortly after God had delivered the Israelites from Egypt by parting the Red Sea. The people of Israel had only journeyed a week or two in the wilderness and had come to a place where there was no water. Becoming thirsty, they complained to Moses: "Why did you lead us out into this wilderness just to perish? Where is God? Why isn't He taking care of us? Why hasn't He provided water for us?" Just days after the parting of the sea, the people demanded that God prove Himself again.

So Moses said to God, "Lord, what shall I do? The people are quarreling and complaining until they're about to stone me!"

God said, "Strike the rock, and water will come out of it for the people to drink." Moses did that, and water flowed from the rock—not just a trickle but a gushing stream! There was enough water to satisfy all the people—more than 600,000 men plus an unknown number of women and children, along with all of their cattle and sheep.

Moses gave the fountain that flowed from the rock two names: Meribah and Massah. In Hebrew, *Massah* means "testing" and *Meribah* means "quarreling." Moses gave the fountain these two names because it was the place where he was tested by the quarreling of his people.

Moses was vexed by the quarreling of the people, and so was God. After all, the people had seen the hand of God when He had parted the waters of the Red Sea before them. They had walked across a seabed that was utterly dry beneath their sandals. The waters of the sea were like solid walls on either side of them. Then, after they had crossed to safety, God had collapsed those walls of water onto their pursuers, drowning the Egyptians. Immediately afterward the people of Israel sang a great song of triumph.

Yet just days after that astounding demonstration of God's power, the Israelites quickly fell to murmuring, quarreling, and complaining just because they were a little thirsty. The psalmist is saying that true worship involves learning, growth, and change. If we worship Him week after week but quickly begin quarreling and complaining the moment things don't go our way, then we are not growing and learning. Outwardly we are going through the motions of worship, but inwardly we are not being changed—*because our hearts are hardened.*

A hardened heart cannot change and cannot genuinely worship. A hardened heart does not listen to or learn from God. A hardened heart complains and slips back into unbelief when God doesn't act the way we want Him to act. This principle is as true today as it was three thousand years ago.

The psalmist is saying to us, "When you come together to worship, listen to God's voice. Don't harden your hearts—open your ears! Pay attention to what God says to you. Listen to His message for your life. Learn from Him, grow in Him, and be transformed by Him. Whenever God does not answer you as you expect Him to or want Him to, learn the lesson that He wants you to learn through this waiting experience."

The Lord Jesus constantly dealt with His disciples about this very issue. Repeatedly they saw Him healing people with leprosy or paralysis, casting out demons, feeding multitudes with a few loaves and fishes—incredible, amazing demonstrations of His authority and power. Yet they continually slipped back into doubting and unbelief. So Jesus had to rebuke them several times with the words, "O you of little faith!" (see Matthew 6:30; 8:26; 14:31; 16:8; 17:20; Luke 12:28).

In other words, He was saying to them, "Why don't you learn from these experiences? Why don't you grow in your faith? Why don't you change and advance in your walk with Me?" It was as if their hearts were hardened like those of the Israelites in the day of Moses.

And if we are honest with ourselves, we have to admit that the same is true of us. We go to church week after week and hear stirring reports of what God is doing in so many lives. We see people being liberated from enslavement to sin, bad habits, drugs, and alcohol, and we say, "Praise God! What an amazing work He's doing!" Yet the moment things don't go our way we panic or become angry with God, and it's as if we've learned exactly nothing. In fact it's as if our hearts are hardened!

May God grant us willing ears to hear what He is saying to us. May He grant us hearts that are soft and eager to respond to the life-changing lessons He wants to teach us.

His Ways Are Not Our Ways

Next God speaks and reveals both His anger and His great patience. The psalmist writes:

> For forty years I was angry with that generation;
> I said, "They are a people whose hearts go astray,
> and they have not known my ways."
> So I declared on oath in my anger,
> "They shall never enter my rest" (vv. 10–11).

Here is a great revelation of the patience of God. He does not immediately condemn the people of Israel because of their unbelief. He patiently works with them for forty years. Throughout those forty years, He pleads with them as if to say, "O that you would listen to my voice! O that you would not harden your hearts against Me as you did at Meribah, at Massah."

Understand, please, that when God says, "For forty years I was angry with that generation," He is not saying that He held a grudge against them. The original Hebrew word that is translated "angry" has a different connotation from that. God is actually saying that He was constantly vexed and grieved by His people during those forty years. His anger was mingled with sorrow over their unbelief.

God analyzed where His people went wrong and concluded that their hearts had gone astray—that is, their hearts were set on the wrong things. Their priorities were all wrong. When you read the Exodus account, you can clearly see why God came to this conclusion about His people. Whenever a problem arose, the Israelites would start wishing they were back in Egypt. They were ready to go back into slavery—and for what? Fish! Melons and cucumbers! Leeks, garlic, and onions! Would you sell yourself into slavery for a grocery list? That's what the Israelites were willing to do:

> *The rabble with them began to crave other food, and again the Israelites started wailing and said, "If only we had meat to eat! We remember the fish we ate in Egypt at no cost—also the cucumbers, melons, leeks, onions and garlic. But now we have lost our appetite; we never see anything but this manna!" (Numbers 11:4–6).*

Here was a generation of people who thought only of their bellies. God said that instead of thinking of their bellies, they should have worried about the hardening of their hearts. As the apostle Paul wrote, "Set your minds on things above, not on earthly things" (Colossians 3:2).

This doesn't mean we should go around thinking of heaven all the time. The "things above" that Paul speaks of are the important matters of life: righteousness, truth, justice, love, grace, and forgiveness. These are the highest values in life—not onions and garlic!

You may think, "How foolish those ancient Israelites were! I would certainly never wish myself a slave for the sake of onions and garlic!" I'm sure you wouldn't. After all, you can buy these things by the pound at any supermarket. But you might be doing something just as foolish without even realizing it. There are many ways that we set our minds on earthly things while forgetting the things of God.

Many of us get caught up in chasing wealth and status. We become obsessed over "keeping up with the Joneses"—a futile effort that someone once described as "using the money you don't have to buy the things you don't need to impress the people you don't like."

Is that how you're living right now? Then your heart is set on the wrong things.

God also says in verse 10, "And they have not known my ways." In other words, people do not understand how God works, what His plans are, what His goal for our lives is. It's vitally important for us to understand God's ways, because His ways are the ultimate reality. On the natural level, His ways are not our ways nor are His thoughts our thoughts. His ways are higher than our ways as the heavens are higher than the earth. So we must make an effort to learn His ways and to think His thoughts.

You may have discovered by now that God does not always behave the way you want Him to. He doesn't answer your prayers as quickly as you want or in the way that you expect. You have your goals and you lay them out before God and tell Him how you'd like Him to achieve them for you, but God seems stubbornly determined to do things *His* way instead of *your* way! Isn't that maddening?

You had better get used to it, because His ways are not your ways. Instead of getting upset with God, spend time in prayer and studying His Word so you can learn His ways and think His thoughts.

Enter into His Rest

God saw that the hearts of His people continually went astray. They ignored His plan for their lives. As a result God came to a decision: "So I declared on oath in my anger, 'They shall never enter my rest'" (v. 11).

The supreme thing to understand about authentic worship is how to rest in God. What does that mean? It means that we learn to depend on God's activity, not our own. As the New Testament book of Hebrews defines it, "Anyone who enters God's rest also rests from his own work" (4:10). In a real sense, rest is really mental health, peace of heart, and peace of mind. It means trusting God to do everything that needs to be done for our own salvation and righteousness.

To enter into God's rest means that you come to the place where you have stopped trying to save yourself and you simply let God do all the work. You look to the Lord Jesus and say, "If He has taken my place on the cross, then that is all I need." You cease your own work and you rest on His.

This doesn't mean you don't need to live a holy life. You do! But you live it in His strength, not your own. As the apostle Paul says, "So then, just as you received Christ Jesus as Lord, continue to live in him" (Colossians 2:6). Live in dependence on Christ for your way of life. Live in Him, and He will live through you. If you step out upon that promise, the result is rest. Wonderful rest! No more worrying, straining, and feeling frustrated in the Christian life. You simply rest on the One who is wholly adequate to do through you everything that needs to be done.

If we insist on living by our own effort, what is the result? God says, "They shall never enter my rest" (v. 11b). You can try worshiping God your own way in your own strength for forty years, and what will you have to show for it? A heart so hardened that God can only shake His head in grief and say, "You shall not enter into my rest."

If you want to worship God truly, then you must listen to His Word and hear His voice. If you want to know His ways, if you want to think His thoughts, then you must hear His Word. That's the only way to find the rest He offers you. There is no alternative path. There is no drug you can take, no secret formula you can follow, no mental discipline you can practice that will bring you God's peace.

There is only one path: Hear His Word. Listen to the Word of God and let it teach you, guide you, correct you, and make you wise. Sit under the judgment of His Word. Let it search you and transform you.

Then you will be able truly to worship the God who made you, the God who redeems and saves and shepherds you. Then you will be able to give unto Him the glory due His name.

18

A Song of Enduring Love

PSALM 107

George Matheson's sight began to fail when he was a child. By the time he was a student at the University of Glasgow in the early 1860s, he was almost completely blind. Despite his handicap he was a brilliant and accomplished student, and he looked forward to marrying his fiancée and serving God as a pastor. His plans for a happy marriage were dashed, however, when his fiancée broke their engagement, telling him, "I've decided I do not wish to be the wife of a blind preacher."

It was a devastating wound that George Matheson would carry for the rest of his life. Still, he continued to pursue his plan of entering the ministry. Ordained in 1868, he became a parish minister in the little waterfront village of Innelan on the Firth of Clyde in Scotland.

For years Matheson thought he had put the pain of his fiancée's rejection behind him. But on June 6, 1882, when George Matheson was forty years old, an event that should have been a joyful celebration tipped him into a deep depression. That event was his sister's wedding. Though he was genuinely happy for his sister, the activities of the day reminded him of all he had lost when the woman he loved rejected and abandoned him.

That evening all he could think about was a love that had wounded him, rejected him, and failed him—a love that had let him go. Those thoughts, he later recalled, "caused me the most severe mental suffering."

Yet even in the depths of his depression, God softly spoke to George Matheson and gave him a song. It was a song about a different kind of love: a love that never wounds and never fails, a love that would not let George Matheson go. It was a song about God's love.

There was something miraculous about the song that came out of George Matheson's suffering. "I had the impression," he later recalled, "of having it dictated to me by some inward voice rather than of working it out myself. I am quite sure that the whole work was completed in five minutes, and equally sure that it never received at my hands any retouching or correction . . . It came like a dayspring from on high." God gave these words to George Matheson:

O Love that wilt not let me go,
I rest my weary soul in thee;
I give thee back the life I owe,
That in thine ocean depths its flow
May richer, fuller be.

O Light that followest all my way,
I yield my flickering torch to thee;
My heart restores its borrowed ray,
That in thy sunshine's blaze its day
May brighter, fairer be.

O Joy that seekest me through pain,
I cannot close my heart to thee;
I trace the rainbow through the rain,
And feel the promise is not vain,
That morn shall tearless be.

Out of the pain of abandonment came a song of a love that will never let us go. Out of the darkness of George Matheson's physical blindness came a song of a "Light that followest all my way," enabling us to "trace the rainbow through the rain."

As we come to Psalm 107, we read another song that God gave, a song of a love that will not let us go. This folk song of faith begins with these words that become a recurrent theme throughout the psalm: "Give thanks to the LORD, for he is good; his love endures forever" (v. 1).

The Restless Ones

Psalm 107 introduces the fifth division of the book of Psalms, consisting of Psalms 107 through 150. The fifth division echoes the themes of the book of Deuteronomy in the Pentateuch. Deuteronomy declares the "second law," and that is what the name *Deuteronomy* means. *Deutero* means "second" and *nomos* means "law."

The first law is the law of sin and death, the law that condemns us and covers us with a sense of guilt and fear. The second law, says the apostle Paul, is the law of the spirit of life in Christ Jesus that sets us free from the law of sin and death. It is God's way of redeeming His people. By the operation of the second law, He buys them back, or redeems them. It is the second law that this psalm addresses.

This final section of the Psalms deals with the power of God's Word. In this section we find the longest of all the psalms, Psalm 119. Every verse of Psalm 119 contains a reference to God's Word (such as "Your Word," "Your decrees," "Your commands," "the law of the Lord," "His statutes," "His ways"). The fifth and final section of the Psalms is made up entirely of thanksgiving and praise, from beginning to end. It sounds one triumphant note all the way through, and the closing psalms resound with a shout of "Hallelujah! Praise the Lord!"

Here in Psalm 107, we see the recurring theme of God's steadfast, enduring love. This unfailing love breaks the back of our sinful rebellion and sets us free from guilt and shame. God's love accepts you just as you are and enables you to become what you long to be, what God created you to be.

Psalm 107 is simple in its structure. It begins with an introduction (vv. 1–3), then divides into two major sections that we might call "The Works of God" (vv. 4–32) and "The Ways of God" (vv. 33–43). Here is the psalmist's introduction:

> *Give thanks to the LORD, for he is good;*
> *his love endures forever.*
> *Let the redeemed of the LORD say this—*
> *those he redeemed from the hand of the foe,*
> *those he gathered from the lands,*
> *from east and west, from north and south (vv. 1–3).*

The introduction establishes Psalm 107 as a song of those whom God has delivered and redeemed from captivity and bondage. If God has saved you from your sin, if He has brought you safely through a time of trial and testing, then this is your song. This folk song of faith is dedicated to all whom God has redeemed and delivered from bondage or peril.

Next the psalmist describes the works of God as they have been displayed in human history. He describes four different kinds of trouble from which God has delivered His people in times past. The first trouble: hunger and thirst. The psalmist writes:

Some wandered in desert wastelands,
finding no way to a city where they could settle.
They were hungry and thirsty,
and their lives ebbed away (vv. 4–5).

Who are these people who suffer from hunger and thirst? We might call them "the restless ones." They wander about from place to place, from job to job, from city to city, and from marriage to marriage seeking answers but finding no rest. There are many such people today. They are looking for something, but they cannot find it. They wander from one experience to another, seeking something that will satisfy. The psalmist says they are looking for "a city where they could settle."

Many of us live in metropolitan areas with crowded freeways, high crime, high taxes, and crabgrass, and we wonder why anyone would want to live in a city. We'd rather live in the country, away from the noise and smog. But the Bible indicates that God designed human beings to live together in communities. Hebrews 11 tells us that Abraham "was looking forward to the city with foundations, whose architect and builder is God" (v. 10). Why would Abraham want to live in a city? What makes life in a city desirable? A city has two qualities that people seek.

First, a city has excitement. Whenever people gather together, there is excitement, entertainment, activity, and fun. We all hate to be bored, and a dull life is almost unbearable. God never intended life to be that way. He intended for life to be interesting and enjoyable. Cities provide excitement.

Second, a city offers security. If you are going to meet trouble, it is better to have others around. If you need defense, you want to be able to call upon your neighbors or the police. In ancient times cities were surrounded by thick walls, an added measure of defense. God intended life to be secure and restful. Cities were intended to provide security.

So the people described in Psalm 107 are looking for the things a city has to offer: excitement and security. They hunger and thirst for the things a city has to offer, but they cannot find them. So what do they do?

> Then they cried out to the LORD in their trouble,
> and he delivered them from their distress.
> He led them by a straight way
> to a city where they could settle.
> Let them give thanks to the LORD for his unfailing love
> and his wonderful deeds for men,
> for he satisfies the thirsty
> and fills the hungry with good things (vv. 6–9).

You may identify with this experience. You may know what it feels like to be restless, wandering, hungry, and thirsty for life but unable to find it. You've tried everything. Finally, when you reached the bottom, you cried out to the Lord in your trouble. When you did He heard you and began to lead you "by a straight way." You went from wandering to moving steadily ahead by a straight way.

God leads these restless people until they find a city to settle in, a place of both excitement and security. Finding our place of belonging in the world does not happen overnight. It takes time. But as God leads us, we find that place where life is good, where we feel secure and safe.

When God's people reach that city, the destination to which He is leading them, what is their response? Thanksgiving! The psalmist records their thankful response for satisfying their thirst and hunger and giving them "good things."

The Rebellious Ones

The psalmist goes on to describe another group of people—a hostile and rebellious people:

> Some sat in darkness and the deepest gloom,
> prisoners suffering in iron chains,

for they had rebelled against the words of God
and despised the counsel of the Most High.
So he subjected them to bitter labor;
they stumbled, and there was no one to help (vv. 10–12).

Notice the condition of these hostile and rebellious people. They sit in darkness and gloom. They are imprisoned, suffering in chains because they have rebelled against God and His counsel. Their imprisonment is a biblical symbol for hopeless ignorance. They cannot figure out what is wrong with their lives or why they live in such gloom. So they are in chains.

They are chained down by habits and attitudes that hold them in an iron grip. No matter how hard they try, they cannot break free. When people rebel against the Word of God, the counsel of God, they invariably end up in chains. We can see this principle at work in the lives of people all around us.

God's Word tells us not to be intoxicated with alcohol, and in principle this counsel would include intoxicating drugs as well. Yet people rebel against God's counsel. They like the feeling of being high. And the result? They end up imprisoned by an addiction they cannot control. Caught in the grip of alcoholism, they end up dead from drunk driving or cirrhosis of the liver. Many who succumb to drug addiction turn up dead in an alleyway with needle tracks along their arms.

Those who rebel against God's counsel regarding sexual purity find themselves slaves to sexual immorality. Some are addicted to promiscuous behavior, others to homosexual behavior, others to various perversions, and still others to pornography. They are wrecking their lives and destroying their families, yet they can't break the habit. They are in chains that they themselves have forged by their own rebellion and sin.

Some rebel against God's counsel regarding forgiveness and a tolerant spirit. They choose to hold grudges and bitterness. A resentful and critical spirit imprisons them. They don't know how to forgive or to love. They only know how to tear other people down and how to lash out at anyone who hurts them. Their lives have become dungeons of hatred, rage, and bitterness, and they don't know how to break free.

What is the reason for their imprisonment? They "rebelled against the words of God," says the psalmist, "and despised the counsel of the Most High" (v. 11). How tragic it is when people rebel against the words of God! People often decide, "I don't like what God says about life. I don't have to do what God says! I want to live my life my way!" They ignorantly fail to understand that God tells us the truth because He loves us. When we rebel against the words of God, we rebel against reality and we inevitably hurt ourselves.

And yet the grace of God is always available, even to those who have rebelled against God and despised His counsel. God does not say to us, "You made your bed; now lie in it!" He is always ready to receive us when we turn to Him. The psalmist writes:

> *Then they cried to the* LORD *in their trouble,*
> *and he saved them from their distress.*
> *He brought them out of darkness and the deepest gloom*
> *and broke away their chains.*
> *Let them give thanks to the* LORD *for his unfailing love*
> *and his wonderful deeds for men,*
> *for he breaks down gates of bronze*
> *and cuts through bars of iron (vv. 13–16).*

God opened the eyes of these rebellious people and showed them that they were not merely rebelling against God but against reality. God's moral law is not an artificial standard He imposes in order to squelch our fun. His moral law is a statement of reality: If you do the things that God says are wrong, then you will hurt yourself and others.

So when people finally become aware that they are imprisoned by their own sin and rebellion, when they finally turn to God, He lovingly responds. He brings them out of darkness. He breaks their chains and sets the captives free.

God does not enjoy our pain. He does not hurt us in order to get even with us. He grieves over our waywardness and rebellion. He weeps over us. He loves us, and when we turn to Him, He showers us with His grace and forgiveness. When we are ready to lay our chains before Him—the drugs, alcohol, sex, bitterness, whatever it may be—then He will break those chains and set us free to truly live, as in the words of the hymn by Charles Wesley:

He breaks the power of canceled sin,
He sets the prisoner free;
His blood can make the foulest clean,
His blood availed for me.

When God sets us free, we are free indeed—free to thank Him and praise Him for His wondrous work on our behalf. So the psalmist writes,

Let them give thanks to the LORD for his unfailing love
and his wonderful deeds for men,
for he breaks down gates of bronze
and cuts through bars of iron (vv. 15–16).

If you are struggling with habits you have not been able to break, go to God. He has the power to set you free.

Sin-Sick People

Next the psalmist speaks of people who are either physically or emotionally disordered. They are sick because of their sin:

Some became fools through their rebellious ways
and suffered affliction because of their iniquities.
They loathed all food
and drew near the gates of death (107:17–18).

Here the psalmist speaks of people who are either emotionally or physically sick because of emotional problems. I don't pretend to be an expert in mental health issues. But I think it's safe to say that many of the mental health problems and emotional problems that people struggle with today are rooted in feelings of guilt, shame, regret, anger, and bitterness. In other words, when people are emotionally unhealthy, there is often a sin component to their emotional problems. For example they are unable to forgive themselves for some sin they committed, or they are unable to forgive someone who hurt them.

I go back to a statement that a British psychologist once made to evangelist Billy Graham, which I mentioned earlier in this book. The psychologist told Dr. Graham that seventy percent of the people in mental hospitals could be released if they could find forgiveness. Sin is clearly a factor in many of the emotional problems that afflict people today. Millions of people are suffering afflictions because of their iniquities.

When the psalmist describes people who loathe all food and nearly die, he is speaking figuratively, not literally. He is saying of these people that they refuse nourishment—not just physical nourishment but spiritual food that the soul requires. They do not want healthy, nourishing things in their lives; they reject that which would give them health and strength.

Food, then, is a metaphor. The people the psalmist speaks of do not want to read good books that feed the mind. They do not want biblical teaching that feeds the soul. They do not want good music that strengthens the spirit. They reject what is good and feed themselves only junk books, junk ideas, and junk music, so they get worse and worse, sicker and sicker, and they draw near to the gates of death.

Here the psalmist gives us a picture of emotionally unhealthy people who are unable to handle life. They are fearful, anxious, and afraid to face reality because of guilt and shame or because of an ongoing sinful habit. As a pastor I have met and counseled hundreds of people who struggle in this area. They don't like to be told that their problem is sin. Yet they can't find healing until they recognize that their root problem is the sin problem.

The renowned Christian counselor Dr. Henry Brandt, author of *The Heart of the Problem*, tells of a woman who came to him with deep emotional problems. Dr. Brandt listened and observed her closely as she told her story for about half an hour. Finally he said to her, "You're not a very peaceful woman, are you?"

"Why do you say that?" she asked.

"Well," Dr. Brandt said, "I notice that you've been chewing on the edge of your handkerchief. You're upset and distraught, and you describe terrible things that happen to you all the time. Even though you're a Christian, you are not very peaceful, are you?"

"What does that have to do with anything?" she asked defensively.

"You know," he replied, "in Isaiah 48:22 God says, 'There is no peace for the wicked.'"

She sat bolt upright! "Are you calling *me* wicked?" she asked.

"There are different degrees of wickedness. If a man robs a bank at gunpoint for a hundred thousand dollars, that's one degree of wickedness. If a little boy swipes a nickel from his mother's purse, that's a different degree of wickedness, but it's still wicked. If you plunge a knife in someone's heart and murder that person, that's one degree of wickedness. But it's also wicked to gossip about people and murder their reputations—a different degree of wickedness but still wicked. In each case God says there is no peace for the wicked. If you do not have peace right now, it's because there is wickedness in your life."

Though resistant at first, this woman gradually began to acknowledge that her emotional troubles all had their root in some sin that she had been denying. Only as she began to acknowledge and repent of these sins in her life was she able to deal with the forces that kept her from experiencing the healing that the psalmist speaks of in the next few verses:

> *Then they cried to the* Lord *in their trouble,*
> *and he saved them from their distress.*
> *He sent forth his word and healed them;*
> *he rescued them from the grave.*
> *Let them give thanks to the* Lord *for his unfailing love*
> *and his wonderful deeds for men.*
> *Let them sacrifice thank offerings*
> *and tell of his works with songs of joy (vv. 19–22).*

When these people cried out to the Lord, He saved them from their distress. People often wait until they are in deep trouble, then they cry out to the Lord. When they do, God saves and delivers them. How does He accomplish this deliverance? He sends forth His healing Word.

I love the phrase "He sent forth his word and healed them." Here's an exciting truth to understand: When the psalmist says that God sent forth His Word, it does not mean that God gave them a Bible to read. This statement is actually a prophetic announcement of the coming Messiah. This statement means that God identified with us by sending His Son, Jesus, the Living Word of God. Remember the opening lines of John's gospel:

In the beginning was the Word, and the Word was with God, and the Word was God. He was with God in the beginning. Through him all things were made; without him nothing was made that has been made. In him was life, and that life was the light of men (1:1–4).

The Lord Jesus is the Living Word of God to us. He came to earth to live among us, to identify with us, and to take the punishment for our sin. So when the psalmist says that God sent His Word and healed these people, it means that God's Word descended to where the people were.

Jesus didn't reject these emotionally wounded people just because they were difficult to live with or because their lives were riddled with sin. He put His arm around them and said, "I understand why you are hurting. Let me show you what's causing this pain in your life. Let me show you how to find healing." And He set them free. As He once said, "If you continue in My word, then you are truly disciples of Mine; and you will know the truth, and the truth will make you free" (John 8:31b–32 NASB).

When these people experience freedom from their emotional hurts, what do they do? They give thanks! And they joyfully serve God and others out of gratitude for what God has done in their lives. The psalmist writes that they make sacrifices of thank offerings. The word *sacrifice* is often used in the Bible as a picture of costly, sacrificial service to others, service that is done in a spirit of joy and gratitude to our loving and liberating God.

Down to the Sea in Ships

Next the psalmist speaks of those brave souls who (in the poetic language of the King James Version) "go down to the sea in ships, that do business in great waters," who "see the works of the LORD, and his wonders in the deep" (vv. 23–24). There is a mystique to the oceans, these vast expanses of water that are several miles deep and thousands of miles wide. The image of a ship sailing the seas has long been a vivid poetic metaphor to describe the journey of life, as these lines by the poet Longfellow illustrate:

Build me straight, O worthy Master!
Staunch and strong, a goodly vessel

That shall laugh at all disaster,
And with wave and whirlwind wrestle!

The dangers of life on the sea are easy to understand. If a ship founders far from shore, what chance of escape do the sailors have? Those who find themselves shipwrecked and cast adrift have little chance of avoiding the perils of storms, sun, hunger, thirst, sharks, and drowning. As Samuel Johnson once observed, "Being in a ship is being in a jail, with the chance of being drowned." The psalmist writes:

For he spoke and stirred up a tempest
that lifted high the waves.
They mounted up to the heavens and went down to the depths;
in their peril their courage melted away.
They reeled and staggered like drunken men;
they were at their wits' end (vv. 25–27).

Down through the centuries many sailors have faced crises at sea like those described by the psalmist. One such man was John Newton, born in 1725, the son of a sailing ship captain. His godly mother taught him the stories of the Bible when he was little, but she died while he was still a child. By the time he was in his teens, John Newton had given up all faith in God.

At the age of nineteen, Newton was "impressed" into the Royal Navy—forced to serve against his will. Working in wretched conditions aboard the HMS *Harwich*, he deserted, was captured and flogged, and put back aboard the ship. At his own request, he was transferred to a slave ship that plied the Atlantic between Africa and the Americas. He was often abused and beaten.

When Newton was twenty-three, a friend got him a job as a sailor on a different ship where he received better treatment. Newton quickly rose through the ranks and became the captain of another slave ship.

While returning home after transporting slaves to the New World, Newton and his crew encountered a violent storm. As the storm raged, Newton lost hope. At one point this man, who had given up his faith in God, shouted to the heavens, "Lord, have mercy upon us!" Within hours the storm blew over and the seas became calm. There was no doubt in John Newton's mind: God had answered his desperate prayer. That day he gave his life to Jesus Christ as Lord and Savior.

Soon afterward John Newton left the slave trade and married Mary Catlett, a woman he had loved for years. He bought books and educated himself by reading. He took a job as a surveyor of tides in Liverpool, England, where he came to know the great evangelists George Whitefield and John Wesley. Discipled by these two great men of God, Newton learned Latin, Hebrew, and Greek and was eventually ordained as a minister.

When John Newton preached, the crowds were so great that the church wall had to be knocked out and the building enlarged. Newton befriended the poet William Cowper, and together the former slave ship captain and the poet began to write hymns, including "How Sweet the Name of Jesus Sounds," "Glorious Things of Thee Are Spoken," and the most famous of all of John Newton's hymns, "Amazing Grace":

> Amazing grace! How sweet the sound
> That saved a wretch like me!
> I once was lost, but now am found;
> Was blind, but now I see.
>
> 'Twas grace that taught my heart to fear,
> And grace my fears relieved;
> How precious did that grace appear
> The hour I first believed!
>
> Through many dangers, toils and snares,
> I have already come;
> 'Tis grace hath brought me safe thus far,
> And grace will lead me home.

That's the testimony of a sea captain and sinful slave trader who was converted when he called out to God in the midst of a great storm. Fearing for his life and for his immortal soul, John Newton cried out to God, and his life was forever transformed.

John Newton lived through the experiences that are described in Psalm 107. Tossed on waves that "mounted up to the heavens and went down to the depths," Newton and his crew "reeled and staggered like drunken men" (vv. 26–27). In his terror and despair, he cried out to the heavens, "Lord, have mercy upon us!" And he was delivered from the storm and from his sin. That's the scene the psalmist now describes to us:

> *Then they cried out to the* LORD *in their trouble,*
> *and he brought them out of their distress.*
> *He stilled the storm to a whisper;*
> *the waves of the sea were hushed.*
> *They were glad when it grew calm,*
> *and he guided them to their desired haven.*
> *Let them give thanks to the* LORD *for his unfailing love*
> *and his wonderful deeds for men.*
> *Let them exalt him in the assembly of the people*
> *and praise him in the council of the elders (vv. 28–32).*

While what we have read was literally true in the life of John Newton and other men of the sea, the psalmist is actually speaking to us in figurative language about a truth that applies to all of our lives. The Scriptures often picture life as a stormy sea. We all go out to conduct our life's business upon the great waters. Usually the waters are calm and the winds are steady. But every so often, the winds rise and the seas become rough. We sail into one of life's storms, and we find ourselves in crisis.

It's interesting to note that the psalmist says the source of the crisis is God. It was the Lord Himself who "spoke and stirred up a tempest that lifted high the waves." As John Newton wrote in "Amazing Grace," these crises in our lives, as painful as they are, often come to us by God's grace. " 'Twas grace that taught my heart to fear," he wrote, "and grace my fears relieved." Newton believed it was not only the relief of fear that came from God but the fear itself. If God had not brought that storm into his life and taught his heart to fear, Newton never would have turned to God for deliverance.

When the storms of life come our way, our courage, self-confidence, and self-reliance melt away. We reel and stagger like drunken men. We come to the end of ourselves. Out of our hopelessness and despair, we cry out to God. At that point we have come to the place God wants us to be—a place of complete dependence upon Him. At last we realize that we are powerless before the towering forces of this life, and God alone is capable of delivering and saving us. Then we are able to thank Him for His enduring love and His wonderful works on our behalf.

The Ways of God

As we discussed at the beginning of this chapter, Psalm 107 is very simple in its structure. We have looked at the introduction and at the first of the two major sections, "The Works of God." Now we come to the second major section of the psalm, "The Ways of God," verses 33–43. The psalmist writes:

> *He turned rivers into a desert,*
> *flowing springs into thirsty ground,*
> *and fruitful land into a salt waste,*
> *because of the wickedness of those who lived there (vv. 33–34).*

God often uses adversity to accomplish His purposes in our lives. He deliberately sends trouble into our path when it is the only way He can get our attention. God knows that you need to hear His Word more than you need a life of ease and comfort. So as C. S. Lewis once put it, "God whispers to us in our pleasures, speaks to us in our conscience, but shouts in our pains: It is His megaphone to rouse a deaf world."

But God doesn't always have to bring trouble into our lives in order to get our attention. Sometimes He speaks to us through the good things He showers upon us. The psalmist continues:

> *He turned the desert into pools of water*
> *and the parched ground into flowing springs;*
> *there he brought the hungry to live,*
> *and they founded a city where they could settle.*
> *They sowed fields and planted vineyards*
> *that yielded a fruitful harvest;*
> *he blessed them, and their numbers greatly increased,*
> *and he did not let their herds diminish (vv. 35–38).*

When you take God at His word, you walk in the fullness of His strength and supply. You experience the joy of fellowship with Him and the rewards of His presence. He meets your needs, satisfies your heart, and fills your life with good things. Your prayers do not go unanswered, for God moves to meet your need. He supplies abundantly.

All of this does not mean, of course, that those who walk with God will never experience sorrow. Nor does it mean that those who experience trials and losses are necessarily under the disciplining hand of God. At some point trouble comes into every life, regardless of whether we are walking with God or running from Him.

But we can be confident that whenever trouble comes, God is with us. He is there to protect us and defend us and to raise us up out of our affliction. The psalmist continues:

> *Then their numbers decreased, and they were humbled*
> *by oppression, calamity and sorrow;*
> *he who pours contempt on nobles*
> *made them wander in a trackless waste.*
> *But he lifted the needy out of their affliction*
> *and increased their families like flocks (vv. 39–41).*

The ways of God are diverse and appropriate for every individual person, for every individual need. God uses both adversity and prosperity to accomplish His purposes in our lives. And when people see all that God has accomplished in their lives, they respond with rejoicing:

> *The upright see and rejoice,*
> *but all the wicked shut their mouths.*
> *Whoever is wise, let him heed these things*
> *and consider the great love of the* LORD *(vv. 42–43).*

Those who are wise are able to see the great love of God in every circumstance. When times are good and we experience God's abundant provision, we thank Him and acknowledge Him as the source of every blessing. When times are hard, we continue to trust in God to deliver us from our troubles. That is what the apostle Paul means when he writes:

> *I am not saying this because I am in need, for I have learned to*
> *be content whatever the circumstances. I know what it is to be in*
> *need, and I know what it is to have plenty. I have learned the secret*

*of being content in any and every situation, whether well fed or
hungry, whether living in plenty or in want. I can do everything
through him who gives me strength (Philippians 4:11–13).*

The last word of Psalm 107 is a word of admonition: "Whoever
is wise, let him heed these things and consider the great love of the
LORD" (v. 43). Have you stopped to think about God's great love for
you? Have you considered how He accepts you, provides for you,
protects you, and restores you to service every time you fail?

Maybe you have failed God in a big way. Perhaps you have gone
through a shameful, humiliating experience of having your worst
secrets exposed. You feel that your usefulness to God is over, that
He has placed you on the shelf. But God's love doesn't depend on
whether the world sees you as a failure or a success. God loves you
even if the whole world hates you. His love restores you to usefulness and service to Him.

Your boss won't give you unconditional acceptance. Neither will
your mother-in-law, your next-door neighbor, the finance company,
the IRS, or anyone else in your life. But God's love for you is unqual-
ified, unconditional, and unfailing. "Give thanks to the LORD, for He
is good; his love endures forever" (v. 1). May we be wise and give
heed to all He has done for us and "consider the great love of the
Lord" (v. 43).

19

When You Are Falsely Accused

PSALM 109

In the winter of late 1691, Reverend Samuel Parris noticed that his daughter Betty and his ward, Abigail Williams, were acting strangely. They spoke to each other in nonsense words, crept around on the floor like animals, and hid from sight. Reverend Parris decided that there was only one explanation for such behavior: The two girls were possessed by the devil. Parris demanded that the girls name those who had "bewitched" them, and the children accused three women of the town.

One of the three was the town beggar, a mentally ill woman named Sarah Good. The second was a sick and elderly woman named Sarah Osborne. The third was Tituba, a slave from Barbados owned by Reverend Parris. On March 1, 1692, the three women were charged with witchcraft and put in prison. Because the village had no government, the women couldn't be tried right away.

Soon other children of the village started making accusations. They accused Sarah Good's four-year-old daughter, Dorcas, of being a witch. They accused Rebecca Nurse, a woman everyone had known as a godly, grandmotherly woman. They accused Abigail and Deliverance Hobbs, Martha Corey, and John and Elizabeth Proctor. All were arrested and put in prison without trial. In May Governor Phips arrived and a court was convened, though too late for some. Sarah Osborne had died in the prison. Sarah Good had given birth to a baby girl who also died in prison.

In all, nearly eighty people were accused, imprisoned, and awaiting trial. The trials were held over the summer of 1692. The villagers of Salem seemed determined to believe the worst of their neighbors. Anyone the children accused was presumed guilty. Every case ended in a guilty verdict and a sentence of death, and there were no appeals. The only way for an accused person to avoid execution was to plead guilty, then accuse some previously unsuspected neighbor of witchcraft.

During the summer of 1692, nineteen men and women were hanged, including a Christian minister who protested his innocence to the end. Another was the village constable, who was accused of witchcraft when he refused to arrest his accused neighbors. Thirteen were women; six were men. In addition to those convicted and hanged, an eighty-year-old farmer refused to enter a plea, so he was crushed to death under a pile of stones.

In 1697, five years after the hysteria broke out in Salem village, many of the children who had made these deadly accusations admitted that their accusations were false. With the passage of time, they realized that their accusations had put innocent people to death. Some of the children struggled with illnesses due to unresolved guilt.

But for those who died in prison or on the gallows or under a pile of stones, it was too late. They were accused, judged, condemned, and executed by their neighbors, the very people they went to church with every Sunday.

Their lives were destroyed by false accusations.

A "Problem Psalm"

What do you do when you are falsely accused? At some point in their lives, most people experience the pain and humiliation of a false accusation. Psalm 109 speaks to a problem that is common to the entire human race. This psalm, written by David himself, describes the response of a man who has been lied about by people who seek to destroy him without cause.

Let's be candid: This psalm is a "problem psalm." It is troubling and painful to read. The spirit of this psalm is hostile, vengeful, and even hateful. Why would God allow such an angry and bitter piece of writing to be included in the book of Psalms? If we study this psalm with care, I believe we'll find an answer to these difficult questions.

First, we must ask ourselves what happened in David's life that caused him to write down such hostile and bitter feelings? As we look at the story of his life in Scripture, we can't be certain to which experience this psalm refers. Still, I think this psalm probably reflects David's emotions after an experience recorded in 1 Samuel 25.

This event took place before David became king of Israel while he was hiding from King Saul and living in the desert with some loyal men. Those were dangerous times, and there were bandits and thieves roaming the desert, so David had his men keep watch over the property of the law-abiding people of the desert, including the herds and flocks of a wealthy rancher named Nabal.

After weeks in the desert, David saw that he and his men were running low on provisions, so he sent ten of his men to Nabal with a message. On behalf of David, they told the wealthy rancher, "Long life to you! Good health to you and your household! . . . Please give your servants and your son David whatever you can find for them" (1 Samuel 25:6, 8).

Nabal responded with a torrent of insults against David, then he sent the men away empty handed. When the ten men reported back, David was outraged. "After all I've done for Nabal," he said, "he has paid me back evil for good!" And David made plans to attack Nabal's ranch and kill him.

Nabal had a wise and beautiful wife named Abigail. When she heard that her husband had insulted David, she and her servants gathered bread, wine, meat, and fruit, loaded the food on donkeys, and took it out into the desert. When she reached David's camp, she fell at his feet, offered the provisions to him, and begged him to spare her husband's life. David was moved by her pleas and agreed to forego his revenge. He accepted the food and sent Abigail home in peace.

Ten days later God Himself avenged David. Nabal's heart failed, and he died. When David heard that Nabal was dead, he praised God because God had kept him from doing wrong and seeking his own revenge and had brought Nabal's wrongdoing down on his own head. Afterwards, Abigail became David's wife.

The harsh and angry words of Psalm 109 are certainly a fitting expression of the outrage and hostility David felt when Nabal mistreated him. Though there were other times in David's life when he was unjustly treated, this psalm best fits the occasion of Nabal's offense.

Unjustly Accused

The opening lines of Psalm 109 lay out the issue that confronts the psalmist David: the issue of mistreatment and false accusation. He writes:

O God, whom I praise,
do not remain silent,
for wicked and deceitful men
have opened their mouths against me;
they have spoken against me with lying tongues.
With words of hatred they surround me;
they attack me without cause (vv. 1–3).

Here is the complaint of a man who is under attack by unscrupulous enemies. David describes them as wicked and deceitful. They attack him without cause. You and I know that there are such people in the world, people who seem to derive a twisted satisfaction from hurting people for no reason at all.

That's how the Bible describes Nabal. In 1 Samuel 25:3 we read that he "was surly and mean in his dealings." Nabal's own wife, Abigail, told David that Nabal was a "wicked man" who was "just like his name—his name is Fool, and folly goes with him" (1 Samuel 25:25).

Perhaps there are people like Nabal in your own life. Maybe someone who seems irrationally bent on destroying your reputation has unjustly accused you. Perhaps you don't even know why this person has singled you out for mistreatment. "I never did any harm to this person," you think. "What have I done to deserve this?"

In the next few verses, we see that David has tried to behave kindly and cordially toward the person who now attacks him. He has tried to live at peace, but the attacker is not interested in peace. The psalmist observes:

In return for my friendship they accuse me,
but I am a man of prayer.
They repay me evil for good,
and hatred for my friendship (vv. 4–5).

The apostle Paul once wrote, "If it is possible, as far as it depends on you, live at peace with everyone" (Romans 12:18), and that is how the psalmist has tried to conduct himself. But even though you do your best to live at peace with others, some will attack you, hurt you, undermine you, and destroy your reputation just to be mean.

In the Sermon on the Mount, Jesus says, "You have heard that it was said, 'Love your neighbor and hate your enemy.' But I tell you: Love your enemies and pray for those who persecute you, that you may be sons of your Father in heaven" (Matthew 5:43–45a). Even though David was a man of the Old Testament, he clearly understood this New Testament principle. His friendship is returned with accusations, but he remains a man of prayer, and he prays for his enemies. Even so, they continue their cruel attacks on him, repaying evil for good.

The Most Disturbing Section of All

The next words we read are steeped in rage and bitterness. But as we read these words, the question arises: Whose words are these?

> *Appoint an evil man to oppose him;*
> *let an accuser stand at his right hand.*
> *When he is tried, let him be found guilty,*
> *and may his prayers condemn him.*
> *May his days be few;*
> *may another take his place of leadership.*
> *May his children be fatherless*
> *and his wife a widow.*
> *May his children be wandering beggars;*
> *may they be driven from their ruined homes.*
> *May a creditor seize all he has;*
> *may strangers plunder the fruits of his labor.*
> *May no one extend kindness to him*
> *or take pity on his fatherless children.*
> *May his descendants be cut off,*
> *their names blotted out from the next generation.*
> *May the iniquity of his fathers be remembered before the* LORD*;*
> *may the sin of his mother never be blotted out.*
> *May their sins always remain before the* LORD*,*
> *that he may cut off the memory of them from the earth* (vv. 6–15).

This is the most disturbing section of this psalm. This angry, vengeful, vindictive language marks Psalm 109 as one of several Imprecatory Psalms. An imprecation is a curse—the act of calling down destruction and judgment on another person. Other imprecatory psalms include Psalms 5, 6, 11, 12, 35, 37, 40, 52, 54, 56, 58, 69, 79, 83, 137, 139, and 143. I chose Psalm 109 to study because the language in this psalm is the harshest of them all.

How do we explain language like this in the Psalms? The answer may surprise you: I don't believe that the words of verses 6 to 15 are the psalmist's own words. I don't believe the psalmist is calling down curses on his enemies. Instead, as we carefully examine the text, it seems clear to me that these verses should be in quotation marks. The psalmist is not cursing his enemies; he is quoting them.

In the original Hebrew language of the psalms, there's no way to indicate a quotation. We use quotation marks in English, but there are no quotation marks in Hebrew. The only way you can tell if a Hebrew passage is a quotation is from certain internal clues and from the context. So let's look closely for those clues.

First clue: A remarkable change of attitude takes place between verse 5 and verse 6. In verse 5 David says, "They repay me evil for good, and hatred for my friendship." Yet with verse 6, the psalmist appears to launch into a long, vile stream of horrible curses. This seems completely out of character, given what the psalmist wrote in verse 5. Why would a man move so abruptly from expressions of goodwill to a spate of curses?

Second clue: The psalmist makes another abrupt transition beginning at that same point, verse 6. Previously he was speaking of his enemies in the plural: "*They* have spoken against me." "*They* surround me." "*They* attack me." "*They* accuse me."

Beginning with verse 7, the language becomes, "Let *him* be found guilty." "May his prayers condemn *him*." "May *his* days be few." "May another take *his* place." "May *his* children be fatherless." The abrupt switch from plural to singular is significant. The psalmist is not expressing his own feelings here; he is quoting his enemies. These vile curses are the imprecations that his enemies speak against him. This entire section should be set in quotation marks because they are not the psalmist's own words.

In these harshly worded verses, the psalmist David reveals what his enemies have said about him. When we read these lines, we can see why the psalmist cries out before God. We can see how hateful and relentless his accusers are, and we can better understand the psalmist's pain. This interpretation of these lines is confirmed by verse 20, which reads: "May this be the LORD's payment to my accusers, to those who speak evil of me."

Verses 6 through 15 reveal the strategy that the psalmist's accusers have devised against him: They want to rig a false trial. They want to drag him before the law on a false charge and then arrange for false witnesses to accuse and condemn him.

These are diabolically clever people. They aren't going to waylay him and murder him in an alley. They're going to attack him openly in a courtroom and pervert justice so that the law does their dirty work for them. They intend to destroy him *legally.*

Their goal is his death. "May his days be few! May another take his place of leadership," they say in verse 8. We should note that many Bible scholars consider this to be a prophetic reference to Judas Iscariot, the disciple who betrayed Jesus. In Acts 1, Peter stood up among the believers and called for the casting of lots to choose a successor to Judas, who had committed suicide after his act of betrayal. Peter said, "For it is written in the book of Psalms, 'May his place be deserted; let there be no one to dwell in it,' and, 'May another take his place of leadership'" (Acts 1:20). The two passages Peter quoted were Psalm 69:25 and Psalm 109:8.

Because Peter applied verse 8 to Judas, some Bible scholars conclude that all of Psalm 109 applies to Judas and is a prediction of the betrayer's terrible fate. In other words, the wife and children of Judas would be left desolate, and Judas himself would spend eternity in hell. Jesus seems to support this view when He says, "But woe to that man who betrays the Son of Man! It would be better for him if he had not been born" (Matthew 26:24). This view may be accurate; however, I think the evidence is too slim to take a definitive position on the matter.

One thing is certain: Those who accuse the psalmist are bent on his destruction. They want him sentenced to death, but death alone is not enough to satisfy them. They want to hurt him by destroying everyone he loves, including his children and his wife. And they continue, curse upon curse.

These wicked people don't care how many innocent people they hurt. They just want to inflict the maximum amount of suffering on the psalmist by seizing his possessions, destroying his family, and taking his life.

You might think there is nothing more you could do to a man than this, but there is. David's enemies descend to the worst and most blasphemous level of all: They ask God to eternally damn the psalmist and his family. Their evil prayer before God is this: "May the iniquity of his fathers be remembered before the LORD; may the sin of his mother never be blotted out. May their sins always remain before the LORD, that he may cut off the memory of them from the earth" (vv. 14–15).

To put it bluntly, they are blaspheming and saying, "God, damn him and his family!" We hear this same oath today. When people feel intense anger or hatred toward another person, they are quick to say, "God damn you!" or "Go to hell!" A heart full of hate seeks the complete and eternal destruction of other people. When a person is in the grip of hate, it's not enough that one's enemies die; one's enemies must suffer intensely and eternally in hell.

It's a dangerous thing to curse another person in this way. Jesus said, "Do not judge, and you will not be judged. Do not condemn, and you will not be condemned. Forgive, and you will be forgiven" (Luke 6:37). And He says, "For in the same way you judge others, you will be judged, and with the measure you use, it will be measured to you " (Matthew 7:2). If we condemn others to hell for some hurt they have caused us, how should we be judged for the hurts we have caused others?

How dare we stand in the place of God and judge the souls of other people as if we were as holy and righteous as God Himself? What arrogance! What blasphemy! Those who are quick to condemn others to hell should think soberly about their own sins and their own souls.

Why Are They So Hateful?

Next the psalmist lists the reasons his enemies give for their vindictiveness and hatred:

For he never thought of doing a kindness,
but hounded to death the poor
and the needy and the brokenhearted (v. 16).

Here we see the strange twisting of reason that takes place when people decide to do evil. They rationalize to make themselves appear to be victims of injustice, even though they know, deep down, that they are perpetrating evil. In verse 16 the psalmist is still quoting his accusers and revealing their thoughts to us. The evildoers make themselves out to be victims of injustice, and they blame the psalmist for their problems.

What we see here is a psychological phenomenon called projection, the act of blaming others for the very aspects of ourselves that we can't tolerate or accept. These accusers project their own evil deeds onto the writer of the psalm. They are the ones who hound a poor, innocent, needy, brokenhearted man to death, yet they accuse him of the very thing they are doing! People do this all the time; they blame others for their own sins.

Predators commonly project their own evil onto their victims, blaming the victims for the crimes they themselves have committed. Child molesters and rapists commonly blame their victims: "She seduced me!" Blaming the victim is a way of rationalizing guilt and avoiding shame.

We saw projection on a massive scale during the Holocaust, when Nazi war criminals blamed their victims for their own crimes. The Nazis spread rumors that the Jews committed ritualized murder of German children, stole German wealth, and plotted to wipe out the German people. In the end the Nazis were guilty of everything they falsely accused the Jews of doing. They murdered Jewish children, seized Jewish property, and plotted the destruction of the Jewish race.

We human beings have a hard time accepting blame for our own sins. Until we are ready to accept blame, we cannot accept forgiveness.

Next we see another reason the psalmist's enemies had such a vicious hatred of him. The psalmist quotes his enemies:

He loved to pronounce a curse—
may it come on him;

he found no pleasure in blessing—
may it be far from him.
He wore cursing as his garment (vv. 17–18a).

Here again we see David's enemies shifting the blame for their own sin. As we have seen, they have cursed the psalmist, blaspheming and asking God to damn him. To justify their own cursing, they say that the psalmist actually loved to pronounce curses and took no enjoyment in blessing others. They are like children who are caught in a sin and say, "Well, he did it first!"

This is human nature, isn't it? Childish, but human. Ever since Adam blamed Eve for giving him the fruit and blamed God for giving him Eve as his wife, human beings have been accusing others for their own sins.

The psalmist's accusers go on to intensify their blaming and cursing against him:

It [cursing] entered into his body like water,
into his bones like oil.
May it be like a cloak wrapped about him,
like a belt tied forever around him (vv. 18b–19).

It is amazing to me how serious a thing cursing is and how lightly and thoughtlessly people engage in it. People seem to forget that there really is such a thing as being cursed, as being damned, as spending eternity in hell, cut off forever from God. People take it upon themselves to pronounce damnation on one another so lightly, as if it means nothing. Only God has the right to pronounce eternal judgment, and people who would carelessly say, "God damn you!" or "Go to hell!" need to be reminded of the seriousness of their words.

The Reaction of a Wrongly Accused Believer

The psalmist is in a terrible situation. His enemies seek to kill him and destroy his family. He has tried to respond in a righteous way, but his enemies have only become more vengeful. So he cries out to God: "May this be the LORD's payment to my accusers, to those who speak evil of me" (v. 20).

What should David's response be? He does something beautiful, something amazing. He maintains a godly attitude. He commits the whole matter to the Lord in prayer. The closing prayer of this psalm is a marvelous picture of the attitude we should have whenever we are unfairly accused:

But you, O Sovereign LORD,
deal well with me for your name's sake;
out of the goodness of your love, deliver me.
For I am poor and needy,
and my heart is wounded within me.
I fade away like an evening shadow;
I am shaken off like a locust.
My knees give way from fasting;
my body is thin and gaunt.
I am an object of scorn to my accusers;
when they see me, they shake their heads (vv. 21–25).

The first thing the psalmist does is to commit himself and his cause to God, asking Him to deal well with him for His name's sake. Here is a man who understands the nature of reality. He understands the biblical principle "It is mine to avenge; I will repay" (Deuteronomy 32:35). Vengeance belongs to God.

History is littered with the bodies of those who took vengeance into their own hands and got swept up in the cycle of "getting even." God is the only One who understands the true causes of conflict and injustice. He's the only One qualified to judge between two opposing sides. He's the only One who knows who is righteous and who is wrong. Leave vengeance in His hands and commit your cause to Him.

The psalmist understands that God will deal justly with these accusers for His name's sake. David says, in effect, "God, this is your problem, and I trust You to deal with it. Your reputation is at stake here, so please handle this crisis for Your name's sake."

That is a perfectly Christian response to a trial of mistreatment. It's the same response Jesus made when He was unjustly accused, falsely convicted, and crucified without cause. As the apostle Peter wrote, Jesus "committed no sin, and no deceit was found in his mouth. When they hurled their insults at him, he did not retaliate;

when he suffered, he made no threats. Instead, he entrusted himself to him who judges justly" (1 Peter 2:22–23). Jesus is the ultimate example of how we should respond when we are falsely accused. As Dr. F. B. Meyer once observed:

> We make a mistake in trying always to clear ourselves. We should be wiser to go straight on, humbly doing the next thing and leaving God to vindicate us. "He shall bring forth thy righteousness as the light and thy judgment as the noonday." There may come hours in our lives when we shall be misunderstood, slandered, falsely accused. At such times it is very difficult not to act on the policy of the men around us in the world. They want to appeal to law and force and public opinion. But the believer takes his case into a higher court and lays it before his God.

That is what the psalmist has done. He has taken his case to the highest court in the universe and laid it before God.

Next the psalmist prays for strength to go through this ordeal of mistreatment and attack by his enemies:

> *For I am poor and needy,*
> *and my heart is wounded within me.*
> *I fade away like an evening shadow;*
> *I am shaken off like a locust.*
> *My knees give way from fasting;*
> *my body is thin and gaunt (vv. 22–24).*

Even after we commit ourselves to God, it's not easy to endure false accusation. It is painful. It wears us down. It takes something out of us. Whenever we accuse people of wrong behavior, this is how they feel. They are wounded and shaken and feel that their strength is failing. It's a serious thing to accuse someone of wrongdoing, and we should consider carefully before we ever speak a word of accusation against another person.

The psalmist cries out to God for help in his physical weakness and his humiliation. He asks God to vindicate him:

> *Help me, O LORD my God;*
> *save me in accordance with your love.*

Let them know that it is your hand,
that you, O LORD, have done it.
They may curse, but you will bless;
when they attack they will be put to shame,
but your servant will rejoice (vv. 26–28).

The psalmist asks God to vindicate him in such a way that everyone knows that God Himself is the One who vindicates. "Let them know that it is your hand," he says, "that you, O Lord, have done it" (v. 27).

Then he adds, "They may curse, but you will bless" (v. 28). In other words, "I can't stop them from cursing me and tearing down my reputation, but Lord I ask you to bless me anyway. Let everyone see that while my enemies curse me, you bless me."

He goes on to say, "When they attack they will be put to shame, but your servant will rejoice" (v. 28). When he says he wants his enemies to be "put to shame," he is not saying he wants them publicly humiliated. Rather, he wants his enemies to be ashamed of themselves. He wants the facts to come to light so that his enemies will be sorry for what they have done, so they will repent and live a godly life. That's the same principle Peter wrote of: "Keeping a clear conscience, so that those who speak maliciously against your good behavior in Christ may be ashamed of their slander" (1 Peter 3:16).

If you are in this situation, if you are being falsely accused, keep your conscience clear. Don't strike back, don't curse, don't revile, don't attack. When you are slandered and you accept it without complaining as Christ did, count it as a victory. As the apostle Paul wrote, "But thanks be to God, who always leads us in triumphal procession in Christ and through us spreads everywhere the fragrance of the knowledge of him" (2 Corinthians 2:14).

This is the note on which the psalmist closes—a note of triumphant affirmation, of ringing confidence in God:

My accusers will be clothed with disgrace
and wrapped in shame as in a cloak.
With my mouth I will greatly extol the LORD;
in the great throng I will praise him.
For he stands at the right hand of the needy one,
to save his life from those who condemn him (vv. 29–31).

Remember that in verse 6 the psalmist's enemies wanted to appoint an evil accuser to stand at his right hand and condemn him. But here the psalmist says that it is God Himself who stands at the right hand of the needy! It is God who makes their cause His own. It is God who brings truth to light and establishes the facts so that even the wicked accusers will be silenced and ashamed that they ever perpetrated such an injustice.

May we always be more concerned with glorifying God's name than vindicating our own. May we be more concerned with spreading love and forgiveness than getting our pound of flesh. And may we always commit ourselves and our cause to God whenever we are falsely accused.

20

Who Am I, Lord?

PSALM 139

In his 1980 book *Peter Sellers: The Mask behind the Mask*, biographer Peter Evans chronicled the life of actor Peter Sellers. Sellers's best-known roles included Inspector Clouseau in the *Pink Panther* films, roles in both *The Mouse That Roared* and *Dr. Strangelove*, and his Oscar-nominated role as Chance the gardener in *Being There*. In fact, said Evans, Sellers performed so many different screen roles that he was sometimes unsure of his own identity.

One day a fan recognized the actor on the street and asked, "Aren't you Peter Sellers?"

"Not today," Sellers answered, and walked on.

Many people today find themselves going through an identity crisis. They look in the mirror and ask themselves, "Who am I? Why am I here? What does my life truly mean?"

Psalm 139 describes a man who is asking himself who he is in relationship to his Creator. If you are struggling with your own sense of identity, if you're not sure of your place in the grand scheme of the universe, then study this marvelous psalm with me—and discover yourself!

"O Lord, You Dig Me!"

Psalm 139 is laid out in a simple yet elegant structure. It is divided into four paragraphs of six verses each, which makes the outline of this psalm easy to follow. In each paragraph the psalmist faces a question about his personal relationship to God. In the first paragraph he asks, "How well does God know me?" The first sentence gives us his answer: "O LORD, you have searched me and you know me" (v. 1).

The Hebrew word translated "searched" comes from a root word that means "to dig." Literally the psalmist says, "O Lord, you dig me!"

Isn't it amazing how God's Word connects with our own culture in such interesting ways! Ever since the Jazz Age of the 1920s and '30s, the slang word *dig* has meant "understand, enjoy, and appreciate." In the 1950s, TV's Dobie Gillis had a beatnik friend, Maynard G. Krebbs, who would often use that word as in, "Man, like, dig that crazy music!" And in the late 1960s, the chorus of a popular rock song was, "I can dig it, he can dig it, she can dig it, we can dig it!" Even today's rappers, punkers, and metal heads still say "I can dig it," meaning, "I'm into it; I grasp it; I love it; it's cool."

And that's what the psalmist David was saying in this psalm: "O Lord, you dig me! You know me; You understand me; You love me; You appreciate me; You dig into the depths of my soul and search through me and turn me inside out and X-ray me! You know everything there is to know about me, and You still love me! You dig me!"

The psalmist carries this theme forward in the next few verses:

You know when I sit and when I rise;
you perceive my thoughts from afar.
You discern my going out and my lying down;
you are familiar with all my ways.
Before a word is on my tongue
you know it completely, O LORD (vv. 2–4).

Here he says, in effect, "Lord, you understand and know me in the realm of my thoughts. You know when I sit down—my quiet, reflective, passive moments. You know when I rise up—my busy, active, working moments. You understand all my moods, feelings, and states of being."

What's more, the psalmist says, God is aware of his habits and choices. Our "going out" and our "lying down" speak of the routines of our lives, our work habits and sleep habits. This is reinforced in the next line, which says that God is familiar with all our ways. Our "ways" are the things we do on a regular basis: our ways of self-expression, our likes and dislikes, our favorite foods, our favorite books, our favorite music. God knows all your ways, your choices, your habits—all the things that make you distinctly you.

The psalmist also notes that God knows what he will say even before he says it. David acknowledges, "You even understand my subconscious thoughts—that level of my mental activity that is below the surface of my awareness. You understand my thoughts before I am even able to form them into words. You know how I think and feel. You understand the language I use to think and communicate."

During my boyhood in northern Minnesota, I lived for a time in a Swedish settlement. The Swedish Christians teased the rest of us, saying, "You know, we Scandinavians are going to have a wonderful time in heaven while all the rest of you are learning the language!" Well, the Swedes may think that Swedish is the language of heaven, but I'm convinced that God has a pretty good grasp of Hebrew, Greek, English, Spanish, Russian, Italian, French, and every other language and dialect spoken on this planet.

Next the psalmist speaks of the fact that God is active in the psalmist's past, present, and future:

> *You hem me in—behind and before;*
> *you have laid your hand upon me.*
> *Such knowledge is too wonderful for me,*
> *too lofty for me to attain (vv. 5–6).*

The psalmist is saying that God has been active in his life in the past and will be in the future. And he says, "You lay your hand upon me." God is active in his life in the present, in the here and now.

The psalmist is overwhelmed by the fact that God knows him better than he knows himself, better than anyone else knows him. God knows his past, his present, and even his future destiny. The hand of God is always on his life.

In an age of alienation and depersonalization, it's wonderful to know that God knows us so intimately and personally. We are His; He is ours. We are immensely important to God.

We Can't Hide from God

In the second paragraph of Psalm 139, the writer explores the question, "How near is God to me?" "Where can I go from your Spirit? Where can I flee from your presence?" (v. 7).

How many times have we asked ourselves that question? "Lord, how can I get away from You? Can my sin and guilt separate me from You? Can my moods and depression keep me away from You?" The psalmist asks this question in a rhetorical fashion. Clearly the answer, though unspoken, is a resounding no. There is no place we can go where God is not there.

The psalmist continues:

If I go up to the heavens, you are there;
if I make my bed in the depths, you are there.
If I rise on the wings of the dawn,
if I settle on the far side of the sea,
even there your hand will guide me,
your right hand will hold me fast (vv. 8–10).

No destiny can separate us from the presence of God. Obviously if we go to heaven, God is there. But even if we go to the depths of hell, we cannot escape Him. Of course the Scriptures also tell us that there is a vast difference between an experience of heaven and an experience of Sheol, or hell. In heaven we will experience the fullness of the love, compassion, and glory of God. In hell we can experience only judgment and wrath.

But God's presence is inescapable. God owns and operates His universe, and there is no running away from Him. This thought holds no fear for those who love Him, but it should trouble the sleep and waking hours of those who have never said yes to His love and forgiveness.

The psalmist goes on to say that no amount of distance can separate him from God. "If I rise on the wings of the dawn," he writes, "if I settle on the far side of the sea, even there your hand will guide me, your right hand will hold me fast" (v. 9). That is such a beautiful poetic expression: "the wings of the dawn." If you have ever watched the sun come up, you have seen how the rays of sunlight burst forth, piercing the clouds, igniting the sky with their radiance, spreading out like the wings of a seagull from horizon to horizon. That is the imagery the psalmist invokes.

"If I could travel with the wings of the sunrise," the psalmist says, in effect, "if I could shoot across the sky at the speed of light, from one end of the earth to the other and even to the uttermost extent of the sea, even there I would find you, Lord. Even there your hand would guide me and hold me."

When I was about twelve years old, our family moved from Minnesota to Montana. The night before we left, I knelt beside my bed for my evening prayers. "Good-bye, God," I prayed. "We're going to Montana." I was sure I wouldn't find Him there. But when we arrived I found out that God was even in Montana! What's more, I have found Him everywhere I have lived since then. There is no place we can go where God has not gone before, whether to the farthest corner of the world or to the moon or even beyond the farthest star.

The psalmist continues:

If I say, "Surely the darkness will hide me
and the light become night around me,"
even the darkness will not be dark to you;
the night will shine like the day,
for darkness is as light to you (vv. 11–12).

Children sometimes try to hide from God by crawling under their bed covers or by hiding in a closet. They think that because human beings can't see in the dark, God can't either. This may seem like a silly notion, but there are many grownups who try to hide from God in the dark.

Some darken their minds. "If I don't think about God," they tell themselves, "then He won't think about me. I'll just ignore God, pretend He's not here, and I can commit this sin without God being any the wiser."

But God can see through any darkness because the darkness to Him is as light. We can't hide from God. He knows us and sees us even in the dark.

The Psalmist's Case for the Reality of God

At this point you might be thinking, "Psalm 139 is beautiful poetry, describing how God knows me and is always with me, but how do I know it's true?" The next section of Psalm 139 is dedicated to answering this question. David writes:

For you created my inmost being;
you knit me together in my mother's womb.
I praise you because I am fearfully and wonderfully made;
your works are wonderful,
I know that full well (vv. 13–14).

Here the psalmist makes a powerful case for faith in God, based on deduction from the design of the human body. He is amazed at the intelligently designed, intricately complex systems that maintain his physical life. He says, in effect, "By just looking at my own respiratory system, my circulatory system, the marvelous functioning of my eyes, the workings of my ears, my sense of smell, my sense of hearing, the wonder of human reproduction—these are complex organic systems that work together so beautifully that they couldn't have possibly arisen by random chance. There's an immense intellect behind it all!"

The psalmist would no doubt be even more amazed if he could have understood some of the bodily systems that we take for granted: the working of the body's cells, the amazing way that genetic information is transmitted by DNA, the fact that the brain is made up of a hundred neurons that enable the miracle of intelligent thought. Even with the psalmist's limited scientific understanding, he knew enough to be in awe of God's creative power, as evidenced by our own human bodies.

Have you ever stopped to think how much of your life is dependent upon forces at work in you—forces over which you have no control? What if you had to control the activity of your lungs or your heart consciously? What if you had to will your heart to beat at a rate of seventy-two beats per minute or if you had to tell your lungs continually, "Breathe in, breathe out. Breathe in, breathe out."

Fortunately we are not required to consciously operate our bodies to keep them alive. Someone else is running our life-support system. That's obvious from the design of our bodies. The psalmist is amazed at how life forms in the womb. He is amazed at the startlingly complex workings of the human body. He is so amazed that he must praise God and acknowledge Him as the Author of life.

How does a human being come into existence? The process is so mysterious! Again the psalmist speaks of the wonder of his Creator-God:

My frame was not hidden from you
when I was made in the secret place.
When I was woven together in the depths of the earth,
your eyes saw my unformed body (vv. 15–16a).

The imagery the psalmist uses is that the human body was liter-ally woven together, even knitted or embroidered, pieced together with fancy stitchery. He makes the point here that the human body was not merely thrown together but was beautifully woven like an intricate and costly tapestry. The human body, David implies, is a work of art, a thing of beauty and wonder.

This metaphor of God's "embroidery work" on the human body suggests another important truth about how God created us. The body is created in such a way that one organ supports another. The lungs need the heart, and the heart needs the lungs; the liver needs the kidneys, and the stomach needs both. All the various parts of the body are amazingly embroidered together.

This fact, by the way, raises one of the unanswered questions of evolution: How can an organ, which is only helpful to the body when it functions as a complete and mature structure, develop in stages over a long period of time? Astronomer and cosmologist Rob-ert Jastrow once observed, "The eye appears to have been designed; no designer of telescopes could have done better . . . It is hard to accept the evolution of the human eye as a product of chance."

And physicist-engineer Wernher von Braun asked, "What ran-dom process could possibly explain the simultaneous evolution of the eye's optical system, the nervous conductors of the optical sig-nals from the eye to the brain, and the optical nerve center in the brain itself where the incoming light impulses are converted to an image the conscious mind can comprehend?"

Even Charles Darwin, in *The Origin of Species,* admitted that explaining the complexity of the eye posed a daunting challenge to his theory of evolution: "To suppose that the eye, with all its inimi-table contrivances for adjusting the focus to different distances, for admitting different amounts of light, and for the correction of spher-ical and chromatic aberration, could have been formed by natural selection, seems, I freely confess, absurd in the highest possible degrees." Darwin went on to say, however, that mutation plus natural selection plus millions of years of time should be able to explain how the eye evolved.

Unfortunately for the evolutionists, there isn't that much time in the history of the planet. Trilobites, which are among the simplest, most primitive animals in the fossil record, have well-organized, complex eyes. How could trilobite eyes have evolved at such an early point in the evolutionary process?

Zoologist Richard Dawkins, a leading proponent of atheism, makes the astounding claim that the eye, though it appears complex, happens to be very easily evolved by random chance mutation. "It has been authoritatively estimated," he writes, "that eyes have evolved no fewer than forty times, and probably more than sixty times, independently in various parts of the animal kingdom." He concludes, "Eyes evolve easily and fast, at the drop of a hat."

Does the fossil record show that eyes evolve at the drop of a hat? No. Is there one single fossil showing a partially developed eye? No. Is there any evidence whatsoever to support his belief that eyes evolve so easily? No. His argument is essentially this: Eyes exist; God does not. Therefore the existence of the eye can be explained only as the result of random mutation and natural selection.

That is not a very logical argument, but it's all an atheist has to work with. By contrast the psalmist looks at his own body (with his intelligently designed and divinely created eyes!) and praises God for the wonderful way he has been made. That is a rational statement made by a man who understands reality.

Note too the phrase the psalmist uses in verse 16: "Your eyes saw my unformed body." In the original Hebrew, the phrase translated "my unformed body" literally means "my rolled-up substance." Here is a picture of a human embryo. If you've ever seen photos of an early-stage embryo, you know that it has a "rolled-up" look. The head is large, the body is curled around, and it appears to end in a curled tail. God sees us and knows us as distinct individuals from the moment the sperm penetrates the egg and conception occurs. He watches over us throughout the gestation process as the embryo becomes a fetus, then as the fetus emerges as a baby.

Today people often ask, "When does life begin? When does an embryo become a human being?" The psalmist's answer is, "Your eyes saw my unformed body, not as a clump of tissue or a collection of cells, but as *me*, an individual human being with a soul and a destiny, all rolled up in an embryonic state."

The psalmist goes on to make an astounding statement about God's view of human destiny:

> *All the days ordained for me*
> *were written in your book*
> *before one of them came to be (v. 16b).*

David is not only impressed by the argument for God's existence from design and creation but also by the evidence of determination, of predestination. The psalmist has gone through an experience that you may have seen in your own life: Every once in a while, we notice that certain seemingly unrelated factors seem to miraculously fall into place to produce a result that can be viewed only as the work of God's own hand. We weren't aware of what God was doing in our lives. Only after all the pieces of the puzzle came together did we realize that our lives were being orchestrated as part of a wonderful plan.

The apostle Paul explains it this way: "And we know that in all things God works for the good of those who love him, who have been called according to his purpose. For those God foreknew he also predestined to be conformed to the likeness of his Son, that he might be the firstborn among many brothers" (Romans 8:28–29). God is actively involved in our lives, arranging events and circumstances, causing them to dovetail together in order to achieve His perfect plan for our lives. His ultimate plan for our lives is that we become more and more like His Son, Jesus Christ.

There is an amazing and beautiful paradox at work in your life and mine: We have completely free will, yet God has complete sovereignty over our lives. Free will and predestination seem like contradictory ideas, yet they actually complement and complete each other: We are free to make our own decisions, yet God has planned our lives since before the beginning of the world. All the days ordained for us were written in God's book before one of them came to be! The psalmist is so awed by this truth that his mind can hardly contain it. My mind can't contain it either, but I know it's true!

This concept that we call determinism or predestination is, in fact, the basis for all biblical prophecy. For example, there are over three hundred messianic prophecies in the Old Testament that were fulfilled with amazing accuracy and specific detail in the life of our Lord Jesus. These predictions were made anywhere from five hundred to a thousand years before Jesus was born. They were not made by only one prophet but by many prophets, speaking and writing as the Spirit of God moved them.

After the passage of centuries, a series of seemingly unrelated circumstances and events fell into place. One man, Jesus of Nazareth, became the answer to centuries of waiting and wondering. The reason those prophecies are so uncannily accurate is simple: All the days ordained for Jesus the Messiah were written in God's book before one of them came to be. His arrival on earth, His miracles, His suffering, His death, and His resurrection were all predestined by the plan and will of God the Father.

Next the psalmist makes note of one more profound truth that convinces him of the reality of God:

> *How precious to me are your thoughts, O God!*
> *How vast is the sum of them!*
> *Were I to count them,*
> *they would outnumber the grains of sand.*
> *When I awake,*
> *I am still with you (vv. 17–18).*

The psalmist is impressed by the abundance of revelation God has given to humanity. We would never understand who God is if He didn't reveal Himself through Scripture. Even though we have the evidence of the intelligent design of our bodies and of the universe, without the revelation of God's Word we would never understand God—or ourselves.

Dr. John McIntyre, professor emeritus at Texas A&M University, committed his life to Jesus Christ in a home Bible class when he was a physicist at Stanford. He once told me, "The thing that impresses me about the Christian faith is the fact that the Bible is the same kind of a cohesive system as nature. The more you examine the Bible, the more complex it appears and the deeper and more unfathomable its thoughts. It's the same with nature. It appears simple on the surface, but the more you study nature, the more complex it becomes until it staggers the mind and seems incomprehensible in its complexity." The perfect harmony between the revelation of

nature and the revelation of Scripture was one of the most important factors in Dr. McIntyre's conversion to Christ.

That is what the psalmist says as well: How precious are God's
thoughts! How vast is the sum of them! How wide-ranging and far-
reaching is God's revelation of reality in His Word! When you think
you come to the end of it, you discover even wider vistas and more
profound depths to His Word. How incomprehensibly great are His
thoughts!

Our Authentic Humanness

In the fourth and final paragraph, verses 19 through 24, the psalmist
takes an abrupt turn:

> *If only you would slay the wicked, O God!*
> *Away from me, you bloodthirsty men!*
> *They speak of you with evil intent;*
> *your adversaries misuse your name.*
> *Do I not hate those who hate you, O LORD,*
> *and abhor those who rise up against you?*
> *I have nothing but hatred for them;*
> *I count them my enemies (vv. 19–22).*

Why does the psalmist suddenly interject these dark and bloody
thoughts? Death and hate! This section of the psalm is troubling to
us because it seems so far from the New Testament standard: "Love
your enemies, do good to those who hate you" (Luke 6:27; see also
Matthew 5:44). How do we reconcile this section of Psalm 139 (and
other similar passages in the book of Psalms) with the words of our
Lord Jesus?

First, we need to recognize that many of the feelings expressed
in the Psalms do not necessarily reflect God's will. We're reading
the honest emotions of Old Testament believers, and they do not
always reflect God's truth. While the Bible may in places provide an
honest mirror of the human viewpoint, we shouldn't assume that
those passages accurately indicate how God would have us respond
in situations of conflict or persecution.

The psalmist, having described his close relationship to God,
now comes to a point where he asks God to act on his behalf. This is

a familiar experience for most believers: When we draw near to God, we tend to make requests of Him in prayer. And for what does the psalmist ask God? First, he asks God to take care of the problem of wicked, blaspheming people. Like most of us, the psalmist is not shy about suggesting to God exactly how He should deal with the problem: "Lord," he says in effect, "wipe them out! Destroy the wicked, God!" Does the psalmist really think that such an obvious remedy has never occurred to God?

You have probably prayed a prayer much like the one the psalmist prays here. I have to confess that I have had such feelings myself from time to time. I remember hearing a pastor say of some troublesome people in his church, "There are some people I know who are going to heaven someday, and, oh how I wish they'd hurry up!" His tongue was in his cheek, but there was an underlying truth to his words.

One of the refreshing things about the psalms is that they honestly express feelings we all have from time to time. They may not always reflect our most Christlike impulses, but they do reflect our humanity.

It is important to note as we examine these verses that they do not merely fall short of the New Testament standard of Jesus, they even fall short of the Old Testament standard. The words "Love your neighbor as yourself" do not originate with Jesus but are first found in the Old Testament book of Leviticus (19:18).

People often make the mistake of thinking that the New Testament and the Old Testament are opposed to each other. "The Old Testament is all about the law and judgment," people often say, "while the New Testament is about grace and forgiveness." That's not true. The Old and New Testaments are two parts of a consistent revelation of God and His standards for our lives. The two testaments are not opposed to each other; they are in harmony with each other.

The problem in Psalm 139 is that the psalmist speaks from a human perspective, not God's perspective. In his honest anger he says, "Lord, the solution to the problem of evil is simple: Just slay the wicked!"

Notice he does not say, "Lord, let me slay the wicked for you." He recognizes that vengeance belongs to God. If anybody is going to slay the wicked, God must do it. So he says, "Lord, the problem of wicked people is Your problem! Why don't you solve it?"

Notice too that the psalmist's motives are selfless. He is not concerned with how evil people are mistreating *him* but how they offend and blaspheme *God*. He writes, "They speak of you with evil intent; your adversaries misuse your name" (v. 20). The psalmist's hatred is directed not at his own enemies but at those who are the enemies of God.

Who are these people with whom the psalmist is so upset? Are they atheists and infidels? Are they worshipers of idols and demons? No, they are people who claim to worship God! When the psalmist says, "Your adversaries misuse your name," he is saying that certain religious people have defiled God's reputation by doing ungodly acts in God's name. They are religious hypocrites, pretending to serve Him and speak for Him.

There's nothing more disgusting than a religious hypocrite. In fact the sharpest words Jesus ever spoke were His words of condemnation against the hypocrisy of the Pharisees, a group of intensely religious people who did great evil in the name of God. So the psalmist is correct in identifying religious hypocrisy as a serious sin, worthy of condemnation.

But the psalmist is incorrect in one respect: Though he shares God's hatred for sin, he has not yet learned to share God's love for sinners. While God hates sin, He loves sinners. Unfortunately, in this passage the psalmist fails to make that all-important distinction.

I believe this is why the psalmist concludes with these words:

Search me, O God, and know my heart;
test me and know my anxious thoughts.
See if there is any offensive way in me,
and lead me in the way everlasting (vv. 23–24).

In other words, "Lord, I don't understand the problem of evil. It seems to me that the easiest way to deal with evildoers is to eliminate them. But then it occurs to me, Lord, that I am also a sinner. If you eliminated everyone who does evil, you would have to slay me as well. So Lord, please search me, test me, remove any offensive and sinful habits from my life, and lead me in the path to everlasting life."

This should be your prayer and mine, especially when we are confronted with the evil actions of others. Instead of praying, "God, wipe them out!" we should pray, "Lord, search me! Know my heart!

Root out the sin from my life and cleanse my ways! Make me worthy to be Your servant!" After all, the wicked people we want God to slay are the very people for whom Jesus died. The most innocent man who ever lived was slain so that the guilty, including you and I, might live.

Next, notice how the psalmist's plea in verse 23—"Search me, O God, and know my heart"—is a prayer for God to continue a work that He has already begun in the life of the psalmist. The first verse of Psalm 139, after all, reads: "O LORD, you have searched me and you know me." Now the psalmist wants God to continue searching him and to reveal to him his hidden flaws and faults. The psalmist wants God to rebuke him, humble him, correct him, and keep him on the path of life.

The question that confronts us in the closing verses of this psalm is a painful one: "Who is the biggest sinner you know?" Is it the atheist down the street? Is it the religious hypocrite in your church? Is it the person you've never been able to forgive? Let me tell you how I would answer that question: The biggest sinner I know is Ray C. Stedman.

God has given us a wonderful treasure in the book of the Psalms. It is a source of comfort for troubled souls. But the psalms were not merely written to comfort us. They were written to enable us to see reality. Through the lens of the Psalms, we see ourselves from God's perspective, including our hidden sins.

O Lord, this is my prayer: Search me and know my heart. Leave no sin hidden and unconfessed. Test me and see if there is any offensive way in me. And lead me, Lord, in the path of everlasting life.

Thank You, Lord, for the gift of the Psalms. Thank You for all 150 of these folk songs of faith. In the book of Psalms, we see You, Father; we see Your Son; we see Your Spirit; and we see ourselves as we truly are. You created our inmost being. You search us. You know us.

How precious are Your thoughts, O God!

Note to the Reader

The publisher invites you to share your response to the message of this book by writing Discovery House Publishers, Box 3566, Grand Rapids, MI 49501, USA. For information about other Discovery House books, music, or videos, contact us at the same address or call 1-800-653-8333. Find us on the Internet at http://www.dhp.org/ or send e-mail to books@dhp.org.